Act of the Damned

by the same author

Elephant Memory

South of Nowhere

Getting to Know the Inferno

An Explanation of the Birds

Fado Alexandrino

Return of the Caravels

Treatise on the Soul's Passions

The Natural Order of Things

António Lobo Antunes
Act of the Damned

Translated from the Portuguese by Richard Zenith

First published in Portugal in 1985 as *Auto dos Danados* by Publicações Dom Quixote

This translation first published in Great Britain in 1993
by Martin Secker & Warburg Limited,
an imprint of Reed Consumer Books Limited,
Michelin House, 81 Fulham Road, London SW3 6RB
and Auckland, Melbourne, Singapore and Toronto

A CIP catalogue record for this book
is available from the British Library
ISBN 0 436 20148 8

This publication was produced with the assistance of the
European Commission. The publishers gratefully acknowledge their help

Photoset in 12/15 Perpetua
by Deltatype Ltd, Ellesmere Port, South Wirral
Printed and bound in Great Britain by
Mackays of Chatham plc, Chatham, Kent

To Thomas Colchie, my agent and friend,
whose faith and encouragement were crucial
throughout the painful writing of this book

and to Miguel Sousa Tavares,
companion of my rediscovered childhood

For my daughter Isabel

Those who are good
are always dirt poor;
and I always, therefore,
do not what I should
but what profits more.
The glory of man
on earth is money
and he must, if he plans
to amass a good sum,
be as cruel as he can.

Gil Vicente, *The Fair*

two days before the festival:

Nuno All Day Long

Morning

On the second Wednesday of September, 1975, I arrived at the office at ten-past nine. I remember this not because I have an exceptional memory or keep a diary (I stay away from pussyshit nonsense like diaries and poems) but because it was my last day of work before we fled to Spain.

Right after the revolution, in April of the previous year, bearded civilians and long-haired soldiers camouflaged in ragged jeans were posted on the main roads to inspect passing cars, or they marched in the streets and the squares, commanded by the unintelligible microphones that Marxism-Leninism-Maoism had recycled from a defunct carnival. Like dogs on the beach following the trail of an imaginary scent along the water's edge, they went into the country to bark about socialism to farmers they'd herded before dusty projectors; they scoured the length of Portugal in ramshackle trucks, threatening the shopkeepers with their squinty-eyed machine guns; they broke into houses with the butts of their rifles, brandishing arrest warrants under stupefied noses. And we had the pleasure, every Sunday, of visiting the remnants of our shipwrecked family: a few aunts and uncles, "economic saboteurs," imprisoned in the fortress at Caxias. There, between cell bars and the armpits of guards, they watched

3

the Tagus River rise and fall against the stone wall. The only one not taken was the cancerous grandmother, who navigated at random in a wheelchair, her transistor radio pressed against the thin white hairs of her ear. She smiled dumbly at the democrats who periodically banged on her door and poked through what was left of the silver with their guns, repeating the strange speeches of the carnival loudspeakers.

Since April, 1974, the Army and the Communists had been stopping before every other building, lifting their penises like animals to urinate, and coating the walls with their *Long Live This* and *Down With That*, excrements which contradicted and cancelled each other and which in a week's time would be buried under placards urging strikes, placards announcing rallies, photographs of generals, ads for rock concerts, swastikas, anti-government slogans and toilet-stall rhymes—a love affair of intertwining alphabet fingers, slowly fading in the autumn of time. In spite of the police jeeps patrolling the streets, gypsies with chairs and tables and pots and pans invaded the abandoned apartment units. Ravaged buildings gave birth to orphanages in which children sat on the bare floor, munching on rubble sandwiches. Charcoal Stalins scowled at us on the corners. And the river swooned at the port of Caxias, suffocated by the bird-wings, while impassive tankers stood still beneath the bridge.

At eight a.m. on the second Wednesday of September, 1975, the alarm clock yanked me up out of my sleep like a derrick on the wharf hauling up a seaweed-smeared car that didn't know how to swim. I surfaced from the sheets, the night dripping from my pyjamas and my feet as the iron claws deposited my arthritic cadaver on to the carpet, next to the shoes full of yesterday's smell. I rubbed my fists into my battered eyes and felt flakes of rust fall from the corners. Ana was wrapped, like a corpse in the morgue, in a blanket on the far side of the bed, with only her broomhead of hair poking out. A pathetic shred of leather from a dead heel tumbled off the mattress. I went to the bathroom to brush my teeth and the heartless mirror showed me the damage the years had wrought, as on an abandoned chapel. There were bottles and tubes lined up on glass shelves, a hairdryer exhaust pipe, and the tormenting light, which at least was less bright in the steam of the shower, behind the curtain with red and blue fish. The soap escaped as usual, three or four times, ricocheting off the tiles or forging a lathery trail to the sink while I went slipping and sliding after it, practically on my knees, blinded by shampoo, banging my shins into the toilet bowl and waving my arms in search of the balance I'd lost. I grasped on to the chrome-painted towel racks to save myself from the ortho-paedist, and finally I made it back—shivering but with the pink lanolin fish in my palm—to the consoling jet of warm water. Ana was propped up on a pillow, smoking, watching me. The trees of the Bolivian Embassy waved in the window. The sparrows hung upside-down from the branches. Daytime and the smell of darkness mingled in the disorder of the sheets. I opened the drawer to take out a shirt and tie, and was met by enough socks for an army of ankles. Ana kept smoking, and men with sombreros, moustaches, belted pistols and the dignity of Emiliano Zapata strutted on the dawn-lit balconies of Bolivia. I took cover in a pair of socks and underpants, and as I buttoned my waiscoat the voice of Ana, who lit a new cigarette from the one that was dying, emerged from the pillowcase:

"My God, Nuno. With a purple mark like that on your thigh, you could at least have the decency not to display it." I put on my trousers. It had been two weeks since I'd heard from Mafalda.

"I bumped into something or other," I said, pulling at my shoelaces. "Into a fender, or a table, or—Jesus, I don't what it was. How am I supposed to remember every frigging thing I bump into?"

Ana stretched out on the bed and smiled, her forearm supporting her tilted head. One good thing about the divorce: for five years now I've been free of her sarcasm.

"Your girlfriends have awfully peculiar habits," she said with a carefully measured dose of acrimony. "Not that it's any of my business. But aesthetically speaking . . ."

"I bumped into something," I repeated, sighing, while I tied my tie on inside-out. Mafalda had broken off with me for the hundredth time for the usual reason: I still hadn't left Ana.

"You're so nervous talking about it that you can't even tie a tie on straight," Ana brayed in triumph as her liquid body spread over the sheets.

Spidery ships plodded along the Tagus. A bolero on the radio carried me dancing toward the door: I grabbed on to the chest of drawers to avoid being swept away by the torrent of flat notes.

"Nervous my ass," I said. "It's this bullshit silk that slides every which way."

The maid was brewing coffee in the kitchen. Her room was a closetless cubicle at the opposite end of the apartment, next to the metallic tree of a fire escape whose steps, like leaves, rustled and groaned in winter, in the dark. Ana bought her a trunk for her clothes and a white enamel nightstand which my mother-in-law, hopelessly addicted to doctors and auctions, no doubt picked up at a hospital sell-off. The taps on my new soles sent echoes throughout the building, from the tiles of the roof to the catacombs of the garage, where cars grazed with their grille teeth on their own shadows. The maid served me coffee and inserted two postcards of bread into the mail slots of the toaster.

"I'm not hungry," I announced to get back at Ana. "A cup of coffee and I'm out of here."

From time to time I heard coughing and spluttering from the children's room. The paediatrician treated their systems with drops and syrups, and today—every Sunday—I'm startled when instead of those thin, pale creatures, wrapped in nappies and chewing cigar-pacifiers, two teenage boys with Martian helmets and pre-moustache fuzz appear in the gloomy hall of a building where my parents once lived and I live now. They rev up their motor bikes to an angry pitch and then demand money, as if they were robbers and I were a bank.

"At least eat a spoonful of jam, Dr Souza." The maid set out a jar of the stuff. "Working on an empty stomach will make you dizzy."

Her eye make-up consisted of a permanent sty, and she did not smell like night (like the rest of the house) but like afternoon weariness (it leaked out of her uniform), as if it were already dinnertime. She smelled like when she cleared the table after dessert, turned on the dishwasher and disappeared into her cubicle without bothering to take a bath, nonchalantly emitting her melancholy goat smell. She smelled like how she smells today, almost ten years later and no longer calling me doctor or sir. Nowadays she drowns under chain-store necklaces and rides next to me on the leather-upholstered seat of my car, gripping on with both hands to her steering-wheel handbag. But in those days— the days of this book—I pushed away the jam, rejected her toast and sipped a solitary sip of black coffee. The kitchen clock read twenty-five to nine. The maid reached up to pull down a box of vanilla cookies from the top shelf; her fragrance intensified.

"A cookie for the road, Dr Souza?" The trees of the Bolivian Embassy shook off their shadows.

"No thanks," I said, pulling back my elbows like an offended fan folding shut. "If I get hungry there's a snack bar next to the office."

7

I crossed the hall to the bedroom to say goodbye to Ana. She was sitting up against the pillow and still smoking, meditating on the spirals of the console table. Her fingers occasionally rose to her mouth, a red point glowed, the smoke blurred her face, and her hand dropped back to a fold in the sheets where a glass nest accepted ashes. The chrysalises of my children were squirming in the room next door, enclosed in their bunk cocoons. I stood still for a moment with my thumbs in my pockets, hesitating. Ever since the anonymous caller had told Ana about Mafalda, it seemed I no longer existed.

"See you later," she said, staring sideways into the mirror that reflected the blinds and, flowing behind them, a toy Tagus River with toy packet boats. I would have liked to pull a dozen paper seagulls from my pocket and sprinkle them on the docks to make the mirror water stir. I found the fretful face of the maid framed between the African horns of the hat rack, and I was on the farm, under the elms that towered above the fence, in summer, when we were small.

"Dr Souza, there's still some sponge cake left over from yesterday."

The elevator carried my No thank you to the ground floor. The concierge, who was watering the plants at the entrance, also smelled like night, and I could hear the night's insects and crickets quavering under her apron. And the soil in the pots smelled like night—not the night of childhood but that clearer, porous night, wet with foetuses and water. Every minute or so the concierge would set down the watering can and yell insults at the boys riding their bikes through the archway.

"Morning, Dulce," I muttered, about to walk down the front steps. I was still thinking of the cake and spitting out spongy pieces with my tongue.

"They peed on my geraniums, Dr Souza," she said mournfully

8

as she lifted a leaf that drooped like a dead rabbit's ear. "If it weren't for his asthma, I'd have my husband go after them with his gun. Come over here and just get a whiff of this ammonia. All that work and fertilizer, and then these hooligans come and piss over everything."

The boys rode past and whistled suggestively at the concierge, who started after them with the watering can, and the elms and aroma of night evaporated. Mounds of parked cars radiated in the sun. What has Ana done to the house? How has the neighbour-hood changed? Still as ugly and polluted as ever? A little better? A little worse? Still inhabited by the same engineers, the same doctors, the same divorced women wearing the same fur coats? Still the same shanties of blacks and gypsies visible from the bedroom window? I pulled the car out of a long row of somnambulant snouts with headlight eyes and had to dodge rocks, sewer pipes and boards, wondering Why don't they clean up this fucking shit, until I reached the avenue that leads to the park, past the police station and the semblance of a plaza, whose plane trees were bathed in the khaki-coloured dust of building sites. I cruised through the trees and slopes of Monsanto Forest Park and past a new shanty town where women who looked like the concierge were emptying out clay pots, then past a soccer field and over a bridge, till finally I arrived at the office—not the one I have today, in Loures, with little more than grazing sheep to entertain me between patients' gums, but the old majestic one on Braancamp Avenue, in a building with a Greek temple entrance, flanked by a pub and a clothes shop.

The patients were leafing through wilted magazines in the waiting room. The dental chair occupied the middle of my office like a gallows. The tools waved their edges, the dentures their fangs. The dental assistant, passed on to me by her predecessor

9

along with a broken toilet, was lining up the files of that day's patients and reeking of efficiency and disinfectant.

"Morning," I said. I hung up my coat on a wire hanger and donned my torturer's smock. The assistant set out clamps and rolled cotton balls. She turned on the video: a fox was chasing a bird in a landscape of dunes. Outside, September's grenades of heat were razing the city, façade by façade. The service-station mechanic, reduced to charred bones, agonized over a dismantled engine. The sun's cannons uprooted plants and patches of turf in the park. The tables at the pond-side restaurant had surrendered: they lay face-down on the stones of the terrace, dripping the blood of their paint.

"Ready for number one?" asked the assistant, obsessively rearranging the bottles and tubes and compresses while I put on rubber gloves and tried out my drill like a pilot his propeller. On the wall there was a cartoon of an old lady dentist with huge sagging breasts exultantly clasping a molar with her monkey wrench. The fox, now on crutches and covered with bandages, was stretching a gigantic net across two high rocks to trap the bird that whizzed back and forth over the desert floor. Summer was bursting the buildings as if they were acne pimples.

"Ready," I said, sticking out my navel like a posing toreador. The two phones next to the files and the coat closet broke out ringing in stereo, the dental assistant railroaded in a woman jingling bracelets, and the fishing net did a flip-flop, snagging the fox and hurling him into a cactus tree. The phones bleated like hungry lambs until appeased by the assistant. "Eleven o'clock on the 17th is the only opening I have," she said. I turned off the television (a light flickered, shrank and died in the centre of the screen) just as the bird whizzed into the foreground, stopped short, beep-beeped and was gone. I inserted another cassette. A pulsating grey snow filled the screen and, after a white strip that followed a red one, I turned up the volume to hear the fanfare for the film's title credits. The assistant put down the first phone and talked to the second. "Hello, Admiral, fine thank you, what can we do for you?", and standing next to the chair was Leslie Caron, smiling, her feet pointing outward in the form of a V. "Your crown fell out?" asked the assistant, "Then by all means we can squeeze you in today, Can you come at six o'clock? I'll be sure to mark it down on Dr Souza's schedule."

The sun continued its crematory slaughter in the plaza. My smock turned into a striped waistcoat and the office became the backdrop of a Paris street, with lampposts, trees and bridges painted in, along with the Eiffel Tower, the Moulin Rouge, the Vatican and as many other European landmarks as could fit. I took two steps towards her, pirouetted back and stepped forward again, in time with the orchestra that played in the hall, and it was Gene Kelly who danced on the office carpet, jumping over boxes of gauze, ignoring the laughing dentures, and skipping down plywood steps to a cellophane Seine lit by coloured spotlights and embellished with cardboard barges at anchor, kiosks on the bank and neon café signs, while in the back, near the window, a dance troupe of tray-carrying waiters and handbag-twirling hookers traced an intricate choreography between Versailles and the Prado.

"This is one of Dr Acacio's patients," said the assistant as she in her turn stepped down to the Seine in the resolute style of the American heiress who for the last fifteen minutes of the film had been insisting I accept a painter's studio that looked to me like a courtesan's boudoir.

"Dr Acacio told me to call you if I had any problem while he's away," said the woman, her image brought into sharper focus by the wide-open, unblinking eye of the dental lamp. "Aren't you the one who fills in when he goes on holiday?"

The pyorrhoeas chatted with parakeets in the waiting-room cage or picked up the hair-salon literature which the girl at the switchboard offered them monthly, in the hope that the passion between the Italian racing-car driver and the daughter of the Greek shipping magnate would take their minds off the pain. A colleague hammered away in the next office down, pulverizing an exposed nerve. The dental assistant whirled from cabinet to cabinet and chained the napkin around the woman's neck. The building opposite, collapsing from the heat, silently crashed to the ground. On the video Gene Kelly, with an air of resignation and his hands in his pockets, ambled along to his artist's garret. Leslie Caron, her head reclining under a trellis of drill bits, pulled down her skirt to cover her knees or what showed of her thighs. "I'm leaving tomorrow for the Algarve with my kids, and who knows where I'd find a dentist down there."

Gene Kelly painted hideous figures while outside his window a neon *Pigalle* appeared and disappeared, pulsing like a freshly dissected frog heart. A drunk and ugly friend sporting a crumpled suit and a glass of whisky extolled the work. The dental assistant was putting clamps in the sterilizer. Leslie Caron crossed her legs and looked me in the eye. Thistle blossoms sprouted from my bones and birds flew out from my torso to flutter their wings over the beach of my tummy. "Last night at dinner I spat something hard on to my plate, probably part of a filling or a chip from a tooth," and I thought, Like hell you did, Jesus how I'm tired of hearing what people can make out of a puny pebble in their lettuce salad, and I said, "It's probably nothing." The music on the video became sombre. Gene Kelly held on to his brush, fell on to the patchwork quilt he used as a bedspread, jumped up and threw back his head to lead into his next number:

"Open your mouth."

He made a complete tour of her gums, enlarged by the little

round mirror. He checked the fillings, stumbled on a missing wisdom tooth, scraped off some tartar and felt her ankle pressing against my lower leg, and more birds flying across my stomach, more blossoming bones, more tides stirring my deepest self as they flowed over a twilight of unending sands. If I stretch this examination out, he thought, if I fix her pebble with the drill, then I'll be able to observe her more closely, closer to her breasts. But I straightened up, turned off the lamp, laid down the mirror and assured her: "Everything looks fine, you can go to your Algarve with nothing to worry about." And again her leg against my leg, until I realized that the phone was ringing, until I heard the assistant say, "Who's calling?" and tap a pencil against the desk and announce, "Miss Mafalda for Dr Souza," and her thigh pulled away from me:

"Where do I pay?"

"The woman in the outer office will bill you," explained the assistant, her back turned, while Gene Kelly performed a lonely tap dance on the bank of the Seine River.

"Nuno?" chirped the goldfinch voice of Mafalda. "What are you doing for lunch? I've got to talk to you. You can't imagine how upset I am."

Out of the corner of his eye he saw Leslie Caron thank the assistant before leaving the stage, while the statue on the traffic circle melted on its pedestal like a rotten smile. ("Olivia," the assistant squawked over the intercom, "thirty-five dollars for a woman with bracelets who's about to float through.") I could feel in my leg the absence of the woman's, the way a slab in a museum still holds the imprint of an insect centuries later. A bronze arm was sliding slowly down the sidewalk.

"The last time we met you screamed me out of your apartment," I said, and I remembered the cutesy flat in Lumiar: the hibiscuses on the rugs in the bedroom, the foyer with arrows and a leopard-stamped shield, and your screams that drove me from room to room out of the door: "I don't ever want to touch another married man," "If you don't have the guts to leave Ana then you can go straight to hell," etc., etc.

"I found a lump on my breast, Nuno. I've made an appointment with the doctor, but that's not till Monday, and—" and I translated, You've run out of drugs, as her kitchen resurrected and I smelled the eternally popping popcorn and those repugnant French cheeses laced with herbs. Her laundry smacked against the porthole of her washing-machine. "Can you take half an hour for lunch between teeth?"

"That's the most I can manage," I said, judging by the stack of patient files on the desk. "All the cavities in the world have descended on me this morning. One o'clock at your place?"

"I'd rather we meet at the café," peeped the goldfinch. "It seems you've forgotten our last conversation. Until you leave Ana, if you ever do, we can stay friends but that's it."

And we didn't even stay friends. How stupid it all was: the arguments, the silences, the rubber bones of our petty grudges we gnawed with such fury, the countless burned-out cigarettes and our heads side by side against the headboard, looking straight ahead past the sheets: serious, stubborn, enraged, intractable, the crease in the middle of each forehead bisecting the angle defined by our feet. You've probably aged faster than the calendar has turned, with skin grown incurably leathery and dry. You're probably still single, still driving your minuscule car impregnated with the smell of tobacco, still ignoring the stop-lights of the world on the other side of your dark glasses and your bubble-gum bubbles, still eking out a living with half-baked schemes (working vaguely in tourism, vaguely promoting concerts, vaguely translating vague French novels), still gulping down frantic cups of coffee and sucking on nauseating lollipops in your ever-failing attempts to quit smoking, still sitting barefoot on the floor when you call up friends to go to shopping malls, to see movies, to eat fish in the Old Quarter, to play cards, to plan excursions by jeep to the Algarve, to go to fashion shows, costume parties, flea markets. You probably lose weight impetuously, feel impetuously sad, become impetuously uglier, and slovenly, and in need of a bath, until the night of my forgetting closes over you in an irrevocable sigh of dried-up waters.

"I have a shitload of work to do before I can get away, so I'm not sure I'll make it."

I could see Leslie Caron in the snack bar opposite the office. She was drinking one of those juice things, apple or pineapple, which I used to slurp down with straws, and I thought about skipping down the stairs to meet up with her, but at that very moment an old lady came in to have her denture adjusted and then a man in a suit who started sweating as soon as he heard the drill, so that the end of the film left me with an acid despair in my stomach and the conviction that our pursuit of happiness is forever doomed by the cavities which, at the very last minute, come between us and a pair of fleeing sandals.

"Is your call finished, Dr Souza?" asked the dependably testy switchboard operator, intruding on our conversation like a cyst in the eye. "All the lines are busy, and Dr Saldanha asked me to put a call through to Santarem."

"I'll be finished in a minute," I said, and I was surprised not to hear a click.

"Please do your best to make it," said Mafalda. "And do something about that idiot on your way out."

"You're the idiot, lady," the operator butted in, "plus a few other things I won't mention. Unlike you, I work for a living."

"Then do your work," I said. "You've got a lot of nerve listening in on our conversation."

15

"I only do what my job requires," she lied, indignant. "I don't give a hoot about yours or anybody else's private conversations."

"I can't believe this, Nuno. How can you let that bitch talk back to you like that?"

"Listen to who's doing the barking," shot back the operator, "and judge for yourself who the bitch is. You'd think they could at least keep your kind on a leash when they're in heat."

"Did you hear that, Nuno? Did you hear what that slut said about me?" Mafalda was hysterical.

"And stop breaking up marriages!" threw in the operator at the top of her lungs. "Besides, if he's looking for a plaything, I'll bet anything he doesn't pick you."

I laid down the receiver while the two voices tussled, scratched and bit each other in an electric desert of screws and wires. I patched up the incisor of a teenager whose fingers turned white from clutching the arabesques of the chair whenever I came near. Surrounded by a battlefield of acne, his eyes expressed an animal terror, a frightened pony's uncontrollable fear. The dental assistant carried in tools, took tools away and prepared amalgams, floating in the sunlit aquarium-office. Greenish air bubbles travelled up and down the aluminium window frames. I treated two more molars, wrote in red on the patient files and put Xs on the charts for the teeth I'd filled. I cleaned the canals of a woman whose four urchins lost no time in opening up cabinets, contaminating the compresses, pricking themselves with pincers and clamping each other with clamps in front of their amused or proud or oblivious mother, who gagged on an aspirator while her children kicked the X-ray machine and did their best to destroy my office, and I thought, Just as well Ana and I didn't have any more children, Just as well my semen became an insipid liqueur without seeds, an addled, sterile egg-white in a laboratory test tube, and after my eighth or ninth victim, a brand-new file with a

Braga address: My God, am I so famous that they come all the way from the north of the country to be saved by my miracle-working hands?

"Did you hear that, Nuno?" hollered Mafalda's voice. "How can you allow a bitch like that to work there?"

I went to the cubicle in the hall to urinate, and the switchboard operator stared at me with a deadpan face, impervious to the friendly, almost tender smile I gave her in passing. In the waiting room I noticed an indistinct, coughing shape knocking ashtrays and magazines off the table: the pilgrim from Braga, I thought, and I pictured a glacial monster covered with bristles, thawed by the September heat. I pressed the toilet-tank handle and heard a click in the emptiness as one part got caught on another, washed my hands with the last translucent sliver of soap (it died in my palm), slid back the latch and smiled once more at the switchboard, which returned a savage roar. The man from Braga was presumably in the chair already, as the waiting room was completely deserted and half destroyed. Ten minutes to twelve. I straightened out my smock, pushed on the doorknob and assumed the air of peremptory confidence that patients want. The assistant was organizing dental bric-à-brac in a compartment-filled drawer modelled on a sewing box. Edward G. Robinson was smoking a cigar on the video, looking at me with the saddest sockets in the world, and a profuse belly, dressed in a vest and holding out a hand, collided with me like one whale into another:

"I'm lucky I got an appointment. It's a pain in the you-know-what to find a dentist these days."

In the place of the bronze statesman there was now a smouldering crater, surrounded by a circle of annihilated buildings, and the sky resembled a gigantic yellow phonograph record, turning at the slowest speed, and I thought, If it gets any hotter, by one o'clock the traffic lights will have melted and it may not even be possible to walk on the asphalt.

"So here I am," said the whale, pointing to his cheek, "with a real fucker of a problem."

The assistant's shoulders, shocked by the obscenity, hunched up and retreated like the water in a well when a stone is dropped, and with my nose in the video, where guns were shooting, I realized It's not only Edward G. Robinson's eyes that are the saddest in the world, it's his limp rubber lips, his cadaverous face wrinkles, his lizardy eyelashes, his poignant fragility.

"It's great, isn't it?" the man said, looking over my shoulder. "I bought one of those gadgets for my kids, but I was smart, I got a contraband unit from Spain," and he breathed so full and thick in my face that his words seemed like gelatin going into my ear.

I pointed to the chair and sat down on my stool without a word, took up the dental mirror and found his breakfast— morsels of bread, pastry, bacon and eggs—in the interstices of his gums. "Where does it hurt?" I asked, and he pointed to a plastic plate that looked like it came from a gypsy bazaar where they'd haggled over the price among limping donkeys and kitchen crockery and shouting and music and carousels and fritters and auctioneering and blind men holding out their imperious palms. I water-jetted the denture, so big it's a wonder it didn't crack his skull, which blossomed into tortuous canines next to his tongue. I don't understand why he doesn't rear up and neigh, I thought, horrified by the sight of his horse-sized chops, Why doesn't he kick his way out and trot at liberty down the avenue? Edward G. Robinson exhumed a revolver from his double-breasted coat, the gang that was with him clacked the breeches of their machine guns, and the bank employees, eyes bugging out from under their visors, trembled behind the rampart of teller windows. The dental assistant was getting tools ready for the afternoon appointments, fishing them out of the sterilizer with a pair of tongs, and it struck me that that was the only form of hair removal worth her while.

"Take that thing out," I said to the man from Braga while searching on the shelf for a spatula. "Let's see what you've got hiding under there."

It wasn't only the bronze statesman next to my office but also the rest of Lisbon's squares, promenades, streets and side streets that turned to ashes. At Estefania Circle, for instance, the remains of the fountain were smoking amid the disfigured buildings. On the video, Edward G. Robinson's gang jumped over the counters and stuffed dollar bills into canvas bags. The man from Braga pulled at the plate with both hands, as if struggling with a recalcitrant bottle cork, but the plastic didn't budge. He pulled a second time, face red, a third time, purple, and still nothing.

"It won't come out," he mewed in terror. "It's probably got rooted into my gums, maybe even into the bone, Holy Jesus, now what?"

"Calm down," I said. "If it jammed itself in, there's a way to jam it out."

I introduced a pair of tight-jawed pincers and a small drill, a pink-coloured sawdust piled up on his tongue, the false teeth dropped out from one side and then the other like the beads of a necklace, and finally the wire that fenced the whole thing in snapped and fell. And now the guy's going to buy another piece of shit like that at another bazaar, I thought, from some slimebag that sells them by the dozen, on display in cardboard boxes, whatever size you want and at the price you can afford, there among the goats and shooting galleries and goggle-eyed families eating cotton candy, while the slimebag's quack brother will gladly take care of your incisors, pound! pound! pound!, under coloured tarps. I glanced at the clock, twelve-forty, and thought:

19

I'm up shit creek, no way can I make it to Lumiar on time. I tossed the denture carcass into the bin full of bleeding cotton swabs and shreds of patients' palates, and the man from Braga, taking the part of a grieving orphan, mournfully contemplated the remains of his truelove. Edward G. Robinson fired into the air and ran out of the bank entrance towards a car where a gangster with a punched-in nose waited behind the wheel. I cleaned the hollow left by the gypsy discount special and smeared on mercuro-chrome like a cure-all for the scratches in his gums, for the breath that reeked of country cooking, and for the cavities which the Bakelite and metal had gutted out between teeth. Divested of the plate, the man's face had shrunk by about half, his now thin cheeks gathered into pleats, his eyes aged, and I thought, How he must have loved that piece of shit in his mouth. "Does it still hurt?" I asked, "Doesn't that feel better now?", and the idiot shook his head up and down as if to say Yes, doctor, that's better, all the while looking at the bin, pining after the cause of his suffering and his joy, and like a man possessed he got up to follow the dental assistant, who was about to carry the wastebasket out the door and down the hall to the basement where the rubbish bins were, and thus they would both exit from my life for ever, because I didn't return to the office that afternoon, and I spent that night in the interior, Alentejo, with my wife and eleven-year-old brother-in-law, and five days later we crossed the Spanish border in one of the rafts of the drowned fisherman to escape the Army and the Communists who wanted to kill us all once the party was over, kill us all in the town's alleys, kill us all on the steps of Santa Maria Church, between its beggars and stray cats, our backs to the cellulose factory in the distance, where long before the revolution the government had promised a dam they never built, leaving the olive trees and rockroses to grow wild all the way to the Guadiana River, in September's yellow, the yellow

20

of a bad photograph or of rancid acid. The assistant disappeared with the denture and with the man from Braga who trotted behind her calling, "Miss! Miss! Slow down a second, you've got something of mine in there," while I took off the smock and retrieved my jacket from the closet, alarmed: Twelve-forty-six, and Mafalda's such a stickler about being on time I'll be lucky if she waits for me. I rinsed my hands under the tap like a priest before he blesses the wafers, I saw the smock fall off its hanger to the floor and didn't turn back to pick it up, and I said "See you later" to the switchboard operator, entrenched behind her counter like an under-the-weather owl on its branch, pissed off at Mafalda, pissed off at me, pissed off at the world, and all set to phone Ana, disguising her voice, saying, I thought you might want to know that your husband's been quite the playboy, that's right dear, the scoundrel has a lover, they've been seen all over Lisbon together, and the girl happens to be a friend of yours. I ran down the steps tucking in my shirt-tail, pulling at my sleeves and tightening my tie. "A doctor shouldn't dress like a tramp," my mother had explained, "You're not a Mickey Mouse student any more," and now I was outside again, where the eighteenth-century statesman was in perfect health, and the buildings too, and no doubt Estefania Circle, its fountain once more dripping water over the bronze that was once more bronze, and I wondered as usual where the car was, because I can never remember where I parked the blasted thing, maybe on this street, maybe the next one, maybe one over, and even if I bump into it I'll keep right on going, completely oblivious, a tin box on four wheels just like all the other tin boxes on wheels, it ought to have my full name and date of birth and social security number stamped in big letters on the hood. The man from Braga, now at his wits' end, was following the dental assistant down the stairs at the back of the building, raising a storm to retrieve his choppers. I

21

began aimlessly scanning parked cars when I saw an old lady buried under packages issuing from a taxi on the other side of the street. "Taxi," I yelled, "taxi," racing across the street and grazing the bumper of a delivery van that veered and stopped short, the driver cursing me with proletarian gusto. I reached the door about half an arm's length ahead of a grey-haired gentleman who huffed, "It's mine, it's mine," and I dropped into the vinyl-covered seat, twirled the handle that lifted a safety-glass barrier between me and the huffer, and ordered the driver to take me to Carriche Street like a viscount commanding a train and looking at the conductor with the saddest eyes and non-smile imaginable, ready to pull a gigantic pistol out of his double-breasted coat and fire fake bullets in Hollywood style.

"It's about fucking time, Nuno," said Mafalda from behind a mineral water and a coffee. "I was just about to get up and leave."

The café was in a small square next to some sort of grocery store and a second-rate hair salon with prudish white curtains pulled across the window. The smoke from the grill devoured the blue-collar clientele; only an occasional arm or neck surfaced from the lunchtime brume. Behind the bar, a cripple supporting himself on the Formica moved from bottle to bottle. Storks wearing overalls and perched on stools pecked at shots of brandies or rose their wings in precarious flight towards the door, heavy with alcohol, tripping on the blue steps of air. A woman's elbow was pushing platters and soups through a hole in the wall. "I got stuck in traffic," I said, and Mafalda, stirring the emptiness of her cup with a spoon: "I could really use some pills, Nuno. My sister's shrink can't see me till next week."

A floating white apron appeared, produced a blurry arm that defecated a menu written in primary-school script, and lost itself among bowls of hot soup like a fish lost in seaweed.

"Won't the pharmacist on your block sell them to you," I

asked, deciphering the snippets, "and let you give him the prescription on Monday?"

Next to us, an old lady with yellow-dyed hair was sucking on fishbones while the poodle in her lap kept sticking its snout in her rice, spilling it everywhere.

"They're all such prigs," Mafalda complained. "They double-check with the doctor, they phone the police, they give you suspicious looks. I told the one on my block to go to hell and stay there."

Naturally there was no more talk of a lump, no more anxiety, no more doctor's appointment. I asked for a steak sandwich, since it might give me time, if I wolfed it down, for a quickie at her place in exchange for the pills I had in my pocket. The waiter yelled my sandwich to the kitchen and vanished again: an aproned fairy with dirty nails and a two-day-old beard. "What?" said Mafalda, "You'll give me the pills at my place? Christ, Nuno, I can't believe you'd dare suggest it, though I've learned not to put anything past you." With an upraised fork, the dyed hair was scolding her dog, whose eyes resembled enormous, wet contact lenses. A knife, fork, glass and napkin were laid in front of me, on top of the paper tablecloth. "I'll have a beer," I said, and the fog cleared somewhat: sitting across from the blonde grandma I could make out a bald grandpa with a dusty bow tie, talking about soccer with a fellow fan who listened respectfully, leaning on the table and nodding his head. "I told you," Mafalda lectured, "that until you leave Ana we can be no more than friends," while I thought about your skinny body fidgeting under the sheets, your assiduous lips, your hollow breasts. The cripple barman hobbled over towards the phone. A lonely heart next to the wall was battling a pork chop. "Anyway," Mafalda said, "if you've got it into your head that you're coming to my place, then you can get it right out, because my mother's cleaning woman is likely to be

23

there today, and you can imagine the flak I'll get if we run into her." The sandwich platter and the beer landed safely under my nose, the mug sweating coldly and the French fries gleaming with grease. I took the pills from my pocket and lined them up on the table: six foil-wrapped cylinders stamped with the name in blue. Mafalda's fingers began reaching, automatically, taken by an uncontrollable thirst; her expression changed, her pupils were dilated, something repulsive and ravenous came over her face. "Calm down," I advised, salting the fries, "just calm down, because for the time being they still belong to me." The hand stopped and trembled, jiggling the cigarette that hung from its nails, a few inches away from the pills. A chunk of ash fell on to the table. The yellow-haired lady set the dog on the ground with great fuss and care, and it promptly lifted its hind leg and showered her foot. "We can try going up to my place," Mafalda suggested in a new tone of voice, "but if she's there and tells my mother, then I can kiss my monthly allowance goodbye." "Bad dog!" the old lady scolded, "Is this your idea of good behaviour?" As I chewed on the sandwich I put the pills back in my pocket. "All the better for me if you don't want them," I said, balancing French fries on the fork: "I need them for my patients, to kill the pain." "No, no, we'll go to my place, it's all right," Mafalda spluttered: "My only worry is the cleaning woman, but so what, let's go." The French poodle sniffed the wall tiles apathetically while the yellow-hair cleaned her shoe with a napkin, sighing the sigh of disillusioned grandmothers. "What did that rotten mutt do now, Joselia?" asked the bald head across the table. "You could at least give me one to take with some coffee," Mafalda begged: "I'm sweating, my kidneys hurt, everything's rocking around inside." Through the brume I could see the waiter, guillotined between two tables, talking to a customer, and I called out like a wailing lighthouse, "A packet of cigarettes and a cup of coffee!"

My chronically fast watch read one-fifty-two, which meant it was one-forty-eight or one-forty-nine. "Nothing, nothing," the yellow-hair said quickly, "just a drop or two of pee-pee that happened to hit my shoe, that's all." I set down my silverware, tore open the foil, and slowly, like a magician, produced a blue pellet. Mafalda, her lips contorted, extended the hand with the cigarette, strewed more ashes, dropped the pill, picked it up out of the sawdust on the floor, and flushed it down her throat in a torrent of mineral water. A tendon bulged on her neck. "It pissed on your shoe?" said the old codger, enraged, "That little shit went and pissed on your shoe?" The waiter wrote out the bill with two inches of pencil in the same primary-school script I could hardly read on the menu. Mafalda began to unwrinkle, her gestures became lively, her eyes smiled. I gave her a second pill, which she grabbed as if on to life. "I'll give you the other pills in your bedroom," I said: "Let me pay this bill and we can go." The wiry-haired animal, feeling danger threatening, jumped back up on the woman's lap. "You bugger," the bald man said, standing up, "you nasty little bugger that dirties up the whole frigging house." "Armindo!" the woman pleaded as she shielded the dog with her rings, "Watch your blood pressure, Armindo!" The man came round the table and shook the woman, whose acrylic fur coat fell off her shoulders and into a pile on the floor. The soccer crony, engrossed in his vanilla pudding, looked all set for a shave. "You're being absolutely despicable," Mafalda protested: "What if they cut off my allowance?, What am I supposed to live on then?" The bar and the stools had emptied out like a beach abandoned, with scattered shot glasses and mounds of nutshells: a sunlit expanse of dregs. "I know it's despicable," confessed Edward G. Robinson in my place, sad and full of pity and oiling his pistol, "but then work out another way that I can see you." The bald man raised his knee and kicked hard enough to make the poodle fly away yelping, its green leash following, into the afternoon of the small square, while the woman yammered, "For God's sake, Armindo, for God's sake, why do you always have to torture the poor thing?" Even the cripple behind the bar leaned over, open-mouthed, to watch the animal vanish into the horizon. We saw a trail of dust and heard a loud thump, then the sudden screeching of a motor cycle. "If you had to sleep every single night in sheets that smell like ammonia," the bald head reasoned with the soccer crony, "then I bet you'd do the same thing, You wouldn't believe how many times I've put the pot on the stove, all ready to throw the beast in, I've heard stewed dog is delicious." "Please, Armindo, stop it!" shuddered the woman. The patrons marvelled at the quality of the kick. "He didn't even brush a chair." "Not even a table." "I've never seen such a clean kick."

Mafalda and I left, her short but quick steps leading the way past horrendous buildings, construction sites, trucks and vans, red dust, shrivelled trees and already roasted pigeons flying along the gutters. She lived a hundred or so yards away, where Carriche Street begins and the city ends. Barren fields stretched along a main road under repair: red and white oil drums and African immigrants tearing up the asphalt with pickaxes. Her building: plants at the entrance, five floors and no lift, walls striped with pastel-chalk obscenities, and two women on the landing—one wearing slippers and the other in mourning clothes—talking confidentially and hushing up when they saw us. "My goose is cooked already, Nuno," Mafalda whispered, "The widow is the cleaning lady's godmother, they see each other all the time." We gave them a neutral smile as we passed, and in a voice they could hear I said to Mafalda, "No ma'am, I'm not suggesting that you've been cheating on your taxes, but I have to do my job, and the government has sent me to verify the size of your apartment," and the two biddies hung on the words, their sharp, steely features focusing on me with fearful respect. We reached the second landing, safely out of view, and Mafalda, while rummaging through her denim handbag for the key, said: "Pray to God Conceição isn't here, pray to God her rheumatism was bad today."

And there we were: the flat as I remembered it, tinged a bit more by tobacco and stinking a bit more of stew. There was the glass door to the kitchen, the door to the living room, the hall leading to the bathroom, and in the shadows the room with a bookcase and shell-collection. There were all the usual odours, the pretentious tapestries, the eternal silence. "Wait in here," Mafalda said, shoving me into a minuscule study with God-awful drawings taped on the wall and cushions and newspapers and magazines on the carpet. I stood at the window, my forehead pressed against the frame, looking at the Africans in their tattered shirts, protected by blinking yellow signals as they sluggishly widened the road with the help of primitive machines which looked like miniature locomotives and detonated like wood-burning stoves. Mafalda and the cleaning woman were talking on the other side of the partition. "I didn't realize you were here," Mafalda sing-songed, "What a lovely haircut, it makes you look younger." The Africans filled holes in the asphalt with shovelfuls of dark gravel, a racket of cans rose and died in the kitchen, and Mafalda said, "I brought a friend home so we can discuss the magazine, I hope we won't be in your way," while I examined an Indian or Javanese doll decorated with feathers and wings, wondering, What magazine? What discussion? A windmill turned on a grassless slope beneath a sky the colour of the earth, without a cloud or streak or bird. "I didn't know you were working for a magazine," responded the unfamiliar voice of Conceição: humble, agrarian and subservient. "Oh, it's nothing much," Mafalda said, "just one of those monthlies for women—you know, lots of

27

photographs, recipes, models, actresses." I looked around in vain for a sofa, a chair, a stool, anywhere to rest my backside, thinking, Am I going to spend all afternoon in this goddam joke of a study?, watching Africans in ragged work clothes lay asphalt?, and I finally squatted down on a cushion, feeling the gun pressing against my armpit. The double-breasted coat squeezed me around the waist. "And does your friend work with you on the magazine?" Conceição asked, and Mafalda's cheeriness became confidential: "He's the Editor-in-Chief, and also a filthy rich builder, I'm trying to talk him into giving me a raise, Keep it down so he can't hear us." Their voices softened and an electric mixer began to whirr, beating eggs in a porcelain bowl. "You can talk over your business in the bedroom if you want," offered the cleaning woman, "I'm all done except for the living room and the kitchen." And Mafalda, briskly, "Don't be ridiculous, Conceição, the bedroom is no place to talk business, What would the fellow think?" And giggles, and probably winks, and probably outbursts of laughter muffled in an apron. She's taken the other pill, I thought, Now she's happy, and free of pain, and thoroughly bananas. And in another minute you'll be here, I imagined as I stretched out on the cushion like Edward G. Robinson, shot dead by the police on a corner in New York, In another minute I'll get to hold you tight, and so I took off my coat and began undoing the thousands of buttons on my waistcoat. "The detergent's all gone," announced the cleaning woman, "Do you want me to walk over to the corner and buy more?" I took off my holster and my shirt; my patent leather shoes, after putting up a fight, finally popped off like champagne corks. "There's another bottle in the cupboard in the study," Mafalda answered, "What do you want to go to the shop for?" And then my trousers, socks, and coloured underpants. "I didn't want to bother the editor," Conceição confided, "I know important people don't like to be bothered," and more winking, more nudging, more giggling. "Enough ceremony," Mafalda said, "Let's just go on in," and a pan clanged, slippers shuffled, they opened the door to the study, and there I was lying naked on the cushion, holding on to the gun and observing them with the saddest eyes in the world.

Afternoon

The cleaning woman, with a face as white as her bleached apron, bumped into every possible piece of furniture as she retreated, and I settled into a more comfortable position, like an old dog getting ready for a snooze. The sun spotlighted my navel.

"You have one minute to get dressed and get out of here," Mafalda creaked like an old stair, her hands holding on to the shelves for support as in a raging sea, surrounded by the wind and foam of her hatred. "Sixty seconds, and not one second more."

Edward G. Robinson squirmed around on the cushion, lifting his head and his anchorless, Pekinese eyes. A flaccid paintbrush, lying slumped on his stomach, ding-donged back and forth in the stickiness. "I've never seen anything so outrageous," Conceição whimpered in the kitchen, her hands no doubt clasped before an oratory of pots and pans, rehearsing an impassioned speech for the mother, whose daughter was holding her arm up at a right angle and implacably counting the seconds of her minute.

"I was waiting for you," I offered in excuse as I thought of her bony ankles and her ribs pushing through her flat little tits. "Is it my fault you marched in unannounced?"

"Thirty-nine seconds," Mafalda answered, unmovable.

"It was a joke, an invitation, a surprise," I said. "How was

I supposed to know that you'd barge in with the maid like that?"

"Twenty-five seconds," Mafalda called out, ruthlessly counting down as if for an atomic explosion. "In twenty-five seconds I'm going to call Ana and spill the whole schmeer."

A pottery something-or-other fell on my shoulder as I hunted through old newspapers and rolls of wrapping paper for my shirt, socks, underpants and trousers. Conceição was still in the kitchen, wailing to the dishes about what had happened: "I just wish it weren't true. If I tell my godmother, she'll faint in horror."

"I still have four pills left," bargained Edward G. Robinson on all fours, looking for his underwear. "You won't find this brand in any pharmacy."

The sun's fire swirled along the window frame. A man with his hands clasped behind his back, reminiscent of the drummers who used to keep time for the galley slaves, watched the pickaxe-wielding Africans with ownerly disdain, calling out orders across a wooden match stuck between two greening teeth. Way away in the distance the farms of Loures mingled with the clouds.

"A man with absolutely no sense of decency, getting himself ready to . . . Lord have mercy," Conceição shuddered. "What will the girl's parents think?"

"Ten seconds," Mafalda warned as she put her hand on the phone. "You've ruined my life. I don't give a flying fuck about your pills."

"Just like my uncle when he was dying in the hospital from a stroke," Conceição said, "paralysed and with a plastic tube and bag hanging from his privates, stretched out on the bed like an animal, like a corpse about to be cut open. Her poor mother's going to die of shame, and her father will mutter and scratch himself for hours on end like he always does when he gets upset. That little hussy, that little hussy."

Edward G. Robinson found a sock among the pencil shavings

31

in the wicker waste-paper basket and scoured the floor for the other one at the same time as he buttoned his shirt. Mafalda picked up the receiver and directed her finger to the dial, hesitating; she dialled the first number, dialled the second, and looked at me, distraught. "Don't ever call me again, I never want to see you again!" She slammed the door and in less than half a second began to explain in the kitchen: "He's a lunatic, a sicko, a madman, he pulls this same stunt everywhere, Conceição, He's already been committed twice, he's not someone you can take seriously, so just calm down, I've sent him away, That's just how he is, you have to learn to ignore it." As I lit my gangster cigar I found the other sock next to the bookcase. It took a while to get my feet into the patent leather shoes, as they kept slipping through my fingers like catfish, the shoelaces trailing behind, and I remembered those strange creatures they showed me as a kid, with antennae or whiskers under their mouths, swimming on the other side of the thick glass. I combed my hair, threw the cigar butt out of the window and into the September heat, and one of the Africans in a ragged shirt picked it up as he walked by, extinguished it against his pickaxe and put it into his pocket, presumably to smoke later that evening, in one of those labyrinthine shanty towns teeming with pleurisies, fluttering wicks and pregnant dogs. "My God, Mafalda, if your father ever dreamed!" said Conceição, distorted by the wall tiles: "He might go and kill the man." The other blacks shot envious glances at the one with the cigar stub until the foreman spat out his match and yelled at them to get back to work. "The poor guy, deep down I feel sorry for him," Mafalda said with a suddenly bleeding heart: "There's absolutely no cure for this kind of sickness, Even electric shock therapy is useless." "Shouldn't we at least call the police and get him out of here?" the cleaning woman suggested, "Who knows, he might come in here foaming at the mouth and waving a knife around." The pickaxes began pecking away again at the asphalt. A truck was unloading boards. The concrete mixers blew round clouds into the air. Edward G. Robinson put the holster in place under his armpit, adjusted the brim of his hat, tugged at his sleeves and checked his tie. "He's not dangerous," Mafalda said, "In a few minutes he'll leave as calmly as he came, just like he always does." I walked over to the door and extended my hand; the latch jerked back with its habitual arthritic stiffness. "Here he comes, here he comes!" said Conceição, "Get me the corkscrew from out of that drawer if you please!" And outside the window: scattered farms, a sky formed by layer upon layer of transparent glass, and clots of tall buildings dotting the hillsides. "There's nothing to be afraid of," Mafalda assured her, "Now stop this nonsense and put down the corkscrew, I don't want you puncturing your hand." I passed the kitchen, which was a chicken coop of terrified flurry, full of flapping arms, flapping skirts and fearful squalls. I pulled the pills from my pocket and threw them into the cavern of ceramic tiles: "Here." The dishwasher alternately stuttered, gulped and belched. The votive flame of the water heater paid homage to a rusting, white-enamel god. "Be careful, young lady, those pills might be poison," and once more I passed the widow in black and the lady with slippers who talked confidentially on the first landing, hushed up, then talked again, peering at me out of the corner of their eyes, simultaneously, like a pair of cockatoos. I buttoned up my coat in the entrance hall to better conceal the festering pistol, and the midget trees of the midget square reeled with colic in the sun. The African with the cigar urinated against the building, while on the third floor Mafalda cooked her hatred by contemplating anonymous letters to Ana, debated whether to push the sideboard off the balcony and on to my head, and tried to convince the incredulous cleaning woman that she really did work for a magazine edited by a stark

33

raving lunatic who took off his clothes whenever and wherever he got the urge. She described the articles she was writing (scandals, royal weddings, high-society parties), her deadlines for turning in copy, the sleepless nights spent in the editorial offices at a desk between a deaf-mute typesetter and a receptionist who was just great, also a great knitter and, the funniest thing, she looks like you, in fact the first time I met her I thought Why it's Conceição!, but of course it wasn't.

Leaning against a toyshop window, Edward G. Robinson looked at the time. Three-ten: what excuse will I make at the office? He jogged over to the taxi stand and a bus whizzed by in a whirlpool of dust: the waiting room would already be full and the dental assistant would already be there, next to the chair, rigid in her impeccable cap and uniform. In the middle of the midget square, a hideous bronze boy petted a hideous bronze dog. Wooden benches were sagging in the heat, and the cleaning woman was swearing, "If that maniac rings the doorbell, I'll hit him over the head with a pan, I'll kill him if I have to." There were two vacant cabs, whose shirt-sleeved drivers talked in the shade, perched on beer kegs outside a café, a fat one and a skinny one, like in a comedy film, unwrapping the white paper of their long sandwiches. I walked up to the vehicles and Laurel said, "Sorry pal, it's our lunch break, try somewhere else," and Hardy, laughing and leaking bread out of his overstuffed mouth: "I've only just started eating." "Don't!" Mafalda begged the cleaning woman, who was threatening a petrified old man with a raised frying pan, "This is the upholsterer who was supposed to come at three. How are you getting on with your rheumatism, Mr Pais?, Don't pay any attention, she's been unstrung all day, Let's see, it's the sofa in the living room that needs attending to. Conceição, put that thing down, Mr Pais is a Jehovah's Witness and a pigeon breeder, you don't have to worry about him doing anything crazy at his age. How old are you now, Mr Pais?" "That guy's face looks familiar," said the skinny one, pointing, "He reminds me of an actor, but I can't remember which one." They studied me for a minute, trying to decide, until the fat and funny one said "How about Charlie Chaplin?" with his tongue all tangled up in saliva-drenched bread, and I felt the gun inside my sports coat, opened the door of a taxi and plopped down on the seat. "Hey, what are you doing?" said the fat one, brandishing his sandwich, "Get out of there, buster, before I really get mad." His and Laurel's indignation loomed in the car windows, one on either side, a door opened, a chequered sleeve reached in and grabbed my knees, two or three lonely pedestrians gravitated towards awnings and the shade of buildings, the sleeve took hold of my ankle and began to use force at the same time as an angry voice kept repeating, "Move it on out, you jerk, move it on out!", and Edward G. Robinson's eyes turned suddenly sad: his waistcoat opened up and gave birth to the pistol, which fired, and like an apple falling from a branch the sandwich fell from Laurel's arm as he wrinkled up to the tune of an accordion inside his shirt. Hardy dropped his mouth open and gaped at me. "I'm in a hell of a hurry," I said in an almost meek voice, thinking In this heat the corpse will melt in no time, evaporating from the asphalt into a fleshy mist. I pointed the barrel to the surviving cabbie, who instantly slid into the front seat. The car took off with the lurching movement of an old woman begging alms before a church, and the gear-lever shook, the roof shook, the air vents and the cigarette lighter and all the dashboard gizmos shook, and I shook, like a helpless doll, lighting up a cigar. We headed downtown, and only as we passed through the park of Campo Grande, after dozens of traffic lights, trees, buses and cinemas, did he dare ask "Where to?", convinced I would direct him to an isolated place in the suburbs, to a garage or a patch of woods where I would raise the gun and pull the trigger again, but I put it away in its holster, and without knowing why, forgetting about the office and the dental assistant and the teeth, in the tiniest, most melancholy and helpless murmur in the world, I answered, "To Beato, please," and the fat cabbie's nape and shoulders slackened in relief, and the taximeter whirred faster, and the shadow cast by the brim of my hat hid the sweet agony in my pupils.

We turned left on to the Avenue of the United States, then right on to Airport Road, passing luxury high-rises and a few dozen veterinary clinics where men in white jackets were examining canary tonsils. Then we went through Lisbon's most cheerless and colourless streets and neighbourhoods—Areeiro, Morais Soares Street, São João Hill, Madre de Deus—to reach Beato, and I didn't think of the cavities that were groaning and overflowing in the office, I didn't think of the time, I didn't even think of where I was going; I thought of Mafalda frantically trying to convince Conceição that the magazine editor was nutty but harmless, I thought of Conceição telling Mafalda's mother about the naked weirdo on the cushion, I thought of the mother, slathered with skin creams, telling her husband after they'd brushed their teeth and were still in the bathroom, each with a sleeping pill in hand, that their daughter was bringing perverts home, I thought of the father meeting Mafalda in his office the next day and saying, from behind his desk, in the absurdly solemn tone of parents: "Last night your mother told me about some hanky-panky going on in your flat, Would you care to explain?"

We came to the river and dived under an iron bridge before beginning the ascent to Beato, passing old factories where women in brown uniforms jabbered at the gates. Advertising jingles competed with one another on the radio in the taxi— "Hanky-panky?" Mafalda marvelled—singing about detergents, sewing machines, latex paint and candy bars. The traffic

36

policeman near the church listened so intently to the redhead owner of the linen shop that he forgot about the traffic. "Turn here," and the sweating fat cabbie went up the steep ramp with palm trees, "Now right." "It seems you've been bringing undesirables home to your place," the father said, fishing for a lighter among the papers on his desk, "and Conceição saw a man with a gun lying naked on the carpet," and Mafalda, all huffy, "Undesirables?, You think I'd bring home undesirables at my age?" There in the midst of some plane trees stood the mansion of Viscount Who-knows-who, with big windows and little windows and shutters and balconies and steps and terraces and a red-suited chauffeur polishing a humongous car at the entrance, and then there were some little houses, the old coal merchant's, a neighbourhood of wooden shacks twisting up the hill where children from Timor sucked their thumbs, dirty and mysterious, and finally the blue gate with plaster-of-Paris swans, at which point Edward G. Robinson flicked his ashes: "This is it. Stop the coach."

"No allowance for three months," Mafalda's father decreed, surrounded by stuffed chairs, English prints and leather-bound encyclopaedias. "Three months of good honest work won't do you any harm at all."

Hardy stopped the taximeter. His eyes were dissolving with panic in the rear-view mirror. As the afternoon wore on, the cloudless and birdless September sky descended on the river and on the freight cars abandoned in the grass and gravel of the shoreside tracks. I set the cigar in the chrome ashtray and flipped through the dollars in my wallet.

"It's no big deal since you have the job at the magazine," Mafalda's father said in his inexorably phlegmatic voice, the words hanging from his lips like ailing plant stems.

"No charge, sir," said the taxi driver, his round face

continually giving birth to new wrinkles of fear. "I can wait around for however long you like. Time is one thing I've got plenty of."

"I'm only a freelance," Mafalda replied. "Any day and, zip, that'll be it."

I gently and humbly opened the door, buttoning my coat and smoothing out my hat as Hardy scooted back on the seat, as far away from me as possible. "With your knack for finding jobs, what's there to worry about?" asked Mafalda's father, "It'll be a cinch, In two or three days some multinational firm will make you an executive." After the gate and the plaster swans I came to a bell that hung under a cast-iron lantern coated with dozens of tiny insects and dead moths. I pulled the cord and a goat bleated in the depths of the house. "You know perfectly well that jobs don't appear out of nowhere," Mafalda retorted, "and after what happened the day before yesterday, I'm sure to get sacked at the magazine." Her father put some papers in the top drawer and left, and Mafalda sat there by herself, hating me, thinking, I should have known that bastard would pull something like this, that he'd screw up my life to get even, sitting there and hating me with mounting rage, remembering me wriggling around naked on the cushion, remembering Conceição's horror and all the breath she'd wasted to persuade her it was nothing, sitting there and thinking that she couldn't phone or write to Ana without losing for ever the last person who would lend her clothes and lend her money, who would listen to her, who would go with her to movies, who in spite of everything conferred on her a shadow of dignity, a social status of peripheral but genuine importance. I pulled the cord again and the goat bleated in the viscera of the house, amid the furniture and the pictures. The taxi raced down via Chelas and past the rows of warehouses on the other side of the tracks and finally disappeared around the wall of a church as the driver kept looking behind, half expecting to see machine guns. The goat bleated a third time in the hallway of my parents' house, and I heard the old seamstress ask "Who's there?" as I looked at the petunias and the unkempt lawn, ratty like the hair on a vagrant. And the arum lilies and other flowers whose names I never learned were just as ratty, and dried up, planted in the parched ground like mouths sick with fever, and I asked myself Why the hell don't they water this?, Why the hell doesn't someone give a damn?, and then the door opened and nothing had changed since my last visit except for the off-colour patches on the wall left by a couple of missing plates.

The seamstress smiled. "Good afternoon, Dr Souza." "Hi, Eugenia, is my mother home?", but the question was gratuitous, because I could hear her voice gushing in the living room.

"She's playing cards with Mr Assirio," said Eugenia, and I thought, Assirio? Assirio?, Must be my father's latest solution to pay off his debts, yet another sucker who fell into the trap like a babe in arms. "They play every afternoon until your father comes home," and I said, "Really?", "And sometimes the three of them eat dinner together in the study," and I said, "Really?", as I walked towards the light at the end of the hall, recognizing all the usual smells and knowing beforehand which floorboards under the runner would creak, until I came to the threshold, feeling the seamstress watching me from her cubicle, where clothes piled up on a wicker table next to the sewing machine. I saw my mother and a well-dressed man not much older than me seated at a card table, each with a drink, and saw her low-cut dress and her shoes and her movements and her perfume, and thought This doesn't seem like just another conquest, Apparently my old man's miscalculated on this one, Apparently my mother's fallen in love, and I noticed the ridiculous way she tried to disguise her age under fake pearls and an idiotic hairdo that only accentuated how fast and far she was decaying, and her raised skirt, her bared wrinkly legs, and the cocksure man, convinced that he had her under his thumb, submissive, mindless, transformed by love into a colourful, moronic clown ready to play the fool on command, and I raised my hand to the holster. I touched the cold metal, decided no, felt in my coat's outside pocket for a cigar, and as I struck a match in the doorway my mother lifted her head and saw me among the sofas and cupboards and cabinets and portraits, with my pinstriped, double-breasted suit, my hat pulled down to my eyebrows and my mouth bent into a circumflex accent of disgust. Her red nails glittered a hello, and Assirio prolonged the gesture with eyes that bobbed past *bibelots* and picture frames until reaching me at the door. His haircut was done by a stylist and his sports coat was irritatingly new and expensive and Italian. "Where's the phone?" I asked, and my mother, smiling a whorish smile, "You could at least acknowledge our presence, you naughty boy," and I nodded at her and then him, and she took up the pack of cards again, "Did you look on the armchair or on the table with the glass top?", while I thought Bet she's already showed this prick the room I had before I got married, with the picture of Ana as a teenager, along with my old toychest, my high-school textbooks and the dictionaries with the dirty words underlined, I bet she made him suffer through all my childhood follies, my crazy schemes, the ha-ha-ha of my unfunny utterances, and Look at my son's toy soldiers, and This is the Meccano set I gave him on his twelfth birthday, and He kept his wind-up cars on top of this dresser—rummaging shamelessly around in my vulnerable intimacy, like a troop commander exposing my cold, shivering sex during inspection.

"Dr Souza's office," the assistant intoned in the requisite hangman's timbre of dental offices.

Edward G. Robinson, chewing on a cigar, spoke standing up

and facing my mother, whose glasses dangled from a tortoiseshell chain around her neck as she moved the cards against the light (the willow trees of the garden tapped on the veranda windows), her profile almost as young as my first memory of it. Her left hand rested as if casually in her boyfriend's, stroking it as if absentmindedly, while her right hand shifted jacks and aces with the agility of a hummingbird.

"Judithe? Hello? Judithe?" I yelled into a spate of loud clicks. "Either the phone company is completely fucked up or the girl at the switchboard is so busy eavesdropping that she mixes up the lines into utter chaos. Just this morning I was getting complaints. We're going to have to get rid of her." The clicks growled louder. "I'm not going in this afternoon. I've got a headache, I'm not feeling well. See if you can squeeze the patients into next week's schedule. Tell them I broke a leg, my hip, six fingers. They won't be satisfied unless it's gory. Make up a catastrophe, something tragic, the death of a child for example."

"For heaven's sake," said the shocked assistant, "isn't a bad case of indigestion enough?"

"They like to suffer, Judithe, they like to be hurt, that's why they come to us. So you have to at least treat them to a tragedy. Think about it: who in their right mind would subject themselves to a dentist's drill? They're absolute nuts, potential suicides, masochistic neurotics."

"And tomorrow's patients?" Judithe asked after a moment of silence in which no doubt she wanly contemplated her uselessly sterilized tools. "Do you also plan on breaking fingerbones tomorrow?"

"No, no, tomorrow we'll give them the pleasure of honest-to-goodness suffering. Don't you see, Judithe? They pay us to hurt them, to hammer and extract and drill, and imagine if there were no screaming—the cavities in the waiting room would feel betrayed."

41

I looked at my mother, who studied the cards displayed on the table with the smile of a triumphant vulture: she had aged an irrevocable twenty years in a matter of seconds, and now she looked like the old lady she was, the kind that drinks hot tea bent over a senior citizen's crossword puzzle. I don't know why, but my body felt part of her body, and the youthfulness of the man planted in the chair, whisky in hand, healthy and fit, was an insult to us both.

"I almost forgot," said the dental assistant, "your wife rang and asked you to call her at once."

The clicks intensified, interspersed with whistles, and I distinctly heard a cough—hidden in a handkerchief or a cupped palm—that scurried away, dodging through words like a rat through furniture.

"Olivia!" I hollered as if into a room full of threatening shadows. "Olivia!"

"She must have got scared and hung up," Judithe said. "Or she had to take a call for one of the other dentists. At heart she's not a bad person, you know. There's no reason to get yourself all worked up."

"I want her out by the thirtieth at the latest. She can go to hell and listen to conversations down there."

"I have your wife on the line, Dr Souza," Olivia cut in with submissive sweetness. "Would you like to tell me the number where you can be reached?"

"I'd like to see how you get out of this one, Assirio," said my mother as she removed her glasses, shimmering reflections which were immediately lost in the confusion of necklaces covering her chest. "I'll give you a biscuit if you can work out what to do with the hearts."

Edward G. Robinson spat a bit of tobacco off his lip, dialled home and listened to Ana's breathless anxiety: "We have to leave immediately for Alentejo. My grandfather's in a really bad way."

"I can't believe it," I said, remembering the square by the church in the fortified village: a ship of stone stranded on a hill, close to the cellulose factory and the treacherous rapids of the Guadiana River. "Your grandfather? He'll bury us all and live a thousand years. I can see him now, behind all our coffins, dressed in his hunting jacket and riding boots."

Assirio lit a cigarette and dropped his hand on to the green upholstery where my mother's hand was. Her fingers climbed up his wrist the way crabs climb up rocks at low tide. Her red-painted pincers played with veins, pinched hairs, and nipped long and affectionately in the hollow of his palm.

"They called me half an hour ago," Ana said. "He had a massive stroke after dinner last night. He went into a coma and the doctor in Reguengos said he'd be lucky if he could hang on till today."

I noticed my mother's legs entwined under the table with Assirio's, her shoes shaking and her net stockings moving back and forth between his thighs. "Come by way of Augusto Aguiar Street and pick up my brother," Ana ordered. "We'll take him with us to the village." And suddenly my father-in-law's electric train, which took up an entire room upstairs with its cardboard stations and celluloid trees, sped around in my head on its little tin tracks.

"I'm at my parents', I'll leave shortly," I said while ankles and knees danced a passionate foxtrot beneath the cards. "I wasn't feeling well, I got dizzy at the office, so I caught a taxi and ended up here. As soon as I'm a little better I'll go get the car and the boy, presuming he's not in class or at judo."

"You've changed the cards around," Assirio charged. "The queen of spades doesn't belong here."

Towards where the sun was setting, past the branches of the acacia tree, the cruel hues of three o'clock had given way to the

43

colours one finds in children's drawings: the sky was sky blue, the sun yellow, the wall white: everything as it should be in the simple order of things. Beginning in the second week of August the turtle-doves, defeathered and fried, stop flying from rooftop to rooftop.

"You don't have to give me excuses," Ana said. "I don't give a damn what you do, not any more. As for my brother, I've already called over to the flat and he's there waiting for you."

"Underneath the cabinets, I'm sure," I said, thinking of my brother-in-law, who was already ten or eleven but still hid under the furniture, squatting among adults' ankles as he drove a miniature bus secured by his fingers.

"I misplaced the queen? So now what?" My mother tried to reconstruct the hand, stumbling over suits and being stubborn. "Why don't we quit and start a brand-new round?"

The telephone hung up on the other end like a breaking branch, and Assirio smiled at a photograph of me as a kid that smiled back at him. A row of bronze objects sat neatly on the mantel over the fireplace, my mother dealt cards and the man, chin in palm, looked on with the blind eyes of an animal driving a millstone. Edward G. Robinson took off his hat, loosened his holster and dumped himself into an easy chair. "Not even a kiss?, Not even a how-do-you-do?" his mother whimpered as her wedding-ring hand pawed Assirio's hand, and I thought, When I was little I caught you kissing my father's partner in the hallway one afternoon: you tiptoed to reach his mouth, your elbows cradled his baldness, your buttocks bulged inside your black dress. I remembered how in those days my father didn't come home on certain nights, and for the next day or two they would shut themselves in the bedroom to argue (we lived in Estrela, and in dozens of apartments before and after, in Lisbon and in other towns: Sintra, Cascais, Loures, Fogueteiro, São Domingos de

Rana, Alcoitão), and I would hear my father imploring her, "Please be friendly to the executive, Isabel, I've got to get this contract." So it was actually my mother who landed his deals, and coming home from school I'd find strange cigars in the ashtray and my mother in a bad mood, stretched out on the sofa staring at the ceiling, and the maids whispering in the kitchen, suddenly shutting up when I walked in and being unusually nice to me, going overboard on the chocolate powder they put in my milk. "The captain likes you, Isabel, try to be a little less irritable with him," my father coaxed: "The commission on sixty French helicopters for Angola—imagine what this could mean for us!" We could fill up the dining room with silver and my mother's wardrobe with fur coats, we could buy a new car, even two cars, I'd get a raise in my weekly allowance. "And if the war keeps on going," my father pointed out, "we can make an absolute fortune. What's so hard about inviting him over for tea?" And it wasn't hard on him, but it was on her, at least initially, until she realized that she could pick and choose her lovers without regard to her husband's business deals, and it was hard on me to sit with them at the dinner table after having seen a government official or a general or some important millionaire slipping naked through the hall to the bathroom, especially since most were old fogies with fat ugly bodies and thinning grey hair all dishevelled. It was hard to be there among the lights and the dishes, watching them eating, drinking, talking to me, asking about my teachers, my classes, my grades, having to look at them, listen to them, answer them, and all the while feeling sick to my stomach, until with the passing years I accepted it all and became indifferent and could talk to them without anxiety and nausea. At the time of this book, seven or eight years ago, when people were fleeing to Brazil by the planeload, I would visit them without feeling any pain or anger or affection, calmly witnessing their slow decrepitude, their listless decadence, their controlled, unspoken rage, calmly ignoring the sheets in disarray at three p.m. or the attempts of my father, dolled up with eyeshadow and face cream, to seduce my cousins' adolescent friends and my own friends and shop assistants and cab drivers, inviting them for a spin in his car or for a weekend in the Algarve, hinting with his intimations, his jokes, his giggles—a suddenly and incredibly effeminate father, who waddled his hips, cried Oh dear! and Oh my!, lit cigarettes like a woman, dyed his hair, varnished his nails and used too much perfume, going out at night on mysterious excursions to Monsanto Park or the gardens near the monastery and returning in the morning with smeared make-up, walking as if on a ledge up the stairs to his room. All of which was punctuated by their trips to the shrine at Fatima, their Holy Week penances, their fasts, their Masses, their friendship with the pastor, their inflexible virtue and their Christian piety.

"You never visit us, you never ask how we are, you never think about us," my mother whined distractedly, worriedly, wondering where she could fit in the six of diamonds. The heat was setting fire to the curtains. The gardener's clippers were amputating branches in the yard. In the alternating lights and shadows of the window, Assirio returned to the table, jingling his ice.

"I came to see you today," I said. "In the middle of the week, no less."

Some of the furniture (in the foyer, in the office, in my bedroom, for example) dated from my childhood, but most of it had been upgraded over the years, piece by piece, with antique cabinets, sideboards, sofas and fine prints—an exuberant, excessive luxury, clinched by a battalion of maids.

"It's your turn, Assirio," said my mother, inserting a cigarette into a holder at the same time as an aproned serf pushed a teacart-plough over one and another rug, making the oils and frames tremble.

"I decided to visit you," said Edward G. Robinson, engulfed by the easy chair, "because I had no idea this jerk would be here."

Assirio picked up a card and smiled, my mother shifted around in her seat with the grace of an anxious dragonfly, floating plates of biscuits spilled crumbs, the maid's apron and collar evoked plaster. "Where's Dad?" I asked, and my words slipped off course, falling acidly to the ground. Assirio, leaning over the cards on the table, took care of the spades, then the hearts, and he opened up spaces by gathering suits and face cards into piles. He was losing his hair, and a wax-coloured area was spreading mercilessly around the crown of his head. It'll probably hit me too, I thought, Time is a heartless bastard, Soon it'll be me examining my head with a pair of mirrors, counting my wrinkles, shuddering at my bloated stomach and measuring crease by crease, down to the last millimetre, the distance separating me from death.

"At the office, where else?" my mother said through a frown. "I can hardly remember the last time I saw him."

"We're going to open up an import-export firm together," said Assirio, who'd won the hand and was vaguely lifting his glass to nothing. "What with everyone in Brazil now, we can do handsomely if we're smart and a bit daring."

"Is anyone from Ana's family still in prison?" my mother asked as her fingers pulled at the skin on her neck. "It's terrible what the Communists are doing to those poor people."

Now the teacart maid ploughed the rugs in the opposite direction, rolling away the clinking objects through doorway after doorway to the dark throat of the hall. The sun dissolved in the curtains, in flakes of dust. The pictures near the ceiling disappeared in the shadows. The room smelled of paint and of my mother's aggressive, antiquated perfume.

"Your father says that in six months at the most we'll have

recovered our initial investment," Assirio said with a blank look, calculating numbers and percentages. "With luck, the money will be rolling in by spring."

"Assirio has some British pounds set aside," my mother said, caressing his hand, running her finger over his double chin, squeezing his nose. "A year from now you'll see—they'll both own gold Rolls-Royces."

The reason we kept moving when I was little wasn't because we were getting richer or because my parents preferred a house to an apartment or vice-versa or because they found out about a place in Lapa for next to nothing and wouldn't it be a shame not to buy it or because the cardiologist recommended my mother spend time at the beach or because the paediatrician said the ocean was off limits for me, but because of thick-headed and uncooperative creditors, because of unpaid bills, because my father feared tax officials, scandal, the courts, jail. We moved to gain time, to outwit magistrates, to flee, while my unflappable father kept assuring us with fantastic schemes, intrigues in the stock market, Arab oil, a jackpot lying under our noses in the pocket of a reserve captain ("Be patient, Isabel, I need your help on this one"), worried, relieved, nervous, satisfied, swindling, begging, arguing, absconding, and this went on for days and months and years at a time. I'd get out of the school bus and find the cook there, waiting for me in her Sunday clothes, while the driver and the other children peered down with their curious noses pressed against the windows. "It's the business of the future," Assirio gloated, "Just wait three months and you'll see what I mean." The cook and I would walk along unfamiliar avenues to a new address, passing street after street, parks, theatres and bronze heroes, on long afternoons that slowly darkened into night. "And I don't consider the general to be all that old, Isabel," my father insisted, "A lot of people live to be older than seventy-eight." Until finally we reached an inconspicuous apartment on the north side of town, in Alvalade, or a decrepit set of rooms in Penha da Franca, or a run-down house in Benfica, with suitcases strewn about the floor, newspapers wrapped around candlesticks and plates, towels at random, and all under the depressing luminosity of shadeless lamps. My father, the captain of our junky and disordered ship, hurled commands to my mother and the maids: "This stays here, that goes over there, That whole box can go to the pantry, Hello sport, did you just get here?, Leave the bedrooms the way they are for now, Delfina." My dusty steps would reverberate in the abandoned rooms. "In another month I'll have your jewels out of hock, Isabel, Pretty soon things will be looking up," with promised yachts, chauffeured limousines, and the cave of Ali Baba around the corner, and in the end it was blocked toilets (the plumber pulled out dripping masses of hair with a hand-snake), falling plaster, and lumpy mattresses on the beds. "What a great apartment," said my enraptured father, "If nothing else, you have to admit that the view is super," and he would step into the birdshit on the balcony and look far and wide until finally spotting, wedged between squalid street corners and sooty chimneys, a blurry and improbable bit of river.

"I've never taken you up to my room, have I, Assirio?" my mother asked suddenly, pointing the way like a friendly tourist guide. "Come along and I'll show you my Japanese fans."

Whenever this happened and my father arrived home, he would cock his ear towards the hallway, listening to the noise and understanding, approving, smiling, then sit down to the paper and a cigarette, reading the news like a deaf man. He leafed through the sports section, revelled in the obituaries until his cigarette burned out, complacently noticed a lighter left on the table, skipped ahead to the robberies and assaults, then pulled a

49

mechanical pencil out of his jacket pocket, while I sat before my afternoon snack of chocolate milk and buttered toast, saying "I'm not hungry, I'm not hungry, I'm not hungry" to a cook who was much younger then and who looked at me, from over by the refrigerator, with a sorry, helpless expression.

My father, sitting with his legs crossed and oblivious to the vibrations in the bedroom, filled in the hieroglyphics and tried to discover the seven differences in the two apparently identical designs that showed a young couple holding hands in a field under the watchful eye of the cow-faced mother-in-law, until my mother came out in her bathrobe, sat down on the chair arm, pointed with her middle finger ("The girl's shoes have stripes in this one, mark an X"), took a sip of his whisky, stretched her arms, yawned (someone or other snored in the bedroom) and untied the manes of her hair: "One more serviceman and I'm getting a divorce, Fernando."

"I don't want to leave too late, not for anything in the world," Ana said before hanging up. "It gives me the willies to think of my grandfather dying and us on the motorway when the owls come out."

"Owls?" I asked absently, thinking about the newspaper puzzle.

"There's one less cloud in the top picture," said my mother, quick-witted. "You're no good at all at these things."

White and red mileposts and phosphorescent warts that separated the asphalt from the fields. Small owls in the towns of Montemor and Reguengos. Owls in the cork trees of the Guadiana River. Owls in the deserted houses on the shore, in the walls and roofs half-eaten by the wind of the waters.

"And the sun," my mother crowed, taking hold of the page. "This one has three more rays than that one."

"That's a misprint," my father contradicted. "You can spot it a mile away. These things have been full of misprints ever since the revolution. It's an absolute disgrace what's happened to the newspapers."

Owls in the chimneys, in the rafters, in the nooks of the castle, in the yellow pits in my teeth, drowned owls floating downriver, my father-in-law's electric trains that ran into the dead birds in the attic and fell over, plunk, on their side, kicking their wheels like black beetles, owls that my father-in-law swept out of the way of his miniature locomotives, owls of ill omen that summoned fever, that made grass and drunks shiver, that woke autumn along the high village wall.

"Misprint my eye," said my mother. "Let's turn to the answers, why don't we, and you'll see."

They turned to Assirio, who said, "It may or may not be a misprint. I'd leave the sun for last."

"Give me back that newspaper right now, Isabel," my father ordered, grabbing for the pages, which twisted and tore. "Let me do the damn thing on my own."

"Getting me involved over something so piddly," Assirio complained. "That pisses me off a little, if you want to know."

"Here it is," said my mother, jumping up and down on rumpled news, waving the answer page. "I was right about the sunrays in your bullshit puzzle."

Bullshit, no: the breeze, the light, the hoopoe birds, the afternoon din, the insects, the riverbank moss and Spain only a stone's throw away. We made the descent to the Guadiana by jeep, pitching back and forth over the jutting rocks, bullshit, no, Ana leaning against a trunk, camera around her neck, smiling, "I could have sworn it was a misprint, Did it or did it not look like a misprint, Assirio?, Go on, what's your opinion?" Bullshit, no: the potters of Arrabalde, my mother-in-law sleeping with her husband's brother, Ana's mongoloid aunt screaming in the kitchen, the cousin who got pregnant by her own father, bullshit, no: what's bullshit is this sun, the paper sun hanging from a beam in the attic, and the owls rotting between cardboard train stations, and the gold-laced cap for the station chief of Vendas Novas, land of soldiers and dust.

"Come now, Assirio," my mother said, screwing off the cap of the whisky, "you're pulling my leg, You expect me to believe that you've never read one solitary book?", and my father, his face shining with a perverse gleam of vengeance, "Why be so surprised?, Some people have no interest in books," and lover-boy, his finger stirring the ice in his glass, "I swear to God, even at the military academy I copied the notes from the kid sitting in front of me, Now I buy *Reader's Digest* at the beginning of the month, give it a quick look-through and presto."

Seven years ago, give or take a little, it was raining dead owls in the attic and electric trains were hanging up on the rails and spilling over, while my bald bull-headed father-in-law straightened out the dented cars. Seven years ago Edward G. Robinson said goodbye to his surprised mother without turning around to look at her ("For Christ's sake, Assirio, you waste your time on the dumbest things"), left Beato without a single glance at its buildings or at the Tagus River, where an Arab or Australian or Congolese steamer would be cruising diagonally towards the sea. He walked a way with his hands in his pockets, thinking of nothing, feeling nothing, seeing nothing, with the weight of the gun in his double-breasted, pinstriped coat, and it was seven years ago that he proceeded to the parking lot on a street parallel the office, in search of his car among dozens of look-alikes, so that he could take his wife and kid brother-in-law to Alentejo Province, to the silent, nocturnal octogenarian mourners with their faces of wrinkled stone, like holm oak trees in the summertime.

Evening

He leaned on the doorbell for the usual half-hour, listening to the absence of voices and steps inside, while sparrows covered my car with a thousand faecal scabs and a rickety lift carried tan-shirted delivery men and veiled widows up and down with the panging movements of an upset stomach. Gisela, virtually deaf, lived in the store-room like a worm in an apple, and the boy kept to the floor, crouching dumbly under tables, so that my in-laws' apartment on Augusto Aguiar Street—rooms full of vases and samovars and paintings, enveloped in an unrelenting gloom—resembled a closed museum on a Monday in October.

After forty minutes had gone by and just as I thought This time something must really have happened (a gas leak, rotten meat, pesticides accidentally thrown into the soup), I heard collusive whispers and footsteps coming from far away, strangled by the curtains spanning the doorways. The asthmatic breathing approached and grew louder, keeping time with the slippers that shuffled across the rugs, and a voice shouted, "Stay under the bed, Francisco. It might be burglars." A deformed, short-sighted eye pondered me through the peephole, while I in my turn shouted, "It's me, Gisela, Ana's husband. Open up!" The intensity and volume of her asthma increased. "Come over here and take a

look, Francisco. I can't see a thing without my glasses."
Scampering steps, a pause, and Gisela, impatiently: "Get a chair,
you dummy, if you can't reach the peephole." A dragging chair,
another pause, the asthma and scampering fading towards the
kitchen for a conference, the scamperer saying something to the
asthmatic, who was sceptical: "Are you absolutely sure it was
him? Take the chair away from the door while I get my glasses out
of the sewing box." Gisela died in the unfathomable, cavernous
distance, but she must have needed a second pair of glasses to find
the first, because she didn't come back. "Francisco," I said, "stop
being a little prick and open the blasted door." The maid shook
receptacles whose contents jingled in the depths: "Have you by
any chance seen my glasses, Francisco?" And I could feel my
brother-in-law, only a few inches away from me, debating
whether to obey his sister's husband or scramble into hiding
behind a floor-length tablecloth, clinging to the comfort of a toy
truck. The asthma finally came back, dragging something heavy
that kept banging into furniture.

"Do you swear you're really Dr Souza?" Gisela yelled through
the door. "Do you swear it over your children's dead bodies?"

A porcelain jug crashed to the ground: "Watch out, Francisco,
without my glasses there's no telling which way this pole might
swing." Various keys twisted and turned in the locks, the security
chain dropped, a bolt slid out of its sleeve with the impetus of the
subway that ran under the building and rattled the bed and cheap
furniture of the concierge downstairs, and finally I was met by a
diminutive, apron-clad centenarian armed with an enormous
rusty pipe and by the eyes of my brother-in-law, peering at me
like a terrified rat from behind a Chinese vase. The drapes over
the windows were so thick and so many that I shivered for a
moment, as if it were winter, and the black mould creeping across
the ceiling evoked rainy autumns.

"Didn't Ana ring to let you know I was coming?" I asked from the doormat, while Gisela blinked and squinted to verify my identity. "Didn't she tell you that her grandfather's sick in bed and that we have to go to Alentejo at once?"

The eyes peering from behind the Chinese vase disappeared down the hallway. The shards from the jug scattered across the marble. Gisela dropped the pipe and bent forward on one foot to get a better look. She smelled of old sheets (mildew, mothballs, lavender) and of old age (ointments, lace underpants and puddles of stagnant urine trapped in deep wrinkles), but her relentless pupils gazed through the redoubled fog of her blindness and deafness to scrutinize me with the diligence of a beaver.

"Is Francisco all packed?" I asked. "Didn't my wife talk to you?"

Gisela came closer, trying to comprehend. My brother-in-law was most likely crawling under some desk, his pocket bulging with a plastic Superman missing a leg.

"Say what?" yelled the maid from the marble floor of the foyer, where she was picking up the porcelain remains with her crab-claw fingers, deformed by gout. Perhaps her ears were like an aquarium in which indistinct sounds, like inscrutable fish, swam at sporadic intervals. "Ana," I screamed, "my wife, Francisco's sister—didn't she tell you we'd be taking him to Monsaraz tonight?"

Gisela, fragile and tiny and hectic, gathered up the pieces into her apron pocket without paying the least bit of attention to me. She went to the pantry to fetch a dustpan and broom and swept up the minuscule porcelain slivers, which she also dumped into her pocket, and only then did she turn towards the endless hallway and miaow into the deep afternoon silence of the apartment: "Francisco, come out from under the furniture and get your suitcase." One octave higher and her sulphuric voice would have rent the curtains from top to bottom.

Seven years later, on the verge of falling asleep while watching television after work, dressed in pyjamas and seated in the easy chair where my father fell asleep before me, I still hear her calling my brother-in-law, who was so quirky as a child, always turning his head to the left and jerking up his shoulder, and who now wears beads and rags from Morocco and paints unintelligible pictures and frequents restaurants in the Old Quarter with an unemployed actress old enough to be his mother. I hear Gisela calling, I wake up with a start, wondering where I am (my wife patiently raises her eyes in resignation), and the exasperated maid yells it out again, "Francisco, get your suitcase," while I wait at the door, nauseated by her insect head and skeletal body, by her broom, by her dustpan, by something in the air choking my breathing. I wake up in my flat in Campolide where she never even set foot and say, "He probably can't hear you, he's probably hiding under the bed in Ana's old room," and Gisela, with a hand to her ear, "Say what?", and I, practically hollering, "He's hiding, the way he always does," and Gisela, standing on tiptoe, "Say what?", and I, bending down and pressing my mouth to her hundred-year-old ear and smelling her smells, shouting at the top of my lungs, "He's hiding!" (my wife stares at me in fright and returns to her knitting), until finally the runt rears his head, a thousand miles away, at the other end of the hall, carrying a knapsack, a mutilated doll, and the moronic expression he always carried. "Can't you speed it up? Your sister's waiting for us," I said, while the sparrows of Augusto Aguiar Street polka-dotted my car with their scabs of shit. The shadows of buildings steadily gained ground as the façades and the sky lost their colours to twilight. "Stop being a retard and get a move on," I said then as now, and Gisela could tell from the look on my face that I was pissed off, because she shuffled over to the pole and hoisted it up, heaving and wheezing, to separate me from Ana's queer little brother, who was tripping over the rugs. "Don't you understand that your grandfather's sick?" I asked that ignoramus who never talked, whom I never heard say so much as a single word, and who now plays clarinet and sells black and green doodles to art galleries in Lisbon, and whose name I run across in the back of the newspaper in reviews signed by Old Quarter colleagues which elevate him to the heights of genius, as if he were capable of painting more than three or four randomly placed lines before which bearded aesthetes go into ecstasy. "Put that thing down," I shouted, pointing to the pole, "no one's going to hurt your little troll," and Gisela, "Say what?" until I finally opened the door, tired of fighting her deafness and afraid she might hurt someone or smash into a china cabinet with that monster of a pipe.

I pressed the button of the lift: a senior citizen with white sideburns and a medal on his lapel appeared, jouncing behind the ancient grille doors and clutching the strings of a white bakery box. "Excuse me," I said politely, "are you going up or down?" As his mouth opened to respond he rose upward and out of sight like a tweed angel—his hairless head, his shoulders and finally his suede shoes—and I thought, A perfect example of Lisbon's doddering seraphim, whose hearts beat to the time of kitchen clocks with enamel farm scenes. My brother-in-law stationed himself by my side under the maternal eye of Gisela, whose deafness made her that much more watchful. He pushed the button, it reversed direction, and again the feeble, pie-carrying angel appeared, plunging towards the street in exactly the same pose, like a film going backwards. "God damn it," I protested, and the wrinkled fellow flapped his sleeves in the quivering cage before vanishing into the centre of the earth. "Unless we wait for this fucking elevator to stop and let the guy out, we'll have him and his fruit pie up here again," so we waited on the landing until we heard the clacking of the folding metal door. "Now," I said, and the cables made a lurching start, then creaked more or less steadily. Gisela stepped on to the landing, the porcelain shards jingling in her apron as she held forth the pipe, determined that I not assault or lame or kidnap the boy without her consent. The lift halted at our floor with the seraph still inside, apologizing: "I was about to open the door when this contraption took off again," and Gisela, recognizing him: "Haven't I run into you already today, Major?" She mixed up days, months, names, things; she died after we'd been three or four months in Madrid. "I'm not a major, I'm a colonel," said the offended old codger while I seized the opportunity to slide open the door, throw in the knapsack on top of the suede shoes and step inside with the boy under my arm. "What's going on? What's going on?" said Gisela, laying hold of the pipe and losing her balance under the weight of the iron: "Where do you think you're going?"

The hexagonal box was just big enough to hold me, the kid and the army officer, who was backed up against a corner, but instead of heading down we were transported to the upper floors, where there were more senior citizens, and Siamese cats, and antique sideboards, and rooms in which people were dying alone in beds meant for two, their tired white arms stretched out in surrender. I pressed all the buttons, including the red one, which set off a senile alarm that died out in an embarrassed spiral: baronesses in mourning tried to grasp on to the grille when we passed by, while Francisco crushed the colonel's bakery box with his shoulder, causing a blood of whipped cream and strawberries to drip out of the corners. Gisela's now close now distant voice threatened the boy: "Your mother's going to hear about this, you mark my words." "Are we going to go up and down all day?" the officer asked in a mousy voice as a multitude of women observed us from the landings, accompanied by nose-picking infants of various ages, identical to the ones found in old photo albums buried in the

58

sepulchral drawers of musty chests. "I hope not," I said, hardly able to shift a shoulder, wedged up against a mirror, "We have to make it to Monsaraz before the funeral." "Funeral?" asked the suddenly animated, strawberry-bleeding colonel, "I hope it wasn't anyone in the armed forces, We can't afford casualties these days," and we burst through the rooftop skylight: I heard glass panes shatter and metal frames snap, and then I felt the emptiness of seagulls in the morning, flying across beaches. "Make this motherfucker go," I told my brother-in-law, "or your sister's liable to bite both our heads off," and he slipped through my legs like a lizard to grab on to the control board of our coffin-shaped rocket, which was soaring over the city towards the clouds. The alarm repeated its laryngitic groan, and I was banished from the lofty seagull heights: the pulleys hurled us to the ground floor with the zeal of a teenager drowning kittens in a tank. We whizzed past the face of an outraged man ("What the hell's going on?, I'm going to report this to the management"), past Gisela scolding us with a shaking finger, and past more nose-picking children before reaching the resplendent steps in the entrance hall, where we were met by the concierge's husband, who had a monkey wrench and was fiddling with the screws of the lift, and by a ferocious mob of widows with shopping bags who let me and Francisco through— now definitely earthbound, dripping whipped cream and red gook from our coats and trousers, like a pair of wounded soldiers or stray albatrosses—but who then stormed the lift, trampling the colonel, whose arms waved like a drowning man's as he pleaded vainly, "Excuse me, Could you let me through?, Excuse me, Excuse me," before going down in a whirlpool of skirts. The warrior and the throng of black skirts shot off towards the skylight in the coffin, pushed off by the wrench that turned nuts and adjusted levers, and by the elevator siren wailing its agonizing lament on every floor. The voice of

Gisela careened down the stairwell like a hard glass marble, pattering off warnings and punishments, and as we stepped out on the street we heard the lift exploding against the roof, the falling debris, the squawking tenants and the soft comet whistling of pastry swirls. And I closed the door gingerly behind me, like a terrorist who's just set fire to a government complex.

Francisco, with his knapsack slung over a shoulder, knitted his brows into the frown of an owl before the afternoon sun, which was disappearing behind rooftops and tarnishing the river. The trees, reflecting nothing, distilled the mysterious wispy green that prefaces night. Cleaning staff were turning on the lights in car showrooms where huge coloured sharks hibernated.

"This way," I said, pointing to a parking strip reserved for an embassy or consulate. In between the Mercedes Benzes with special red plates and the black limos with pleated curtains one could see pallid hands and scarlet, gold-trimmed sleeves saluting in file. The sparrows decorated the roof of my Volkswagen with the afternoon's final round of diarrhoea. A gypsy wearing a polka-dot tie was roaming about with an imitation gold pen in his hand. I opened the door on the passenger side and locked Francisco in.

"A hundred dollars," the gypsy offered, shoving the pen in my face and demonstrating with his dirty paws. "*Cien dólares. Ein hundert.* Real bargain. Diplomat likes very much."

Edward G. Robinson glanced sideways at the pinchbeck as he walked around the front of the car. He felt the pistol in his armpit like a tear welling up in an eye.

"Good pen," the gypsy insisted. "*Très bien.* Ambassador has one. For you I make it seventy-five. *Seventy. Siebensetzen.*"

His clothes accompanied his gestures like fish scales in their nearly transparent imponderability. He smelled of a dead mule and snivelling children in some vacant field with squatting women and a supper of thistle soup cooking over an open fire in a rusty can.

"*Made in Hong Kong,*" the gypsy said, proudly showing me the words and maternally smoothing the lapels of my sports coat. "Chinese make top-notch products. Today is your lucky day, my friend. You can't find anything that comes close to it, not even in Germany."

A man wiping his mouth with a handkerchief walked out of a bar and stood on the sidewalk, lighting a cigarette and watching us. Greenish twigs were burning under the rusty can. A paralytic waited for his portion before a tattered tent, surrounded by chickens and food scraps. I opened the door on my side and moved the gear-lever left and right.

"We in Poland," I said with a subtle Warsaw accent, "only write with yellow spray paint. On walls. To honour the Pope."

"But you can use yellow ink," the gypsy said, "and honour the Pope in a notebook. It's much prettier, and your whole family will join together and clap hands."

The women distributed the soup in smaller cans. A mule attached to the shaft of a cart opened its flan-pudding eyes wide and round. Coloured cloths were drying on a clothes line and a man sitting on a stone drew ellipses in the dirt with the toe of his boot.

"Fifty dollars," the gypsy said, trying to force the pen into my pocket. "Fifty dollars for all that nice gold."

The man on the sidewalk, intrigued, advanced with the crooked steps of a lobster, the kind that sneeze seaweed when you crack open their shells. Edward G. Robinson observed his cigar sadly, fondling the holster with his fat fingertips.

"Forty dollars," the gypsy offered. "Two measly twenty-dollar bills and you'll be rid of me for ever. Or would you rather I call the police for illegal parking?"

Francisco was bending and unbending the elbow and knee joints of his doll. The engine seemed to stand on its toes, lose its balance, regain it with a gymnastic manoeuvre, and finally it started, hemmed and hawed and began to swell, while I activated the windscreen cleaner to dissolve the plaster-coloured continent of bird crap.

"I know some of the men on the force," the gypsy said. "I'm an informer. Don't fool yourself into thinking you can get off scot-free. Thirty dollars and we'll forget it all. I'm the one who'll lose out, but that's all right, let's close the case."

The women chewed on the undercooked leaves. The chickens cranked their necks up and down as they walked. There were scattered heaps of litter and refuse and bottles.

"Just one word from me to the inspector," the gypsy said, grabbing me around the neck, "and you'll be fucked good and proper, my friend. I've filled an entire jail with your type. Twenty dollars. Give me one lousy twenty and we'll be pals like before. Cross my heart and hope to die."

The fascinated lobster twitched his pincers and leaned forward to hear better. The elevator car was flying over the trees, with the colonel's arm waving for help among the widows' black scarves. Ana, fuming, would be looking out of the window to see if I was pulling up next to the drugstores and tawdry boutiques on the ground floor. The gypsy's fingernails reached across the steering column, groping for the key to turn off the engine, and Edward G. Robinson's eyes became gentle and understanding under the felt brim of his hat: a revolver emerged from between his suit's pinstripes, the gypsy said "Holy Jesus" and backed up into a tree, the Chinese pen forgotten in his hand like a beggar's coin, and the Volkswagen leaped off the sidewalk and on to Augusto Aguiar Street, heading towards the roundabout below the park, where the elevator boat, coughing whipped cream, hovered over the statue. The last glob of fruit-flavoured birdshit from the colonel's pie box landed on my car, right in front of the windscreen, and strawberry blood dribbled off the fenders for the rest of the way. I found an empty space next to a fire hydrant in front of our building, between a bookless bookshop and an ice-cream parlour that puffed polar breaths on to the pavement. "Bring your knapsack," I ordered the cretin. Seven-twenty, we dashed up the stairs, and Ana was beside herself with rage.

"Are you aware of what time it is?" she shouted. "Are you aware of anything any more?" Without a word to his sister Francisco shrank and ran under the dining-room tablecloth to wallow in peace with the knapsack and his maimed doll. Some of the bedroom lights were already on, projecting an insoluble brain-teaser of trapezoids and rhombi on to the hall wall.

"I couldn't get him out any sooner," I said. "You wouldn't believe all the hassles." (The two maids in the kitchen bickered as usual like cartoon squirrels.) "My finger went blue from pressing on the doorbell, Gisela threatened to clobber me with a gigantic pipe, and then I was accosted by a gypsy con man who attached himself like a skin disease."

My sons were running around in their pyjamas and bathrobes and didn't stop to give me a hug. Ponchos and straw hats navigated on the balconies of the Bolivian Embassy, homesick for Incas and llamas. The clock we were given for our wedding cleared its throat politely and chimed full and benevolent schoolroom sounds.

"A gypsy? A hundred-year-old deaf maid attacking you? More of your fantastic lies," Ana decided. "I phone you at three, you show up four hours later, and you expect me to believe this cock and bull. I'll send down the luggage and we can stop to eat on the way if there's time."

She tilted her head back and threw open her jaws, balancing on her hind legs like a coyote on a cliff, to howl:

"Francisco!"

The still-bickering maids began carrying suitcases and baskets down to the garage. The hair of the tall one formed a coxcomb which bobbed with her head as she walked, like the gypsies' chickens.

"The car's not in the garage," I said. "I found a space out in the street."

The maids' beady eyes, contrasting bizarrely with their tree-root hands, looked at us stupidly, obediently waiting. The hills of Monsanto Forest Park darkened under the pink sky. The sewers slavered under the mud of the river.

"Then you'll have to put the Volks in the garage," Ana said. "I want to go in the jeep. Francisco!"

I figured he was sitting on the floor in the children's playroom, engrossed in a crab-like spaceship that bristled with antennae, or maybe he'd shut himself in the bathroom, where I'd sometimes caught him pawing at his frozen reflection in the mirror.

"The suspension in the jeep kills my back," I said. "I can't take more than ten miles in those seats."

The maids swayed like dromedaries under the suitcases and baskets, kicking smaller items along as they went. My brother-in-law was finally located next to the desk, wound around the waste-paper basket in the company of Superman.

"We're going in the jeep," Ana said. "The only place I'd drive the Volkswagen out of town is to the junk yard."

Edward G. Robinson stepped between the suitcases and the stairs, suckling on his cigar, when the tick-tocking light on the landing died, reducing us all to an obscure constellation of profiles, where bullets could go wild in a massacre of phantoms.

"Turn on the light," I ordered, gun in hand, pointing uselessly to the glowing orange pill of the switch and feeling my voice hesitating and breaking in the darkness. "I don't want any innocent victims."

"Francisco!" Ana said in the middle of a concert of coughs. "Get your butt over here right this minute."

The taller chicken pushed the light switch and abruptly exposed us all, standing dumbly on the pseudo-marble floor like statues posing at the wax museum. There was no hat brim hiding my face, no smouldering cheroot extending my tongue.

"Have you gone deaf?" Ana said to the maids. "Get the luggage into the jeep. And you, Nuno, stop making scenes and move out of the way. The orthopaedist said your bones are just fine. The X-ray report is in the medicine chest if you care to re-read it. It's under the EKG results and all those analyses you had done when you were having a heart attack a day."

Francisco, forgetting about Superman, came running with his body turned sideways, firing water out of a machine gun. The park and the sky blended into a single shade of lilac, the red flashes of the antennae on the hills swelled and subsided, and the cars on the Avenue began turning on their headlights.

"What I complained about was colitis," I said. "I never particularly worried about the heart attacks. Take a look and you'll also find X-rays for colitis, along with the prescription and the special diet the doctor gave me."

"Hand that machine gun over to your nephews," Ana told her brother. "If you think I'm going to let you take that thing to Alentejo so you can shoot it in my ear every waking minute, you can think again."

The maids elbowed me out of the way and went down the stairs, one after the other, slumping down under the weight of their bundles and sticking out their sullen camel lips. Neighbours dressed as Bedouins were frying croquettes for dinner in tents that came out of detective novels and were lit by *art nouveau* lamps. Francisco set the water-loaded weapon on a sideboard, between two plates loaned us by my mother-in-law and propped vertically on wooden stands. The light on the landing tick-tocked off again, and down below, in the cement underground where I always dreamed of finding faded brown-red paintings of bisons and gazelles on Paleolithic walls instead of chalk scribbles and oil-stains, the maids stuffed boxes and baskets into the four-wheeled heap of shit which I blame for the arthritis I have today. "We'll get there twice as late in the jeep." And Ana: "Don't you dare talk to me about being late." There were puddles of water in the floor cracks, and tyres, broken grilles, used batteries and garden chairs in a corner. Ana grabbed Francisco, who had retrieved his doll, and strapped him down with the seatbelt. The big maid and little maid ("If I get a spinal hernia, it will be your fault") jumped back two steps in perfect synchrony, startled by the exhaust fumes, and fixed their sparrowy pupils on us.

"Your test results are ultra-normal," Ana said. "What I'd give for half the good health you have."

The garage door opened in a percussive outburst of undulating sheet metal, and the maids hurried up the stairs to sleep in our bed, drink our good wine, eat our cocktail snacks and call home long-distance. The streetlamps, in spite of the bats, conferred a golden halo on the proprietress of the fabric shop. In the Bolivian Embassy, Indian women with braided hair were chewing down dinners of corn and cured meat by the light of the chandeliers. We bounced our way to the bridge, along the blueness of evening, and between the two banks of the river dwarfish boats rested on a smooth, solid surface. "See what I mean about the suspension?" I said with Francisco's mouth nearly glued to my neck as his feet thrashed around the baskets and suitcases, "You want us all to end up with slipped discs, is that it?" A centipede tanker veered its stomach to the left as I was about to pass, I braked, and something snapped in my back. "Jesus, Nuno, watch what the hell you're doing," Ana said: "If you keep driving like that, our heads will be smashing into the windscreen in no time." And I thought, I married a real bitch, a clone of her bitch mother, If she had her way I'd live tucked away in an attic, squatting in the stench of dead owls and playing with a set of trains. Arrows and the names of small towns loomed and vanished on the highway: soon we'd reach Setubal, and before long Vendas Novas, and Montemor, Evora and Reguengos: clusters of houses that pulled in closer in the darkness. "If you want to drive this bugger, then we can swap places right now," I said, steering clear of another tank trailer, "but don't try my patience telling me what to do." (Edward G. Robinson's cigar returned to my mouth.) "If you think you're going to do to me what your mother did to your father, then stop kidding yourself." The hot air blowing in through cracks in the jeep body tousled my hair, opened wider my collar, tickled the hair on my chest and was gone: the superhighway ended, the headlights pulled buildings on buildings out of the darkness like extra, unwanted teeth and spat them back into the night in disgust, "And just what did my mother do to my father?" Ana asked in a flat voice, adding, "Careful with your answer, we've got my brother with us," and I decided to keep my mouth shut and my mind on the road instead of telling her that she belonged to a nauseating family of sluts and spineless cuckolds who devoured each other in the mansion by the Guadiana River, fighting over inheritances, hating each other, robbing each other, stepping on each other, destroying each other, all under the caustic eye and cigarette-holder of the grandfather, who watched from his rocking chair with consummate satisfaction as his kingdom fell apart, determined that nothing survive him, determined that no one insolently go on living without him, determined to take his property and his people to the unknown underground where he was going, determined to make them die too, to increase the pleasure of his slow dissolution in the amnesiac mists of the past, for now he was bedridden, watching his family through his only good eye, unable to speak and unable to move but still cracking his lips with mirthful cruelty. "What did my mother do to my father?" Ana insisted in the measured, ironic, dictatorial voice of her grandfather. "What did my mother do to my father? Answer me." Stone walls, owls, trees, lost villages: "What did my mother do to my father?", and it was in precisely the old boy's tone of voice, with the syllables rising and falling, getting heavier, sharp and sarcastic, the old boy that sleeps with your mother while your father, his son, switches trains and builds stations among the attic feathers, your mother that sleeps with her brother-in-law who sleeps with all the women in the family, even the retarded one by whom he had a daughter, and by the daughter had a son, it's been five or six years, and it's no secret, the whole town knows who got your cousin pregnant, who visited her in the middle of the night, who took her on trips to Lisbon not as her father but as her lover. The whole town knows why she went to live in Outeiro, in what used to be the priest's house, far away from everyone else, with the cork oak and the fig tree hiding the entrance, and if I opened my mouth about it you probably wouldn't even flinch, because it probably wouldn't be news to you, because the murmurs of insects and of people reach your ear as clearly as they reach mine, but this grandfather living in you, this piece of him that occupies your person, hates me even more than I probably hate you, pitting my weakness against your strength, my naïvety against your sibylline irony, my affair with Mafalda against the metallic, invulnerable, flawless virtue you hold over me, unless your uncle—the husband of your father's sister—also humped you in one of the mansion's countless cubicles smelling of gin and decay, in one of those old beds whose springs creak while the floorboards shake loose like worn-out bones, your uncle whom your grandfather protects and favours because he does to the family exactly what the old man wants, helping to lacerate you all with exactly the same calm, ruthless ferocity until there's nothing left but an out-of-focus dust of family portraits decorating tabletops and dressers. "So spit it out, Nuno, What did my mother do to my father?", and the lights of Setubal doubled right and doubled left and spread out like a Cassiopeia of dots in the night.

"Shall we eat dinner here?" I proposed.

"Are you hungry, Francisco?" Ana asked her monkey brother. The warm breathing against the back of my neck went away, and looking sideways I saw him crawl over the seat to poke his head in Ana's ear. "Let's stop here," she translated. "He's got to go to the toilet and wants some French fries."

"French fries?" I said. "That's no dinner." I went round a little roundabout and parked the jeep in a lot separating the restaurants from the Sado River. A fleet of buses was sleeping in the revolting rectangle of fish odour.

"What's wrong with French fries?" Ana said, getting out. "Does everyone have to like the pig slop you eat?"

The black water of the Sado spiralled up against the bank in intestinal protest, and the fish smell rose and fell. I pressed my shoulder against a storm door with announcements tacked on the frame and posters for bullfights taped up on the inside. A television blared on a high shelf, and the viewers shifted their eyes away from the commercial to the hips and buttocks of Ana, this woman I could no longer see as a woman, who for centuries, it seemed, made my blood run cold. We sat in the diner's less cruddy section, where two or three men in white jackets were clearing tables. "Go do your wee," Ana told her brother, who was staring at her imploringly, his tongue hanging out, like a thirsty dog. He slid under and out from the table, cantering off to a door with a miniature cowboy nailed under the word *Gentlemen*. One of the white jackets brushed the crumbs from the table with a rag, showering our shoulders and laps with flakes of bread dandruff. "You still haven't enlightened me as to what my mother did to my father," Ana said, and at that very instant something in her expression or something in her voice or some inexplicable intuition told me beyond a shadow of a doubt that she'd also been fucked by the uncle, and that she was still being fucked by him during summer trips to Alentejo or at her parents' place in Lisbon, where Gisela's deafness would preclude suspicion as the little bitch fucked away with the stud bull that the grandfather offered all the little bitches, and it surprised me that I wasn't surprised, that I didn't start raving, that I didn't get upset, that I didn't try to discover or visualize the details, what positions, how often, the dates. "And to drink?" asked the waiter, and I ordered her favourite wine and a juice for the kid, who was returning from the Gentlemen with Superman in his fist, after a post-piss masturbation session, if the innocent and satisfied way he drank his orangeade was any indication. There were no other customers except for a solitary man reckoning with a platter of stewed squid next to the washbasin and the toilets. "Eat some bread and butter," Ana said to Francisco, "and the French fries will be your dessert," and I imagined the hands of her pig-faced uncle, his legs locked around hers, fondling her neck and her breasts. I looked towards the Sado River, which couldn't be seen or smelled but which made itself felt by a suggestion of smell, and I met my diffuse reflection in the dark windows and smiled. "What's so funny?" Ana asked, "What dirty joke has occurred to you now?" "Nothing, I just remembered something, Don't worry about it," and I was still smiling, thinking It's possible my sons are actually *his* sons. And even this hypothesis wasn't enough to set me off. In fact there was something appealing in the idea that I might not be related to that pair of epileptic dumbbells who broke lamps and vases, ruined my stereo needle, scratched up my records, constantly quarrelled, drove their teachers crazy, and failed year after year with an arrogant indifference that comes from your side of the family, so that, when someone would ask How many children do you have?, I hesitated before pulling out my wallet photos of the chubby-cheeked beasts with their straight blond hair and diabolic eyes, saying They don't really look like me, They take after their mother, and I'd reinter the wallet in my pocket and change the topic as quickly as possible. I wiped the smile off my mouth with a napkin. One of the buses began moving in the car park like a foetus in a womb, its headlights flashed on, and a sweeping cone of trees scintillated with mystery. "You think I'd worry?" Ana asked, "If I were a worrier, I'd have committed suicide on the day I married you." The bus left and the trees dissolved into the shadows. A piece of house, undermined by the fish stench, appeared on the flank of a high stockade with battlements, and only the lamps and moths and bats remained, buffing the roof tiles with their bellies. I opened Francisco's door. "What did my mother do to my father?" asked Ana across the jeep, her canvas handbag dangling from a shoulder.

Only after Vendas Novas and its grey and ugly barracks that blemished the night like warts, only after I realized that the kid had fallen asleep in the back, clutching on to Superman and a half bag of fries, only after we re-entered the eucalyptus trees and the absolute blackness that reigned in the countryside—only then did I hear her voice, now supremely calm, in the spitting of the jeep, "What did my mother do to my father?", and precisely at that moment, in the middle of nowhere, a red light flashed on the shoulder up ahead, the helmet of a police officer poked through the window like a cuckoo, Francisco shifted around in his sleep, and the hand of the law hovered under my nose:

"Registration and licence, please."

With the engine turned off I could hear the insects' slow gnawing of silence and the grass's interminable, contradictory, nonsensical speech. A second, identically helmeted policeman appeared out of the darkness, straightening his phosphorescent suspenders. A highway-patrol BMW was just barely sticking out its snout from a forest of holm oaks whose tops blocked the moon.

The first cop examined the papers with a flashlight while his partner walked around the jeep with an illuminated red stick, sniffing like a puppy that couldn't remember where he'd buried his bone. The one with the papers went to the front of the jeep to check the number on the plate, came back to my side, checked the tyres, hung a cigarette from his mouth, lighting it with a lighter that split his face in half like a knife, and practically rested his donkey chin on my shoulder to say:

"The address on your driving licence is different from the one on the registration."

"Different?" I said, incredulous and already out of the jeep, fixing my eyes on the printed words while I searched for a foolproof alibi. "Of course they're different. This one has my home address and the other one has my work address."

"There's no way that could happen," the policeman said as he started for the car that was hidden in the trees. "You've tampered with one or the other," he explained, rummaging in a briefcase full of code manuals and blank tickets. A microphone hanging on the dashboard droned orders and alerts. "So," he said, uncapping his pen, "that means I can slap you with a nice hefty fine."

"Hey Matos," the suspendered cop called over, "this piece of junk is chock-full of violations. It's missing the shades, a mirror, a reflector and lots of other goodies. Not to mention the balding tyres and the flat spare."

Matos neighed jubilantly, shook his mane and stamped his leatherette hoofs in the moonlit landscape of Alentejo as the lights of Vendas Novas shimmered behind us and the halo of an unknown village glowed on the left and hundreds or thousands of mosquitoes danced in my ears. A car passed without slowing down and died in the highway's dark-grey curves. "And what's more," continued the other cop, "his headlights are tilted too high. Turn on the high beams so I can see how they are." Matos sauntered a few steps away, sobbing with contentment, and I could tell from the sound of hissing liquid that he was urinating somewhere in the night, overjoyed that he could fine me for ten or twenty or a hundred simultaneous sins. "How long are we going to be stuck here?" demanded Ana's voice, and the policeman with the red stick snorted euphorically, "All night, ma'am, if necessary." A train whistled but remained invisible, its wheels crying as if out of nowhere, going nowhere, and Ana: "Have you explained to these yokels that you're a doctor?, Have you told them my grandfather's on his deathbed?" I walked a few feet away and unzipped to take a leak as well. "Nuno?" Ana said, "Where are you, Nuno?", and I could hear my brother-in-law munching on a burned fry. "You nitwit," said Matos, so close to me I got a whiff of his after-lunch eructations, "don't you realize you're pissing all over my leg?" A concert of crickets echoed through the woods. "I'm a doctor," I said, deflecting the stream, "I got an emergency call in Lisbon to attend that woman's grandfather in Monsaraz." "Matos," said the one who was hunting out infractions, "step over here for a second, will you?" A nighthawk swam in the starless air. Tiny paws galloped in a ditch. "Hold on while I take off my shoe, This bastard pissed on it and inundated my sock." "Arrest him on an assault charge," suggested the radiant partner, "and let the court decide on Monday, Maybe he'll get that judge with balls who throws the book at everybody, That would at least be some satisfaction." Someone turned on the roof-light in the jeep. "Shit, this actually works," said the disappointed policeman, and Ana, at her acid best, "Get your snout out of here, you swine," and the vaguely visible cop, "A little name-calling, eh?" I shook out the last yellow drops, zipped up and walked toward the headlights, hesitating, when I stepped on something soft and Matos's voice said, "Fuck!, I sit down to dry myself and this shithead pulverizes my fingers." "Add it to the list," the partner said, "The judge'll be so indignant even his gallstones will dissolve." "Nuno," Ana shouted, "either get this smelly pig out of the jeep or I'll smack him on the helmet with the tyre jack, My poor brother's having a fit," but I was already quietly jogging away, hands in my pockets, towards Evora, not on the sandy shoulder of the motorway but five or six yards into the woods, stumbling over stumps and on roots and in unexpected dips in the ground, and the arguing voices got farther and farther away until they were nothing more than high- and low-pitched sounds in the night. One of the cops bellowed, "Let go of the frigging screwdriver and tell me where the hell your husband's got to," and twenty or thirty minutes later I cut back over to the asphalt and stuck out my thumb whenever the headlights of an east-bound truck appeared, until finally a semi-trailer pulled over with a kind of muscular effort, and a pygmy-sized man in the cab asked, "Where you headed?", and I answered, "Monsaraz, but you can drop me off wherever's convenient," and the pygmy said, "How about Evora?", and I said, "That's fine, from there I can get the bus in the morning," and the pygmy hauled back on to the road. Soon the highway-patrol BMW passed us in a rabid gust of sirens, we ended up

74

behind a sluggish station wagon with a million cords tying down the load on its roof, and after a while the jeep caught up with us. We were in the middle of a nameless, lifeless hamlet—a dozen grim houses with kerosene lamps in the windows and dogs that barked at us with their lips rolled up over their gums like shirt sleeves over elbows—and I saw the silhouettes of Ana and the kid and wondered how they'd got rid of the police. Ana probably threatened them with sinister reprisals from her grandfather or with her uncle's friends, I thought, They were probably hurrying to Montemor to report me at headquarters. Tomorrow in Evora, on the way from my hotel to the bus, I'll pick up some dark glasses and a hat, I thought, Tomorrow they'll send agents to my office to arrest me, and my dental assistant will get cross and say What right do you have to barge in like this?, Can't needy teeth in Lisbon be treated in peace any more? "Who are you running from?" the pygmy asked calmly, and I answered, "From that jeep and those police that went by a little while ago." The man struck a match, lighting up his features, and his profile burned—like a piece of paper that crinkles, flutters, shrinks and disappears— until it was just a minute tobacco ember. "If I drop you off at the police station in Montemor, we can save the boys some work," the pygmy proposed, and more grim houses, more dogs, that dry, oppressive smell of Alentejo which the pygmy's cigarette stubs pierced like cloth or cellophane, and the chronic cough of the diesel engine. On the other side of Montemor, with the pygmy carcass lying flat on its back and not so much as one insect of a man on the road, I rolled down the window because I was getting sick of the cellar and manure smell left by the cigarettes, and in the night's rotten holm-oak entrails I found an equally thick aroma of cellars and manure, and I finally ended up on a side street in Evora, where a greasy Asian from Mozambique manned the desk of the foulest hotel I've ever seen. I filled in the

75

registration card with jagged, unreadable letters, followed the canvas shoes down a filthy corridor, locked the door and was met by a ramshackle bed, a broken chamber pot, a tapless sink in the corner, hangers hanging from nails, a window that looked out on to another window, equal and unequal, as if cross-eyed, and a cut-glass bottle of water capped by an upside-down drinking glass. I didn't take off my socks or underpants. I folded my clothes, turned off the wall switch (it zigzagged a jittery spark), groped my way into the sandy, sweat-starched sheets, and spent an eternity staring at the nothingness and listening to the furniture groan, waiting for the sleep that never came.

the day before the festival:

Ana at Night

Side 1

Ana and Francisco arrived between eleven o'clock and midnight, right after the doctor from Reguengos had left, shaking his head as he pushed open the gate under the fig tree that wheezed from what seemed exhaustion. We were in the living room, seated before a turned off television as before a fireless fireplace, when she lifted the miniature cast-iron hand hanging from the front door and knocked as far back as I could remember existing. I heard my daughter say, "Put all the bags in my room" in the same bossy tone her grandfather would have used, I heard the claws of the mute bloodhound contentedly scratching the flagstones in the entrance hall, I heard the criss-crossing sounds of the maids and the steward and Francisco, and even the way Ana's steps thumped the floor reminded me of the old man when he would return from hunting and call out to the cook to come and get the game he'd caught, and he smelled of gunpowder and blood—smells that used to fascinate and frighten me—and of cool forest, of rabbit guts, of early June mornings. Like dancers in a chorus line we turned our heads together towards the door, where Ana stood on the threshold, puffing on a cigarette and smiling the unsarcastic, unironic smile she smiled to mock us, while upstairs my husband's electric locomotive circled over the floorboards, pulling dozens of tin cars after it.

"So what's the story?" she asked, plopping on to the sofa next to my brother-in-law, as if she'd asked What are we having for dinner?, as if she'd left her children and travelled a hundred and fifty miles out of mere curiosity, to amuse herself, leaning over her uncrossed knees to reach for the silver-plated ashtray shaped like a sycamore leaf while balancing her cigarette to the drumbeats of her tongue, as if it were a circus act, doing everything she could to prevent the tip of ashes from spilling to the ground, as if not spotting the worn-out rugs had suddenly become the highest priority in the world, conferring comic pomp on the gratuitousness of her feat, Exactly, I thought, like her grandfather.

"The doctor left a few minutes ago," said my oldest sister-in-law, her spherical body tipping forward in her chair. "He gives your grandfather no more than a day or two."

My other sister-in-law, whose tongue hung out and whose weeping willow of grey hair covered half her face, was wrapping a finger in the fringe of her pinafore. "Didn't your mother tell you about the stroke?" my brother-in-law asked gently, and I hated him as I continue to hate him, even when I'm in bed with him, even when he fondles me and shucks off my clothes—the way my mother used to shuck peas—in the room below the electric trains that whistle and accuse me and inhibit my orgasms at the very moment my body's wild roses are ready to flutter. "Where're Francisco and Nuno?" I asked, and Ana got up and walked towards the door without answering. "Wait a second, I'll go up with you," my brother-in-law offered, and she stopped dead in her tracks like a pony obeying its trainer. "Francisco and Nuno?" I repeated, thrusting my knitting needles into a ball of yarn and tossing it all into the basket, "Didn't Francisco and Nuno come with you?" But my brother-in-law was already at her side, the moron was rocking back and forth with a thread of drool hanging from her lip, and Ana, who had started climbing the stairs: "The one is probably hiding under a table, and the other can go to hell for all I care. Go and look for them, Mother, if you've got nothing better to do." The electric trains paused for a second and then started up, and my fat sister-in-law leaned back in her chair, reaching for the box of chocolates on top of the chest with the silver.

"Pardon my saying so," she said, "but you and Gonçalo have to do something about Ana. Next thing she'll be spitting right in your faces."

The mongoloid stood up and wandered aimlessly about, like a chimpanzee, dragging along a saliva-drenched doll, and then went back to squatting on her straw stool. Quick steps could be heard overhead and the train halted. "Hi Dad," Ana must have said to my startled husband, who would be on hands and knees among his cardboard stations, taking off his stationmaster's cap and scratching his head like a crouching animal without ever so much as opening his mouth, while in the room next door the dying old man was getting frailer by the hour, reduced to one of those sets of animal bones joined by wires in museums, with a card in Latin (we should have taped one to the headboard) announcing the name of the extinct species to visiting schoolchildren.

"She's thirty years old, You think she's going to change now?" I said, concentrating on the sounds from upstairs, to see if they were going to the old man's room or to the mattress where my brother-in-law slept with her on the afternoons when Nuno went fishing at the Guadiana River without ever bringing back a single fish, only trees and crags and burbling water in his eyes—the mattress where Ana was covered with caresses and nonsense syllables identical to the ones that got me excited and wet and unable to resist. My fat sister-in-law, a sunken ship in the overstuffed chair, was no doubt just as attentive to the moans I was hearing, but she never stopped smiling and chatting and receiving visitors, and she proved just how agile a meatball could be on the days she walked briskly to the church on the square, where a handful of nonagenarians were sprinkled at random in the forlorn pews. "And right now she's worried sick, You know how much she adores her grandfather," I said as I thought She likes the old buzzard so much that I bet she hasn't even laid eyes on him, and right now my brother-in-law's taking off her bra in exactly the same way he takes off mine, and soon the chandelier will begin swinging metronomically while my sister-in-law and I keep talking as if we heard nothing, blabbing away, scolding the retard, wiping our noses and gripping our chairs until every-thing—the night, the house, the electric train, the knitting needles and the mute dog licking our knees—stops dead in a succession of howling jerks before returning to normal, all things in the places where as a child I knew them. "That may be," said my sister-in-law Leonor as she fought off the amorous advances of a horsefly, "but she's got to learn to have a little respect, for heaven's sake," and the chandelier began to waltz around with force, a clay figure danced on a shelf, the dog grew nervous, and the sounds must have reached my stupefied husband as trains passed through the tunnels of his armpits, and it occurred to me that Leonor despised me not for being Ana's mother but for being the steward's daughter, for having infected the family with working-class blood, the blood of poverty from which I came, the earthy, backward, impure blood of those who grow up on hardtack and lard. "The family always made too much of her," I offered in Ana's defence, "always treated her like a baroness." The mongoloid was clawing at a fashion magazine. "Everyone always gave her whatever her little heart desired, and this is the result," though what really got my goat was to imagine her naked, squirming under my brother-in-law in the same savage way I squirm when I'm with him. "That's no reason to let her get away

82

with her current behaviour," said Leonor as she listened to the coughs, the humps, the whispers, calculating their pleasure by the frenzy of the chandelier and by the plaster dust falling from the ceiling, and she talked louder and louder as they approached their orgasm, which made us all shudder, even the mongoloid and the maids in the kitchen and the mules in the stables. There was a loud gasp, a muffled shriek, and the chandelier came to a standstill. "You have to assert your authority," said my sister-in-law Leonor with a sigh of relief, "rein her in a bit, To tell you the truth I don't see how her husband puts up with her," and in fact not too much later she was left alone with the kids, those two detestable cannibals who never stopped running, fighting and breaking things, whom I won't have near me, not even in the form of photos. "Either you or my brother should lay down the law," Leonor advised. The retard, having destroyed the magazine, was now chewing diligently on the paper shreds: "You know Gonçalo," I said, "He seals himself upstairs with his trains and doesn't want to hear about anyone or anything," and I remembered when he arrived from Evora carrying a cardboard box, removed all the furniture from the room next to his father's and only appeared when it was time for bed, unfastening the buttons of his uniform with the quiet pride of a twelve-year-old. He slept with a horn tied around his neck, vaguely interested in the fig tree outside the window as he dreamed of train stations and level crossings.

"Poor Ana, she's really upset about her grandfather," my brother-in-law said as he joined us on the sofa, smoothing down his rumpled shirt with his palm. "She's locked herself in her room and doesn't want to be disturbed by anyone."

The wind sometimes blew from the castle to the house, and with it came the mooing of the cows and the bull which had been brought in for the festival and were now entrapped by wooden fences as we were by the walls of the old house, sensing the coolness of the river in the September heat while werewolves slunk through the olive trees, and then I heard my husband leave his railway alcove and heard his steps in the hall, his fist knocking on Ana's door, waiting, knocking again, giving up, his railwayman's boots descending the xylophone of stairs, and I saw the mongoloid drop the magazine and scurry like a baboon, tipping over a lacquer table as she went, towards the switchman's uniform, the commanding cap, the cigarette stub perched on an ear, the whistle and the horn and the signal flags hanging from his hand, as if the wind had suddenly, unexpectedly brought him, along with the cows' guttural protests. The mongoloid circled around her brother, jumping up and down like the stray dogs that circled around the fenced-in cows.

"No late arrivals?" my brother-in-law asked with a worried administrator's frown. "All trains leaving on time, Gonçalo?"

"Get down," my husband ordered his sister, swatting her clutching paws and grabbing a fold in her wrinkled neck to break her loose. "All trains running on schedule, sir. Employee performance, flawless. No passenger complaints to report."

"There's a woman—the daughter of an administrator—who's locked herself in one of the compartments and refuses to come out," my brother-in-law explained. "It's a delicate situation, has to do with marital problems. No need for you to worry about it, Gonçalo—the management will take care of it."

The wind shifted course and carried the cows' mooing far away, but the corroded walls of the castle-turned-arena, looming larger in the darkness, towered over the house roofs and leaned towards us.

"As you wish, sir," my husband said, while his pouty-faced mongoloid sister sprawled out on the floor, winding a corner of her pinafore around a thumb.

"Sit down, Gonçalo," my brother-in-law ordered, pointing to a chair. ("I still maintain," continued my immovable sister-in-law, "that it's not too late to teach Ana a thing or two with an occasional box on the ears.") "Take off your cap and have a drink with us." And I wondered, Do they really not see each other or do they pretend not to see?, Do they really not hear each other or do they pretend not to hear, the way the village pretends deafness to the thousand sounds of the night, to the panic of the cows and the bull that's to be killed at the end of the festival, to the troubled creaking of the fig tree's branches, to the snoring of maids and to the silence of the ancient castle cadaver, that corpse of bones and roots and veins of shale disintegrating in darkness's hollow coffin? My husband removed his cap, set it on his knees, respectfully nodded yes and accepted a glass. "Married or not," Leonor said, "she's still your daughter, isn't she? Forgive me for talking this way, but Ana's insolence has got out of hand." "Drink up, drink up, You're among friends," my brother-in-law told my husband, and there was a knock at the door, the doctor was back, timidly directing his eyes into the living room and bringing the tranquillity of summer with him: "I'd almost arrived home in Reguengos when I realized that I left my stethoscope upstairs, Don't bother to get up, I know the way." Soles on the stairs, soles on the second floor, a rummaging among objects, silence, more steps, the angry voice of the doctor: "Get out from under your grandfather's bed and give me that stethoscope immediately!" "And her brother, as you can see, is following right in her steps," Leonor said, "If he's already stealing expensive instruments like stethoscopes, then imagine what he'll be like when he's thirty." "So how's the brandy?, Not bad, eh?" my brother-in-law said to Gonçalo, "How about another nip before you go back to work?" Francisco, upstairs, was apparently ensconcing himself in the farthest corner possible under the bed while the doctor, to judge

by the clomping, was crawling on all fours and shouting, "Give
me that thing right this minute or I'll stab you in the stomach with
this broom handle!" "Didn't I tell you you're bringing up a
perfect thief?" reiterated the overweight know-it-all. "Certainly,
sir, Thank you, sir," my husband said. "My stethoscope!" wailed
the desperate doctor from out of the tempest of a flailing broom,
"Don't press on it, you'll ruin the diaphragm!", and bodies tussled
on the floor amid exclamations and insults. "If you don't watch
out, in no time at all you'll have another Ana on your hands,"
Leonor said as she rescued a knitting magazine from the hands of
the mongoloid, who'd been stirred up by the commotion upstairs.
"Don't chew on the rubber tips," the doctor begged, "This brand
doesn't even exist in Portugal, it's imported, And will you please
get this dog to let go of my trousers." "You have a truly
outstanding brandy, sir," my husband complimented as he
lowered further into his chair, shy and uneasy, never once looking
at me, "It reminds me of the brandy my father used to offer
guests, though his wasn't as good, of course, I've never had
brandy like this before." "Oh my God, don't tell me that's a pair
of scissors in your hands!" shouted the doctor, "Don't tell me
you're cutting the tubes!" "Hear that?" Leonor said, lifting her
eyebrows toward the ceiling, "You've produced not only a thief
but a sadist." "Must you, Leonor?, My subordinate and I are
trying to have a drink," my brother-in-law conciliated as he filled
the glass for the third time, "What's the harm in a young kid
having a little fun?" Once more the wind brought the murmur of
trees, the howling of werewolves, and the dull thud of cows
ramming their weight against the fence posts. The bloodhound
clawed the floorboards, and by stretching my ear I could hear the
water of the river and the silence of the night, as when I was little
and my parents had turned off the light in my room: their steps
would fade in the distance and the silence whirr till it deafened

me. "If you ruin my stethoscope, I'll put it right smack on your grandfather's bill, and tell this animal to stop chewing on my shoe—it's already destroyed the shoelaces on the other one." "What did my father do for a living?" my husband asked, his eyes turning aimlessly, searching for an answer in the emptiness of his brain: "He smuggled textiles across the border—isn't that right, sir?", and I stood up without looking at them and said, "Let's go to our room now, Gonçalo, It's getting awfully late." ("Not the seat of my trousers!" the doctor squealed, "Order this beast to leave me in peace!") "Our room?" Gonçalo echoed with a perplexed look as he shook the moron, who was clutching his belt: "How can we afford to rent a room in this place?" My brother-in-law's laughter chased away the murmuring leaves and the silence of my childhood, full of vague forebodings and the fear of sleep. I grabbed hold of the striped cap, put it on my husband's head and pulled him, over the retard's protesting grunts, towards the staircase, where decorative plates and clay plaques hung on the wall, and Leonor babbled on, in an ever sharper tone of voice: "If I were you I'd put them into a correctional home." "That's enough," said her husband, "They know perfectly well how to bring up their children," and Leonor, shouting: "Do they? Well I guess you ought to know, since you've been Ana's lover for years now, or do you take me for a complete idiot?"

And as we climbed the steps, passing plate after plate and plaque after plaque, the racket got louder both upstairs and downstairs—the doctor crying over his mutilated instrument and my whiny brother-in-law saying "How utterly ridiculous, Where did you ever come up with this load of rubbish?"—until my daughter appeared in the hallway in her nightgown: "As if the cows weren't enough to keep me from sleeping, now the whole damn family has to make as much noise as possible." And her aunt, shouting from the depths of the ground floor: "You think

I'm blind, you lousy son-of-a-bitch?, You think I don't know about all your shenanigans?" "Break the stethoscope into smithereens if you must, but tell your dog to let go of me," the doctor pleaded, "I'll just die if this mutt bites into my varicose veins!" "This is unbelievable," said my brother-in-law, "Your father's on his deathbed, and here you are going on with these preposterous accusations." Gonçalo blew his horn and waved the green flag for the two a.m. express train. "Mother, do you realize what time it is?" my daughter snarled, "Is this your idea of a good example for Francisco?" And again the wind brought the bull and the leaves and the distant sound of water, and I looked through the window that opened on to the yellow fields turned grey in the moonlight, the thin woods, the crooked teeth of the Guadiana gorge and, beyond the river, the Spanish night. "Any time is a good time to discuss important issues," Leonor was saying in the living room, "You can't imagine the humiliation I suffer because of all your messing around." My grandfather coughed weakly as the enraged doctor and the bloodthirsty hunting dog rolled around, overturning bedpans and showering the floor with fur and hair. "This is an absolute nut house," my daughter said, it wasn't clear to whom: "Stop all this commotion, I can't take any more." "For Christ's sake, Leonor, let's not destroy thirty years of happily married life over peanuts," and it wasn't only the bull and the trees and the water that the wind brought, it was also the laughing and talking in the bar, it was the time of night when my father would arrive home, at the other end of the village, when he'd fight for an eternity to get the key in the door, when he'd knock into the furniture, when he'd pick up the porcelain shepherdess—his best man's wedding present—and throw it on the floor, when he'd explode at the impudence of his own shadow that never left him, when he'd explode at my mother, at me, at the cat that leaped out the window. "If I could prove what you're up to," Leonor was swearing, "you can bet your bottom dollar I'd hire a divorce lawyer, Rodrigo, and screw you good." I was just a girl and deathly afraid of shadows, loud shouting, my father, his vomiting, his scowling. "Francisco!" my daughter said in her grandfather's implacable tone, "You have five seconds to get over here, Francisco." My father would kick over chairs, catch his ankles between the legs and crush the straw seats on his way to the bedroom, but it was the doctor from Reguengos who came out, completely dishevelled, with the dog hanging from his coat. My father banged the door in with his shoulder and through his legs I could see my mother, cowering behind raised covers and opening her mouth to scream for help, opening her mouth as when she wept at my wedding, years later, in an elegant dress Leonor had lent her, overcome with emotion and pride that the family we served had deigned to accept her daughter, that I would now live in the village mansion and she could feel part owner of the fields, the livestock, the olive groves, the buildings, and that now she could call herself a lady, a lady of Evora, a lady of Lisbon, a lady who'd left behind her drunk husband with his ridiculous hat and hillbilly shoes and crooked tie and tweed jacket whose sleeves he was constantly pulling because they were too short, a lady vindicated after years and years of humiliation, hunger, and abuse. "What a laugh," said my brother-in-law downstairs: "As if I wanted anything of yours, As if I couldn't survive on my own!" My mother at the altar, standing next to us and the priest and the organ, wearing the only necklace and ring she owned, bought in her youth at a fair in Beja, happier than she'd even been in her life, with her dazed, incredulous husband at her side, travelling by car for the first and last time as they went from the church to the reception. Ana gave the dog a swift smack on the snout, sending it whimpering to the store-room, and Francisco appeared quietly and obediently, hugging the wall and carrying the stethoscopic remains in his hand. With railway vigilance my husband eyed the bottomless depth of the black rectangle defined by the window. "Apologize to the doctor and give him these pieces of whatever, unless you want to get clobbered," my daughter said, looking in bewilderment at the two metal question marks with black olives on the ends. "You'd better keep your mouth shut," Leonor said, "or I'll appoint someone else to run the factory and the estate." "I just want to know who's going to pay for these trousers," the doctor said, still with a panicky glare in his eyes, "I can manage with another stethoscope, but God knows where I'll get hold of this kind of broadcloth." The mongoloid was waddling up the stairs like a duck when Gonçalo, planted in the middle of the hallway, suddenly raised a flag and whistled to give a departing freight train its signal: metal wheels and brakes poured out white steam throughout the second floor, the breeze of the passing freight cars tousled our hair, pallid lights vanished in the bathroom dark, and my husband, standing tall with his cap, watched the cars as they disappeared into Francisco's room, and the cows returned, along with the smell of grass and thick blood, and the olive trees next to the Guadiana River repeated the words which even now, as an old widow living in this huge house all alone and stooped over by arthritis towards the earth's lungs, I can't completely understand. "Don't worry, in the dark no one will notice they're torn," Ana said, to get rid of the doctor, "When you come tomorrow, bring the trousers so we can work out what the damage is." The dog came around to examine the doctor, and the moron lost her balance, grabbed on to a table covered with silver and china, and both moron and table fell headlong in a storm of flying and shattering objects. My husband wedged the flag under his armpit, and without the slightest bit of interest in the doctor or his daughter or his son or his abnormal sister who followed him with the grunting loyalty of a monkey he announced, "Let's get some shut-eye, Lurdes, There's nothing else until the six a.m. mail train." And so I lay down at his side the way I did every night, winter and summer, for thirty-three years, from the day of our wedding to the morning of his death, in October, when I found him in uniform on top of the covers, with the signal horn lying flat on his chest, so utterly dead that at first I thought he was alive and more stationmaster than ever, patiently waiting for the passenger or freight train that wasn't arriving and that wouldn't arrive, that would not cross over the foot of the bed in its usual chaotic haste, for there was no more haste: its steam had run out. Thirty-three years lying at his side, and for most of those years he wasn't even a stationmaster, only a switchman, assigned to an imaginary switch near the Guadiana River, the eccentric son of my father's boss whom they sometimes interned in a special clinic for switchmen in Lisbon, and he'd come back almost unable to move, or he would move like a Virgin Mary carried in procession by the faithful, looking at people with jelly eyes whose pupils reflected no one, until gradually his old obsession returned and he'd instal himself next to the water mill to change trains' courses, the owner's son whom I'd watch in astonishment for entire afternoons, kneeling on a boulder no more than three yards from the river, where he was busy with non-existent trains, making engine noises with his cheeks, spinning his elbows at connecting-rod speed, stiffening his jaw and frightening the geese with locomotive whistles, until one day he noticed me, considered for a moment, his engines on hold (and I wondered Should I run?), called me, dropped his imaginary switch lever, grabbed me by the wrist, dragged me over my protests through shrubs and grass up to the village, kicked the dogs and chickens with his boots, stepped through the front door of the mansion, where a suit of armour greeted us like a carnival dummy, crossed the courtyard

91

without a word to the servants, passed through a storm door, another door, a parlour with women and a priest chatting over tea among pieces of museum furniture, climbed a worn staircase, walked through one room, two rooms, and stopped in the third, where my father's boss, wearing glasses and a tie, wrote at a desk surrounded by stacks of books and papers and files on the floor. Huge and bald and seemingly blind to our presence, he wore a signet ring on his finger and a look of consummate disdain on his face. A flock of storks sailed past the window, like a school of white fish in blue water, far above the fishing boats in the river, and if I'd stood on tiptoe I could have seen the cemetery, flanking the village wall, with its crosses and pompous idiotic monuments to the dead, and further on, beyond a pergola, the garden of the gravedigger, who worked during the week for the electric company, and a man hoeing, minuscule in the distance, bending forward and straightening up as if controlled by a built-in spring.

"I'm here to report that I'm getting married," my husband, still holding my wrist, announced in his chronically insipid voice.

Past the storks there was Spain, with the same olive and the same cork trees, separated from us by only the rapids, familiar waters to the smugglers I sometimes saw in the tavern, leaning over the bar to talk business with the bar owner, their mouths full of cheese and good deals. Gonçalo's father calmly finished the page he was writing, dried it with blotting paper, recapped his pen and regarded us through his spectacles with an enormous indifference. Even if I broke free of the hand that gripped me, I was sure to lose myself in the labyrinth of the house, bumping into more priests and more old ladies sitting in circles and brandishing teacups, or into the maids that prattled in the kitchen, or into a cupboard full of buckets and rags, or into the empty pantry, occupied by a solitary old woman in a wheelchair, her bugging irises gleaming with affliction. My husband switched a track with his make-believe lever and raised the volume of his monotone to repeat:

"I'm here to report that I'm getting married."

My father-in-law sneezed. The dogs in the yard barked the way they do before it rains, when heavy black clouds roll in from the south, and I thought When is this lunatic going to let me go?, When will I get out of this place, When can I return to my boulder near the riverbank to watch the fishermen coming and going with their empty baskets, skipping from rock to rock with the swift grace of frogs? The old man rang a bell, there was a knock on the door, and in walked my father's helper, unsmiling, cap in hand, sullen and obedient, dragging his club-foot across the stone tiles. There were no more storks to be seen through the window. A large drop spattered against a pane. The dogs ran wild around the medlar tree, their pallid flanks grazing the twisted bark.

"Who does this girl belong to, Bino?" asked my father-in-law, pointing vaguely at me with a flick of his pen as he read over the page he'd just written, making changes in the margins. More drops hit the panes, and the rain changed the colour of the sounds I was hearing, turning them thick and dark, heavy like tears, and I smelled a profound dustiness, as if from a trapdoor that had been shut for centuries. Someone whistled for the dogs, whose barks tumbled in unison towards the house. "Quiet," ordered the whistler, "there're enough bones for everyone." "When it's chicken then they really go crazy," said another voice, "Soon I'll have to give that pregnant one a good kick, That's the only way to teach these mutts," and I thought Even the voices are different: steely and impatient, bristling with rough edges. My husband switched a track on the rug, still holding me tight, and the shadow of the midday express blasted between two chairs, rocking the pictures and shelves and books, and drowning the words of my father's helper in a wind of engine noise that made us all bow, like reeds, towards the tracks.

"Say what?" my father-in-law asked the employee, who'd stuck his fingers in his ears. "My God, Bino, you look like Brother Mario during the novenas at church."

The midday express died out in the bathtub, accompanied by a rueful look from Gonçalo.

"It's Dionisio's daughter, sir," repeated my father's helper. "Should I send one of my nephews to look for him?"

"Bring him here immediately," the old man said from behind a huge law book, encyclopaedia or dictionary. "He's probably in the yard next to the hen coop, tinkering with the combine engine. Unless of course he's drunk."

And once the employee had left, we waited for half an hour, or day, or year, standing before my father-in-law, who opened book after book as if we weren't there, stopping only to insert cigarettes into his holder and light them with kitchen matches buried in the desktop clutter of pencils and pens and erasers and clips and jars and an unplugged lamp with a rip in the shade that resembled a scar. We stared at the grey sky, the metallic river and the cork trees of the rain-beaten landscape that no longer had detail or depth or birds or the man hoeing (he'd taken refuge in a niche in the wall), while my future husband directed train traffic on the carpet, tightening his grip on my wrist with his free hand, and I sniffed and measured the space around me and began to get used to the strange sounds and ghostly presences of the house, to the clanging of the pots, to the smells from the stove and to the dogs' bronchitis, until the rain let up and clarity was restored to the Guadiana and the trees and the cemetery and the pitted stone of the village wall, and from the balcony opposite the window I could make out the church of Santa Maria da Lagoa and the square and the ancient women sitting in perfect stillness on stools outside their houses. My father-in-law began another page, his cigarette ashes fell on the paper, and the locomotives never once distracted him from his writing. He only looked up when my father, followed by the helper, appeared on the threshold, wrapped in an aura of alcohol and filth, afraid and nervous, scratching his armpits with his huge, gawky, moleskin hands: "Did you want to see me, sir?", and the dauntless old man kept writing as if completely unaware of my father's alcoholic paunch pressing against the desk and the halo of wine that illumined his words. The rain was now a light pollen of sad things, startled and stirred by my husband's trains. "Here's the man you wanted, sir," said Bino, reduced to an obsequious voice in the hallway, and then the pen stopped, the old man's eyes floating haphazardly behind the cage of his wire-frames, searching for the eyes of the torn waistcoat and the sawdust and shirt stains that were my father. The pen revised a sentence, halted again, and my father-in-law's pupils focused abruptly, and his face became hard like the bust in the community hall honouring him as a benefactor, among other benefactors equally bald and severe. My father brushed nervously against the desk, looked at me in surprise, looked at the switchman who was pulling a pretend lever to send locomotives away from the bookcase, and tried to make sense of it all in his wine-fogged mind, while my father-in-law put down the pen, took off his glasses, and announced with a toothy smile that held on to the cigarette-holder, "Well well, Dionisio, it looks like there's going to be a wedding around here," and my relieved father said, "Just tell me what to do when the time comes, sir," and the old man, who got more amused as they talked on, "The couple's in such a hurry I don't think we can put it off more than a month or two," and my father, "That's plenty of time to get things ready, Are you listening, Bino?", and my father-in-law, waving his cigarette-holder in the air, squirming with glee,

95

"Don't you want at least to know who the two lovebirds are?, Aren't you at all curious?" The dogs had begun barking and jumping again, whining like children, biting at each other and rolling around in the yard, the storks again hovered outside the window, my husband began fixing a malfunctioning locomotive, and my father looked on dumbly, with a half-open mouth, feeling ill at ease in the luxury of the office, where normally he received orders or reprimands. The underling's calf-shaped nostrils puffed in stupid jubilation, and my father-in-law said, "Don't you have things to do, Bino?", and the frightened little bull took off. The old man stood up with his thumbs in his armpits and filled the office, touching the walls with his hips and grazing the ceiling with the thin hair of his head. His buttocks knocked the leather quadruped of a chair to the floor, dead as a doornail: "You're not interested in who's getting married, Dionisio?" The storks crashed into the window and died. "Why, it's the switchman," he said jocularly, pointing his cigarette at Gonçalo, "That's right, the train nut, And the lucky girl is this piece of scum, this rachitic beauty who hasn't seen water since the day she was baptized—I'm sure they'll make a wonderful couple." My father was absent-mindedly rolling a cigarette. A mongrel bayed next to the turkey pen, a puppy tried to imitate it, and the sounds smelled of wet leaves, the humid house and the recent rain. "Fifteen years old is a fine ripe age," my father-in-law continued, "They can live in the switchman's room, scrunched together in the same bed, and hey, that means I'll soon have a grandchild, Let's just pray to God that it doesn't take after the parents, Go ahead and light your cigarette, Dionisio," and he himself extended a match, and for the first time in his life my father smoked in that office and let himself sink in the floral-patterned chair cushions, with a glass of Madeira in his hand, while Gonçalo dispatched the trains to Spain or to Lisbon, forever clutching my wrist with his bony fingers and the stubborn audacity of a kidnapper.

And my sister-in-law Leonor bought me clothes in Evora, made me take a bath and clean my ears and cut my nails, taught me to brush my teeth, to sit without showing my legs, to talk without the crude language of my mother and father and the rest of my family, who lay out on rocky slopes in the sun, looking down at the river, the fields and the afternoon, and she forbade the maids to tease me or to use my first name, insisting that they call me ma'am instead, and even the villagers began calling me ma'am, and my cousins, who now kept their distance out of timorous respect, also said ma'am, and my father-in-law would thrash his mongoloid daughter, who howled whenever she saw me, and my tummy mysteriously began to grow after a night of blood and trains and pain when the horn squawked in the station of white sheets, and months later my bones split open at the hospital in Reguengos and they brought me Ana, frightfully red, and feeling so tired I wanted to die I looked at her, thinking What's this?, Why did they bring me this monstrous larva? And a nurse wearing glasses said, "Let's try breast feeding," and she unbuttoned my gown, cranked the lever at the foot of the bed, placed the wrinkled and repugnant creature on my chest, and pushed its head against my nipple, and I felt a pair of ferocious, cartilaginous lobster pincers sinking into my flesh. After eight days I returned to the village with Ana, and it was only years later that my husband, promoted to stationmaster and outfitted with a blue uniform, his usual tin horn and two tightly rolled flags, a green and a red one, again grabbed my wrist with the violence he'd once used, dragging me to the riverside, to where we first met. Storks watched us from their nests atop crumbling chimneys, and there were other birds, small brown ones mixed in with the mud, identical to the slime-covered brood of swans that hopped and flew, and there were the hopelessly scrawny trees and cankered boats, the echoing mill and the coughing water, coming and going with the monotonous regularity of a lung as the railwayman said "Lie down" in such a neutral tone that I began to cry, and the cork trees and the undergrowth and his face were all a blur through the lens of my tears, "Lie down," just like that, after all those years sleeping at my side without ever touching me, not even in his unconscious tossing and turning, and he lifted my dress, "Lie down," and ripped the elastic of my underpants, "Lie down," crucifying my shoulders against the wet earth, "Lie down," as he reached into his trousers and fumbled around, and three months later (a year before Francisco was born) I miscarried, ejecting a painful dark paste into a bucket, and I don't think my husband ever knew what happened, occupied as he was with passenger and freight trains, sounding his horn in the middle of lunch or waving his red flag during the Offertory at Mass, a paste in a bucket at a clinic in Evora, and then back to the ancient village on top of the hill, with its three parallel streets and a pillory in the square. I arrived in the old man's car, driven by the ministry's chauffeur, who was my father's age and had the same build and the same hungry, miserable upbringing. He took my suitcase into the house, where I found Leonor and my husband arguing, Ana playing on the floor in a corner, and the blank-faced mongoloid scratching her armpits between two tables. My husband rushed past me, motioning to a train that was running late. The chauffeur deposited my luggage in the bedroom like a falcon dropping a load of faeces in mid-air, and I unpacked my things, changed my dress and combed my hair. The day was taking on the yellows and pinks and lavenders of five o'clock in the afternoon, the cook was trying to quiet down the dogs in the yard, and my sister-in-law Leonor was laying into her husband about some maid. I put on my shoes and went down the stairs, and they hushed up to look at me with inquisitive contempt, side by side on the sofa like parakeets on a perch. The mongoloid was hugging the chewed-up remains of a doll. "How are you feeling, dear?" asked Leonor, and I went out the back door without answering, walking with the slow, sore legs of old women. "Absolute repose," ordered the doctor, a country-bred man who wore a green smock and talked with anyone about anything and especially about hunting quail, for the season had just opened, "Keep to your bed, Lots of soup and fruit, Take these iron capsules and vitamin tablets, and drink one of these ampoules every night." The olive trees on the hillside rattled their leaves as I walked out of the village, passing by the last house and finally by the cemetery and the hoeing man that stood out like signs against the high village wall, behind which there was only a huge concave void. I reached the path to the river and followed it blindly, my chest in pain and my muscles stiff from fatigue, until I smelled the aroma of water beyond the hill where there used to be hangings and saw the birds with sludgy wings pecking in the grass, and I stopped in about the same spot where my husband manned train switches before dragging me home to announce our wedding to his supremely aloof and ironic father. I sat on a boulder and observed three fishermen next to the water mill, each one motionless, each with his dog and his empty basket, and the wind whistled in the trees as it always whistled at that time of year, a playful, almost happy, almost childlike sound. One of the fishermen wound his reel and brought up a naked hook while the other two sat as still as the rocks they were on, and I remembered asking my uncle what he fished for in the Guadiana, and he answered, dead serious, "Mostly nothing." I sat on the boulder, amid tall grass and the heat and the cascades of water stumbling downstream towards the sea, and I noticed a couple of fishermen on the opposite shore, with their likewise empty baskets and an inexplicable, cataleptic patience. I remembered the blood-soaked compresses the doctor pulled out from between my thighs, and it was as if he had pulled me out of my own body, as if all my insides and thoughts and remembrances had dropped into the bucket with the embryo of my son or daughter or whatever it was that had existed in me and would have grown in time, like darkness in the evening. A fourth man arrived from the village and sat down on a folding stool a little way upstream, accompanied by a pole and a basket and boots and the same irrational, hopeless patience they all had—six men fishing mostly nothing on an afternoon whose colour was slowly changing to port wine on the Spanish side and white wine towards the castle—and I heard, just then, a train approaching from the south, and the noise grew louder on the invisible tracks, at first just the metallic turning of wheels and the whooshing of brakes and the chugging engine, and then the hissing steam and the friction of linings and the screeching rails, until the train stopped completely, to let unreal passengers get on and off at the unreal station next to the fishermen intent on their fishing, and a horn blew, a green flag waved, a round clock indicated what was no doubt the wrong time, the engine gathered speed and power, and the locomotives vanished on the track bound for Lisbon, on the track bound for the Algarve, on the track bound for nowhere and nothing, with no one ever knowing but me, a solitary witness to the silhouettes in the windows, to the speed of the axles, to the machine that sells candy and cigarettes, to the ethereal employees pushing their dented carts, until nothing was left but the Guadiana River, the wind, the decayed village walls that crowned the summit, and my husband—with striped cap, blue uniform, and eyes of glass—standing tall by my side and signalling to the holm oaks with his coloured square of cloth.

Side 2

Only after I'd locked the door to our room, unpacked our suitcases, lined up my skin creams on top of the dresser, returned from the bathroom still wearing the headband I use when removing make-up, and found my husband stretched out on the bed, his shoes kicked off and his stomach rising and falling as he puffed on a cigarette—only then did I notice the smell of dead cattle in the sheets, and perhaps in the furniture, and perhaps in the night that twitched on the windowsill like a sleeping cat, re-echoing the music and loudspeakers of a nearby fair.

We'd arrived in Evora an hour earlier and begun to decay with the rest of the two-thousand-year-old town in the first hotel we found: a family operation with vinyl couches and a TV in the lobby and flags of many nations planted in a wooden disc on the counter, where a squint-eyed geriatric whose fingers were longer than conductor batons or lobster antennae handed out keys and had guests fill in cards. We dragged the luggage up two flights, the squint-eyes leading the way with a jittery cockroach's energy, we entered the room, the old man's snare-drum skipping faded out in the corridor along with his grumbling about the tip, and within a few minutes we'd discovered that the light bulb in the bedside lamp was burned out, that the window lock was jammed, that pressing the lever on the toilet made its empty stomach swallow the tank ball in vain, and that dozens of insects patrolled the baseboard, probing the cracks in the wood with their feelers.

It was in Brazil, a year or two after the revolution, that I realized Portugal was as fictitious as my father's trains. My Geography and History teachers had invented Portugal, dreaming up rivers and mountains and cities governed by successive dynasties of playing-card jacks that were eventually eliminated from the game by a round of cowboy bang-bang and replaced by the beard-and-pince-nez crowd, helplessly imprisoned in official oval portraits from which they contemplated the Future with the acute myopia of the elected, and so it was perfectly natural that this all dissolve into the perfectly white peace—shapeless and flat—of the Salazar dictatorship, which is when my family began cleaning up like mice on a binge, getting fat on the cheese of factories and estates. In Brazil I came to understand that poor people—the ones who were short and dark and talked just the way I do—were like my History teachers' playing-card jacks minus the bright colours and diamonds and swords, carrying the string-tied bundles of their puny hopes down one of a thousand streets in São Paulo. It was in Brazil that my childhood and its memories (Sunday dinners, merry-go-rounds, the adults' aches and pains, my enormous fears) gave way to a vague nostalgia for a muddy bank where the Guadiana River gingerly deposited boats and suicides under the birds' shrill fury. And now, back in the Alentejo countryside after all those years, the smell of dead cattle made me suddenly aware of my foolish role as the queen of hearts, fleshless and boneless, stretching her ear across the town's old stones in the hope of hearing some waves.

"What did you say this town's called?" my husband asked in the thin bleating voice of a lamb facing slaughter, while an intolerable intestinal vapour rose from his body. Sprawled out on the bed with those dull, drooping eyes, he evoked a steer's carcass I once saw when going for a walk with my mother and my cousin (whom no one likes to talk about on account of her mother being a mongoloid) between the river and the slope leading up to the castle, a steer whose horns, like a baby's teeth, were just beginning to show and whose body was already swarming with flies and those repugnant little white worms secreted by the earth, twisting their way into the cadaverous depths, a steer which even the dogs rejected, smoking a cigarette, scratching his navel and asking, "What's this place called, Ana?", and the stench from each syllable swelled in my ears, like gas in the stomach.

"Evora," I said, disappointed because the water of the river didn't make the walls tremble, because the squint-eyes' emphysema drowned out the lamentations of the poplar and olive trees, because instead of the Spanish horizon there were pale pink buildings with concrete balconies, and bathroom tiles instead of the church and the town walls. "Evora," I said, and the slaughtered flock of lambs, getting more gooey and putrid by the minute, decreed from the mattress:

"I want to get back to Lisbon by tomorrow at the latest. With luck we can get on a flight to São Paulo right away."

I put the small box of cotton balls into my cosmetics case, found a space for my cleansing cream among the dozens of jars and bottles on the chest of drawers, and looked at him with envy: for years and years I'd dreamed of escaping these sombre cork trees and the werewolves of these nights, and when I finally left for Madrid it was because I suddenly had no choice, because the Communists' rifles were at my back.

"We'll leave for Monsaraz at the crack of dawn," I said, "I'll sign the deed for my mother, and by three or four o'clock we can be at the airport, checking in our luggage."

"I'm tired of old things and old places, Ana," the dead lambs complained, in a voice that dissolved on its pillow like the deceased on their mattresses. "I'm tired of monasteries and ruined castles with turtle-doves cooing in the battlements."

My husband undressed and lay naked on the sheet, a dead ringer for the steer in the grass by the river. Maggots and flies entered and exited the stinking corpse. The breath of the Guadiana whistled in the crevices of the water mill. My mother, my cousin and I gaped in horror at the archway of ribs stuffed with lung paste. There was a man walking past with a basket on his shoulder about twenty yards away.

"Why doesn't someone dig a hole and bury it?" my cousin asked, covering her nose with her shirt sleeve.

My grave-ready husband lifted his disjointed collarbones, from which long threads of tendon and bits of underbrush and moss were hanging, to look out of the window at the town—a statue, a café, and a soundless square—unreal and veiled like the scenery in dreams. Cross-winged flies were flying in the room. An army of ants marched single-file along a meandering crack in the wall. In the distance, above the luminescence of the café, I could see Monsaraz sitting squarely on its hill, hiding houses like oysters behind the fortified walls.

"I'll have one of the farmhands get rid of it," my mother said as she poked the corpse with her foot, infuriating the insects and maggots, "right away, before the dogs in the village pick up the scent."

"I never want to hear another word about Portugal," my husband said as he lay back again in his mattress of bushes and plants, waiting for hungry dogs to show. The first one, equipped with a long snout, approached uncertainly. Others were barking in the hotel corridor, where the geriatric's feet periodically skipped through, nimble as the birds by the river, and I felt the dogs' wet breathing, the swiping of their paws, the sweat in their grimy fur. I thought Any minute now they'll be fighting the flies and the maggots for the dead lamb meat of my husband, chewing until they get to his seaweed entrails, whose face and expression and smile are a mystery to me, and tomorrow morning, when they knock on the door to bring in breakfast, I'll wake up to find a few scattered bones and, a little way past them, the water of the Guadiana tripping over rocks on its way to the sea.

"My mother will lose the house if I don't sign the deed," I said. "You think I'm going to let the poor woman beg around for a place to sleep while we bask in our three-bedroom apartment in São Paulo?"

I hung up the last dress and unbuttoned my blouse, but not my bra, because my breasts have sagged since the two children I had. I set the alarm clock for seven, took off my skirt, folded it over a chair, and lay down in bed as far away as possible from my husband and his aroma of dead sheep, which excited the worms in the flowerbeds and wilted the cork trees and the roses stamped on the bedspread. Never had I slept so close to a corpse, nor felt so threatened by beetles, earthworms and the strumming grass.

"Sleeping in your panties?" marvelled my husband, as he inched over from his side of the bed to touch my stomach with his cartilaginous phalanges. His mouth opened and closed with the sound of swishing seaweed.

"My period started this morning," I lied, turning off the light and transforming the furniture and the things we'd unpacked into colourless, unidentifiable shapes, adrift like wreckage from a sunken ship. "All that bumping in the car is making me bleed like you wouldn't believe." Only the window gleamed in the Evora night, which stretched its reflecting wings towards the roads going south, to Ferreira and Beja. The long-snouted dog snarled as it pawed in my husband's belly. Other faint forms barked next to the mattress or scratched themselves in the corners, waiting. The phalanges withdrew and the sheep smell diminished.

"You can stay here in the hotel," I offered from under the sheets. "I'll go to Monsaraz by myself and be back by lunchtime."

I felt him next to me, advancing and withdrawing in the manner of a corpse, ruled by the tides of shadows. I felt his silent disgruntlement, I heard the mongrels picking him apart, and when the sky shifted in the window panes, becoming tentative and heavy like after a bout of insomnia or fever, I groped for my skirt and blouse among the black hulks of the dressers, put on my shoes, found my purse on the wickerwork stool where I'd left it the night before, and trundled down to the front desk, where the squint-eyes had been replaced by a red-haired teenager wearing a badge against nuclear arms or some such thing and reading a comic-book with his feet propped up on the counter. He looked up at me from behind the fountain of flags with the somnolent gaze of a poached fish sleeping on a bed of carrots and greens.

"You're going out now, at five-thirty in the morning?" the astonished boy asked, protected by Popeye's biceps on the back page. The convex skin of the television screen loomed in the half-light. The municipal grounds crew was watering the bushes around the statue in the square, pulling at their green plastic snakes like fishermen the ropes of their boats at the end of the day.

"I like to get up bright and early," I said, suddenly realizing that I hadn't combed my hair and doing what I could with my hands to unscramble it. I set my bag on the counter next to the tennis shoes, which instantly vanished, and plunged my hand into the silt of diaries, cigarettes, passport and crumpled tissues to get to the car keys, while the municipal fishermen talked in the square with voices that were multiplied, divided and splintered in the circular geometry of the building façades.

"If my husband asks for me," I said, trying unsuccessfully to understand the redhead's badge, "tell him I'll be here by one o'clock at the latest."

And it occurred to me that by that time the hotel maids would have already brushed the ashes of his corpse into a waste bin and shooed away the ants and maggots from under the bed. The redhead threw aside his comic-book and wrote down the message with a brisk efficiency designed to make me forget about his tennis shoes perched on the counter. I leaned forward on my tiptoes and was certain that none of us could ever decipher his scrawl.

"I didn't know they used Egyptian letters in Evora," I said as I jangled the car keys and reached my neck out towards the redhead's T-shirt with its ecological button.

"What?" said the kid, who folded up in his chair like a mussel, jealously hiding his anti-nuclear preference with an elbow. A door slammed somewhere in the hotel corridor, blown shut by a gust that chilled my vertebrae.

"Egyptian," I said. The men who had been watering rolled up the hoses on the back of a truck and took off in a deafening motorized clamour. One of them left behind a loud laugh that hovered for a moment before evanescing into a gaseous swirl. "I didn't know that people from Evora wrote in Egyptian."

"Stenography," he said proudly, capping his pen. (Soft purple bands were appearing on the horizon.) "I took a correspondence course two years ago."

And my mother and the cousin whom no one talks about and who stayed behind with the Communists in the hills of Alentejo were there with me, in the lobby, staring frozenly at the vinyl-upholstered furniture that floated in the Guadiana rapids. A table with a vase of flowers went under on its way downstream. The band that was to play for the festival was unloading clarinets and

trombones from old vans with rust-eaten bodies. The cart with
the bull was wending its way towards the village, passing Outeiro,
where my cousin, who always used sandals and weird clothes and
black nail-polish, lived with an Australian diver among the
indescribable clutter of her blanket-weaving shop.

"And for successfully completing the stenography course," I
said to the redhead behind the Bulgarian flag, "they give you a pet
shark that feeds on the pickled testicles of albino chemical
engineers."

We'd parked on a steep street next to the square because my
husband thought there might be a problem with the battery, or
the spark plugs, or the distributor, or the whole tangled schmeer
of coiled, wiry intestines that has always made me feel horribly
ignorant, and while I was hiking over the shiny wet pavement that
transformed my shadow into a scintillating serpent the streetlights turned off, and I began to distinguish the details on façades,
to perceive sounds non-existent only seconds before and to feel
the oppressive, diurnal breathing of Alentejo Province, its heat
and its torment, as of an asthmatic cat, and the roofs of the
buildings became brighter than the walls, while the smell of dead
lambs continued to pursue me until I sat behind the wheel, shut
the door, inserted the key in the slot, and drove down the hill and
far away from my deceased husband, deposited on the shore of
white sheets by an ebbing tide. I shifted into second and pressed
down on the accelerator, the Ford sneezed like a baby waking up,
I took my foot off the clutch, veered to the right around the
statue's pedestal, and could see the face of the redhead observing
me through the glass door of the hotel. Outside the town walls I
found the road to Reguengos and the new morning, in between
rows of tall thin trees, darkened by the agony of the recent night,
and through the trees I saw the fields, already standing in sharp
relief. I passed two small towns that had gaggles of motor cycles

parked before taverns and a feeling of rural awe in the air, I turned on the radio and turned it back off, because the sound bounced in my head as if a cabinet were tumbling down a staircase, accompanied by the echoes of sleepless nights when we rise up from bed in a phantom stupor to search for aspirin. In Reguengos some German tourists—like lonely white poplars, planted firmly in their gigantic Roman gladiator sandals—were taking pictures of the cathedral, and it was probably seven o'clock, to judge by the temperature, when I stopped in Outeiro at my cousin's workshop, if that's the right word for a disintegrating, squalid shack with a crooked brown sign over the door. A stillness as of gas chambers lurked behind the dust-coated windows.

I rang the doorbell three hundred and forty-seven times until an irritated voice broke the silence inside, hesitating in its own sound as if walking in untied shoes: "The sign says we don't open till nine, come back then." I heard chickens clucking in the bushes next to the patio. A goose led a troop of geese behind a plough and out of sight. Rubbish, boards, assorted bundles, cotton scraps and wool scraps were strewn about the yard. The sky began to turn blue from the heat, and the surfaces of things acquired the oily, static sheen of tar. The Australian diver's bubbling English rose to the surface and sank back down behind the voice, and I imagined a human frog with a wetsuit and a pair of oxygen bottles flapping his flippers around my cousin and twisting at the waist like a sea bream. A heavy object fell from the other side of the wall, the voice complained, "See what you've done?, You've fucked up my loom," and soles shuffled forward and retreated, "Oh," the diver lamented, and immediately there followed another cataclysmic thud, and immediately the silence of a repentant Saint Bernard, and immediately the now possessed voice that screamed, "Get away, you bastard, before you fuck up everything," and after a pause I heard defeated steps withdrawing to a room at the opposite end of the house, and the sky's taut, burning epidermis was ready to burst into a spume of microscopic clouds, gliding slowly southward over the stomach pangs of the eucalyptus trees. The voice muttered indignantly, presumably examining the damage to the looms. I leaned on the doorbell and pressed my mouth to the door, "It's Ana, Open up." A strange breeze—strange because I couldn't feel it—made the domino blades of grass bend flat. More objects fell, and there she was, looking straight at me, looking without smiling, wearing a bathrobe that no doubt doubled as a floor rag and dish towel, and she wasn't seven but fifteen or twenty or thirty years older, with wrinkles at the corners of her mouth and eyes, not unlike the old village women, and with skin—like theirs—of dry worn stone, and I said, "Hi there," taken aback, supporting myself against the car, and she scrutinized me in silence, framed by the fragrance of white wine. She probably doesn't recognize me, I thought, She's probably slowly becoming like her mother, crumpled and full of wrinkles, with thin grey hair taking over her scalp, perspiring an odour of dried faeces and dragging about like a sick kangaroo, and I remembered when she was a girl and they sent her to a reform school in Beja with a white dress and pigtails and patent leather shoes—the mongoloid's daughter whom they'd tried to keep a secret, locking her up in the kitchen with the maids; I remembered the car with the two nuns that took her away and the driver that had a crucifix and a heart bristling with thorns embroidered on his uniform; I remembered my grandfather talking ceremoniously into the black swaddles, scratching his belly; and in the evening, as soon as it got dark, the mongoloid began to howl on all fours in the kitchen, clawing at the wall tiles, until my uncle lost his patience, took off his belt and whipped her, and then they called the pharmacist, who gave her a tisane and put her to bed, and she sucked her thumb and became quiet.

And my cousin continued to stand barefooted, flat-footed, on the brick floor of her workshop, as passive as when she got into the car that took her to Beja, with the same dress, the same pigtails and the same doll under her arm, and I, dressed in a habit, approached her and asked, in a simperingly sweet eucharistic voice, "Is this the young lady?", and I saw the obedient silhouette of the Australian diver (or my grandfather?) walking across the square of Santa Maria da Lagoa Church and towards the nuns cocooned in black swaddles, and I saw myself peering from behind the shutters in the room with the trains, wondering Are they going to send me away too?, Are they going to make me eat turnip soup seven days a week in a dining hall crammed with foster-children and pictures of saints? The diver had flippers, goggles, swimming trunks and a forest of freckles and orange hairs on his chest: "Ana," my still unsmiling cousin announced, like a museum guide before a unique item on display. The limping driver greeted my aunt, my uncle, the servants and my mother, who had just come back from the grocer's with a bottle of olive oil, and I didn't see you again until ten years later, when you stopped in Monsaraz on your way to Lisbon, dressed up the way governesses dressed back then. You marched into my grandfather's office, closed the door behind you, and talked as loudly and fiercely and forcefully as the old man, even getting him to shut up for a change, and you rang the bell for my uncle and insulted him too, and neither one dared to answer you back, and meanwhile your mother, who had been relatively calm during your absence, was screaming at the foot of the stairs as my aunt held on to her and the bloodhound licked her legs and knees, and then a door slammed, and then another, and another, still another, and it was only years later that they told me you were living in Outeiro, awash in the bracelets and necklaces that gypsies sell at fairs but that most country women are too bashful

111

to buy, that you were living in Outeiro like a recluse, a foreigner, a disgrace to the family, and then came the blanket shop, which we found out about at the dinner table from one of the maids, and the conversation just kept going as if you didn't belong to the family, as if you weren't you, as if you were as dead as your mother, whose funeral you didn't come to and whose share of the inheritance you never asked for, and it took everyone by surprise when Grandfather got sick and you showed up at the village tavern with the Australian diver, both so scruffy-looking that all the customers turned round to look at you—the granddaughter who'd come for the funeral dressed in carnival clothes, with rings on all her fingers and a hippie boyfriend at her side—and I supposed that this was your revenge for all the years of humiliation and misery, for the screams of your mother forcibly held back by her sister on the landing, for her anguish and her howling that only the pharmacist's teas could alleviate and that only my father didn't seem to notice, busy as he was raising and lowering his stationmaster's flags at the top of the castle.

"Ana," my cousin pronounced on the threshold, without joy or hatred, as the gabbling goose rubbed against my shoes and the diver's head of red hair with a red Triton beard nodded yes, and I realized that I'd ceased to exist for her, just as my first husband and our two idiotic sons and certain old friends and hazy faces from my childhood had ceased to exist for me. I realized that none of us in the family meant the slightest to her, that we'd become transparent to the point where her arm could pass straight through us, that she didn't know us any more than I know all of you, as now I get out of the car at Monsaraz in front of the church, not far from the mansion with its oppressive furniture and religious paintings, where my mother dodders about with the stiff pains of old age, complaining about her neck, her back, her arms, and her legs as she bumps into sacristy chests like a blind beetle.

"Ana," my cousin said to the redhead before shutting the door in my face, "Ana," sobbed my mother as she put her arms around me and hung on in a pathetic display of gushy warmth, and the plaster was falling off the walls, paintings were missing, plates and salvers and photographs were missing, the plaques were coming loose, and naked nails poked out of the walls like a frightened cat's claws, my cousin's footsteps retreated as my mother's came nearer, I pulled out on to the main road in first gear, stuck behind a tractor on my way to Monsaraz, "Ana," said my mother as she sat down at the table to watch me eat, and I saw how the coming and going of the years—like ocean waves—had eroded and twisted and deformed your bones, how the only thing missing from the scene were a few white gulls in your hair and on your neck and some swooshing water in your bronchial siphons, and halfway through my fried eggs, with the cook's curiosity burning two holes in my back, I heard the halting gait of my uncle upstairs, the dragging of his boots and the thumping of his cane as when the curtain is about to rise on stage, and I thought, as I cut the bread, that decrepitude was perhaps your only remaining link, and I thought of my dying grandfather, seven years ago, in the bedroom next to the train room, his mouth turned sideways in dumb agony throughout the festival and the fireworks and the bullfight, until finally they covered his face with a handkerchief to hide the faunish snigger that lingered from the days when he used to fondle the maids, who would squeal, "Let go, sir, Please, sir, If my husband finds out he'll beat me black and blue." "Ana," said my cousin from farther and farther away, from down below, from Outeiro, in the midst of a swirling cloud of woollen dust, and I turned around without warning, without setting down my knife and fork, to meet the hard eyes of the seamstress and clusters of pupils behind the cracked door, "That's the Brazilian," they whispered, "She's here to help her mother ruin the uncle, to take

113

everything away from him—the house and the furniture and the land and the properties in Borba, in Vendas Novas, in Lisbon," my grandfather would wiggle his cigarette-holder in their faces as they protested, "Stop it, sir, or I'll go and tell your son-in-law," the fig tree's fragrance came in through the window and dripped like a leaking pipe, and when I'd finished eating I took her to the notary public in Reguengos, on the second floor of a two-storey building, above a drapery or sewing shop, or a clothing store with obsequious mannequins sporting outmoded clothes in a display window smeared with fly droppings. We were the only ones waiting, a girl hedged in by file folders typed away, finally we were led to an office with a picture of the President or the cardinal or some hotshot Communist tucked away among the filing cabinets, and the notary—whose circular gestures and that indefinable look of perpetual indigestion from too much fried fish and guitar gave him away as an alumnus of the University of Coimbra— lined up two chairs in front of his aluminium desk: "Do please sit down, ladies." He regally accepted the dossier from the typist, whose disdainful deference suggested she'd been sleeping with him for a long time, then read us some interminable, nonsensical sentences, pulled a pen out of his jacket, and asked me to sign on the dotted line, "next to the pencilled X," sign so that the old man's land and houses and buildings now belonged to my mother and my mother alone, sign so that my uncle wouldn't even be entitled to live in the dilapidated mansion in Monsaraz that would soon revert to the creditors, sign even though no one in their right mind would be interested in barren acres of thistles and ragweed and sun-bleached steer-jaws, nor in buildings whose rafters had been devoured by insects and whose ceilings were breeding grounds for lizards and whose floors had been raised by the insinuating muscles of fig-tree roots such that the view outside the window might be at navel level or ankle level,

114

depending on where one was standing, sign so that my mother would have full rights over a flimsy inheritance that smelled of lavender- and camphor-impregnated sheets no one sleeps in any more. The notary shook our hands with his sticky palm after we'd paid, showed us through the outer office to the door, "Good-day, ladies, My pleasure serving you," and we drove back to Monsaraz, passing a few ugly hamlets that seemed to have paused midway in a relentless slide down from the hilltops, and I thought At last, after all these years, we've finally managed to defeat my grandfather, not directly but through my uncle, who now hobbled around in the attic, cane-first, and as soon as we'd reached the village I asked my mother "So when do we kick him out?", and she, flabbergasted, "Kick him out?", and I, "Mother, you became the sole owner of this house the moment I signed that shitload of paperwork in Reguengos, so kick him out, what are you waiting for?", and she, walking without a word towards the front door, and I, shaking her hard, "You mean I did all this work for nothing?", and my mother, in the humble murmur of the steward's daughter that she used to be and that suddenly reappeared in her loose dentures, in her torn sweater, in her worn sandals, in the ancient, congenital, eternal fear of the landowner, "What work?", and I, about to lose my head, "What work?, What work?, After everything I've done you have the nerve to asked me What work?" The customers in the tavern stared at us out of their red-wine aquarium, a band of chickens ran off squawking, and I, rabid, seizing her and shaking her body's wispy bones that crumbled in my fingers, "What work?, God damn it, What work?, I come all the way from Brazil, run my butt off talking to people I know in Lisbon, force my husband to come with me as far as Evora, get you a deed drawn up so it won't be my uncle who turns you out, make you the owner of all this crap—the house, the maids, the porcelain, the silver and whatever else is still lying

115

around—and you, with the look of a silly moron, ask me What work?, and you, with these disgusting plastic teeth falling out of your rotten gums, ask me What work?, Even the mongoloid knows how to look after her things better than you do!", and she, practically in tears, not for my sake or for her sake, but for the sake of my lousy uncle, that invisible rag that still tumbled around in the attic, "If I kick him out, where will he go?", and I, grabbing on to her dress collar, "Let him go and beg!, Let him sleep on the street!, And if he tries to come back, then set the bloodhounds on him!", and she, overcome with anguish, repeating my words, "Beg?, the street? bloodhounds?", and I, more and more beside myself, screaming in the square on the day before the festival what everybody else already knew, i.e., "Do you mean to tell me that you still like him?, Do you mean that after one hundred goddam years you still haven't got that slimy bastard out of your system?", and she, speechless, motionless, defenceless, spineless, looking at me with the droopy red eyes of a mournful dog, a dog that's always beaten, until I shouted, "If you don't know how to take care of your own affairs then I'll take care of them for you in no time at all," and I left her standing there among the other flea-bitten mutts that were her equals, among the chickens and the goat turds, I left her standing there on a corner, where she deserved to be left, the way cheap whores and scabby animals are left, and I went into the mansion, shoving aside the shadows of servants holding out their arms, went upstairs and stopped on the landing, surprised not to hear the usual bird-like hops of the cane followed by arduous steps across the patterns of the rugs. All I heard was the tocking brass suns of pendulum clocks and the scurrying feet of rats in the roof. What's happened to him?, I wondered as I lifted up drapes and wrenched open cabinets in the nightmarish clarity that inhabits ancient buildings like a sidelong smile, and I kicked aside hat boxes, moth-eaten curtains, shoes missing their heels, backgammon boards, and lacework that evaporated into the air when touched, I looked under staircases, in nooks and in corners, startling the spiders, turned porcelain doorknobs that fell off into my hand, and shouted "Uncle" and nothing, not the slightest sound, not the slightest shuffle, the slightest groan, the slightest cough, only my echo in the deserted rooms as I shouted "Uncle, I need to talk to you, it's important, where are you?", because I knew he was hidden somewhere or other, maybe in this cupboard, no, maybe under this table, again no, he was eluding me the way crickets elude slippers out to step on them, and through the window of my grandfather's office I saw my mother sitting on the steps of the church like a beggar, How humiliating, I thought, to be her daughter, to be the daughter of hirelings and smugglers and tramps like her, "Uncle," I yelled from next to the piano, "Come out immediately, Uncle," that lecher I hadn't seen in seven years, since my grandfather's death, that lecher who lied to us all, abused us all, slept with us all, deceiving us with false promises, false moans, false secrets as he pawed and stripped us and penetrated into our thighs like a stem into a vase, and who mounted me on the very evening my brother and I arrived from Lisbon to be there for my grandfather's final hours, mounted me as if I were a mule, in the very next room to the dying man's, while my father's electric trains choo-chooed near by, mounted me like he did all the women in the family, with indifferent brutality, "Uncle," I yelled, "I'm throwing you out of this house, Uncle," and my mother sitting on the steps of the church, engulfed by chickens and stray dogs, while I opened drawers, raised the leather lid of a trunk, lifted a bench seat and found wreckage, residue, shards of plates, corpses of pictures, "Come on out, you old goat," I challenged, "Show the points of your horns, you coward!", and the only place left to look was the main sitting room, where I found the trembling glass tears of a chandelier that dangled by a lone wire, the overstuffed chairs covered with tattered velvet, the deplumed harp leaning against the wall, photos of white-eyed girls observing nothing, the collection of antique guns secured by hooks onto a sort of hanging mat, and bookcases and more bookcases, and I peeked into the hutch, hit my knuckles against the fake arches whose hollowness resonated like empty coffins, knelt down to look under a couch and nothing, and so I kicked in the door to the walk-in closet while holding up one of the muskets from the hanging mat, switched on the light, and found him scrunched up in a corner between two baskets, using his cane as a shield and looking infinitely older, having aged more than I ever dreamed possible in seven years, shrivelled and hunched over, his old boots almost in shreds, there in the corner, inert and impassive, waiting for the first blow, like a sad, bony, resigned ox.

The round clock above the Nepalese flag to the left of the redhead kid in the hotel in Evora said it was four-thirty, which meant that it was either earlier or later (I've travelled enough to know never to trust a hotel clock), and I went upstairs to our room, which was locked, and beat on the door for an exasperating eternity, first with my knuckles, then my palms, and finally with my clenched fists, feeling the dead animal smell drift towards me and watching my cousin bend over my husband who rotted in the grass as my mother's voice forbade her to touch it and hearing the Guadiana rapids nearby, the siphon gurgle of the abandoned water mill, the sun on the rocks and the silence of the trees and, after a rattle of bedsprings ("Just a second"), the corpse appeared in the doorway with a towel wrapped around its waist and meadow flies circling its head, and my cousin poked a stick into the carcass, "What is it?" said my still-sleeping husband in a floating, translucent tone of voice while he tried to guess the time by the tonality of light in the window. "Leave it alone," my mother told my cousin, "Didn't anyone ever tell you that dead animals get their revenge at night by howling in your bedroom, or giving you a skin disease, or charging at you in your dreams with their horns?" "It took a little longer than I thought," I said as I went to wash my hands, brush my teeth, fit all the bottles and tubes in the cosmetic case and pack my clothes in the suitcase, "but if we leave right away for Lisbon I bet we can still make the plane, so let's phone and get them to pick up the car at the airport, and we can be on our way to São Paulo." "I've changed my mind," my husband said, making himself comfortable on the bushes of the mattress as a battalion of ants crawled up his thigh and around his dog-chewed ears, "We'll spend the night in Evora and work out the logistics tomorrow, Today's flights will all have left by the time we can make it to Lisbon." The twilight's first owl flew through the holm oaks while the crickets hidden in the boxwoods droned, afraid. The shadow cast by the castle walls grew like yeast and stretched towards the river. One or two lights turned on in the village high above us, my mother tried to chase away the gnats with her hand, "Time to go," she ordered, "Your grandfather's probably huffing and puffing at the table," waiting for us in that huge dining room full of pictures which I went back to find empty and shrunken, without a trace of its once majestic air. "Don't you want to lie down?" my husband mooed in invitation, "You must be exhausted from dealing with all those lawyers," but his body's dead-cow smell was so nauseating that I leaned out of the window overlooking the square, and in place of the rectangle of houses surrounding the statue I saw a slope that went up and up to the cemetery and, after the cemetery, to the village. I heard my cousin snivel and complain, I heard more nighthawks, I heard my mother scold me and my juvenile breathing, which would accelerate and then tire. My grandfather, who was sitting at the head of the table, put his cigarette-holder in his waistcoat pocket. "I don't feel like eating," said my supine husband, oblivious to the banqueting mosquitoes, "go on without me to the dining room," where three or four gold-buttoned, white-jacketed waiters twirled their trays, a bow-tied manager hugged on to his missal of wines with the fervour of a deacon and, at the table next to mine, a chunky man faced a bowl of tomato soup and read a newspaper. I ordered fish and mineral water and the dead cow smell began to abate, thank God. My fat neighbour smelled of cheap aftershave and his cheeks, spilling into the puddle on his plate, moved like a toad's. I saw the redhead desk clerk and his flags waiting on a Spanish guest. An aproned woman went from table to table, changing the flowers in the vases. The fat man made an inspection of my legs and returned to his spoon, but a minute later he eyed me again, straightened his tie, and folded shut his paper with a swat of the hand, crumpling a train crash. His gestures had taken on the cautious dignity of chameleons, planing over his silverware as if ready to snag a dragonfly. He took less steak off the serving dish than if I hadn't been there, about three feet away, struggling against fishbones with my knife and fork. The manager and his gold-buttoned underlings were talking in a corner, huddled together as in a Church council.

"Is this your first time in Evora?" asked the fat man across the tomato puddle.

The redhead rang the bell on the counter, the waiters turned to look, and the manager, forever clutching his fine vintage bible, hurried over to try to untie the knot of the argument with the too-closely clipped nails of a Spanish for deaf-mutes that consisted of facial contortions, snapping fingers and simulated toreador footwork reinforced by an occasional *Olé!* or *Caramba!* from the redhead.

"I stop here every Wednesday," explained the fat diner as his suckerfish fingers went for more bread. "I'm a sales rep for a textile manufacturer, and when we drew straws I ended up with the south. That Mercedes outside belongs to me."

I craned my neck but could see no Mercedes on the square: only the outlines of trees, the streetlamps that dug monstrous caries into the building façades, the silhouette of the statue in the middle of the square, and beyond it a fountain whose invisible water fell in a curtain of spangles. My mongoloid aunt swung her legs back and forth at the far end of the table, and my father, with cap on knee, stared at the painted still life of apples and hares as if at a train schedule that had to be met at all costs. Whatever happened to the horn?, I wondered. The redhead shouted *No señor* in the lobby, making Costa Rica and Luxembourg flutter.

"Here's a picture of my kids," said the fat man, opening his wallet and treating me to a swarm of smiles protected by a gelatinous coating. "The oldest girl began Agricultural Science just this year, Isn't it something the way time flies?"

And I sank into horrified contemplation of a fat girl with hair in her eyes wedged between a fat mum and dad on the sofa, her mouth wide open as if hungry for gnats. The man put his batrachians proudly back into his coat pocket and leaned a little further over his seaweed dinner:

"Are you here by yourself?"

In winter, after the floods, when the Guadiana River resumed its normal flowing and returned to its usual rocks, showering the abandoned mill with shrub and tree dregs, my cousin and I would crouch by the puddles to look for frogs and December's teensy creatures that slithered around in the soil, springing out unexpectedly into the grass. And now, unexpectedly, another of these creatures born of microscopic eggs had popped out, winking its eyes at me and approaching with a fork-impaled steak morsel:

"If you appreciate Indian clothing, I'd be delighted to give you one of the saris I have upstairs in my room."

He didn't smell of dead cattle: he smelled of rain and mud and the month of March, of my grandfather's cold tobacco and of the perfume my mother sprayed on my hair and neck as she dried and combed me after my bath. After panting his way up the stairs, the fat man rummaged around in a slew of bags crammed with clothes, held up bras, spread out scarves, unfolded skirts and blouses, waved handkerchiefs ("Take your pick!"), and dived under piles of coats in search of the ideal bathrobe while the bloodhound, frightened and enraged, barked at him from far away, and my father, with a war medal from a pawnshop pinned on to his stationmaster's uniform, blew his whistle throughout the mansion. My mother and cousin and I arrived at the cemetery with its sad little monuments and the gleaming vegetables of the gravedigger's garden, we ran to the gate, and when we entered the dining room my aunts and uncles gave us admonishing glances, the cook served my grandfather, who broadened his greasy toad smile while extending a nightgown my way, and only the mongoloid, strapped into her special chair, seemed to be in peace, passing through people and things with the mysterious clarity of her pupils.

Day One of the Festival:

To Lidia, Wherever She is

1

The first thing I heard when I stepped into the house was my father's electric train rumbling around toy tracks in the attic, and even today, darling, seven years later, sometimes I wake up next to you in the middle of the night with the taste of an interrupted dream fading on my tongue and I hear, or think I hear, seem to hear, from an undiscoverable point in the shadowy world of our jumbled clothes and the alarm clock's ringing, the relentless chug of a stubborn locomotive winding past celluloid stations, plastic trees, nativity shepherds, the Three Wise Men, tin soldiers and grey paper tunnels, disappearing finally between two chairs, and as your body lies quietly submerged in the sheets, illumined by the ebbing clarity of the glass of water on the nightstand, I grope for the packet of cigarettes that aren't there, then flap the striped wing of my pyjama up and down in a fruitless search until through the darkness, on the other side of the room, I notice a bald man hunched over a chrome lever, by which he controls the motor of my anguish and my days, obliging me to meander from dresser to dresser, weighed down with the baggage of nineteen summers. And then I lean my leg into your leg, my side into your side, shoulder into shoulder, seeking the calming solidity of your flesh. But I inadvertently touch your face, your nose twitches, you mumble, protest, fidget, and move away, shaking your platinum mane of hair, and again I'm alone, as in that grey September of my childhood, again the bloodhound scratches its claws against the flagstone floor and wets my neck with its snout, again my father's pointless electric train, so alien to me, alien to everything, appears from under a baroque dresser, navigating between porcelain Holy Infants and cardboard Dutch towns.

I light the lighter, my fingers stumble, an object falls and rolls on the floor, and I look for a few seconds at the curve of your nose, your chin, your gaunt neck recalling the queens on paper money, and your wrinkles—like my sister's— fanning out from the corners of your eyelids and your lips: I like your harsh and haughty expression, your big breasts that hang oblivious one to another as if cross-eyed, your raspy, measured voice, your forty years of age decaying in the majestic despair of an ocean-weary tanker. I like living with you on Praça Street in this fifth-floor closet with its minuscule shower, toilet placed next to the stove, floor covered with newspapers and books and typed pages and dirty underwear, virtually no furniture, a few torn cushions, and you with your tape recorder, practising your lines for a dumb radio play, bending at the waist *à la* Phaedra. I like that you chose me, who can't even get into an X-rated film, to go with you to Old Quarter restaurants where unemployed artists wearing greying beards and the colourful rags of opulent poverty wrap their grimy nails not around knives and forks but around saliva-browned reefers, inhaling the doubtful nutrients of a marijuana or hashish dinner. I like your over-effusive embraces, your drinking sprees, and the sincere lie of your love for me. I like when you kiss and hug and fondle me and spread your legs and guide me slowly, sacredly, Body of Christ, Amen, into the contracting silk of your vagina, and I turn my head towards the window shutters, where past the dusty glass and splintered frame I see the nocturnal river, sown with the lights of boats and the shadows of derricks rising and subsiding to my chest's anxious rhythm, while above the river, embedded in a slate-coloured vault, the stars twinkle questions.

In these moments without substance, in this gaseous eternity, in this pure fleeting pleasure, I can almost forgive the runs in your stockings, your worn-out heels, the burned toast at breakfast and the buttons missing from my shirt like keys from a broken clarinet. I only feel a little homesick, when you're not with me, for my mother, my sister, my grandfather, and my father, around whom the maids, at dinner, danced a complex ballet of plates and tureens. And I always feel sure that if I stop for a minute and cock my ear towards the ceiling I'll be able to hear, besides the bed's squeaking and your whispered griefs, an electric hum of non-stop wheels monotonously devouring a set of sinuous tracks.

When the first cars, before daybreak, drive down São Domingos Street and I can barely perceive the outline of my patch-covered coat hanging with other coats and shirts and trousers and handbags on the back of the straw-seated chair, when a cornfield of TV antennas sprouts from the rooftops and the derricks of the Tagus acquire the false depth of a theatre stage, when your body, shrouded in the bedspread's disorder, finally reveals the solitude of a foot, the grey roots of your hair, the dissolved make-up on your cheeks, blanched by the pan-coloured six a.m. cold, then I remember, by some strange somnambulant association of ideas, the afternoon when Nuno yelled for me from the hallway and took me in the Volkswagen to the apartment in Restelo, smoking filterless cigarettes that smelled like a mixture of croquettes and thatch.

My family's homes stood out from other people's for having more china cabinets, more night-commodes and more crystal per acre of carpet, bordered by the tombstone quiet of the sideboards. Even my sister, who was twenty-eight or twenty-nine at the time, was already bumping left and right into sofas and samovars, and she calculated the colour of the sky by looking at the barometers that hung on the walls like mahogany fruits. The mirrors reflected dour couches amassed in a lifeless museum symmetry, and the air seemed ancient and rarefied, like the spent air of caverns, forgotten by the chlorophyll of encyclopaedias and dictionaries. And after dropping some acid and imagining you talking with my grandfather, I lie down again by your side, laughing, while in the light of the fully risen sun our garret on Praça Street resembles the port of Portimao at low tide, clogged with every kind of debris imaginable, beneath a white sky slowly filling with an eiderdown of pigeons.

Forgive me, darling. Forgive me for the upright pianos and the Catholic schools that prevent me from understanding your courage, your independence, your pride, the unpaid bills, the money we owe the grocer, your D & C's, the wine-stains on your threadbare slacks, and the eternally problematic future. When finally we're left by ourselves for the night and you light candles on the tables and turn on the transistor and touch me and pull me by the shirt and your tongue lingers over my collarbones, my ears, and my forehead, then a vegetable peace crawls up my legs to my sex, spreads over my stomach, fills up my ribcage and sails through me like the feathers that blow in from the balcony and sail happily through the rooms without ever once grazing the furniture. Our members free themselves, my penis grows, my mind breaks away from its worries and forebodings, and the bliss of a catechism of questions and answers unrolls its highway of virtuous satisfaction before me. It's thanks to you that I no longer feel the invincible urge to hide under tables—picking my nose and curled up in the form of a snail—as on that afternoon when Nuno took me to Restelo and abandoned me, like a sea wave abandoning an old tin can on the shore, in the hallway, next to my sister, who looked at her watch with the stern expression of a schoolmarm before a pair of late students.

Being seventeen years older, she was entitled to ask arbitrarily, with inquisitorial coldness:

"Did you wash behind your ears, Francisco?"

You, at least, never ask if I've washed my ears, brushed my teeth, shampooed my hair, cut my nails or behaved politely: we share an ardent aversion to water, as evidenced by the bathtub, a depository for all sorts of junk: old scrapbooks, headless dolls, brushes, clothes, pots and pans, and the army boots of your last lover, the sports photographer who lifted weights at the gym. I have yet to find soap on the bathroom sink, or shampoo on the shelf, or cleanser in the kitchen; at times it seems we feed on dung, like desperate vagabonds in a barren land. My sister examined my ears, hands and nose, and pried open my lips with her thumbs to inspect my teeth. A frown of disgust deranged her eyebrows:

"Filthy as usual. Did you bring everything you'll need? Mother wants us to leave immediately for Monsaraz, so don't you dare disappear under the furniture."

I remember that it was almost night, for they'd already turned on the lights and there was silverware jangling in the kitchen. In the dark of the hallway werewolves darted through the olive trees, along the bank of the Guadiana River and past the boats of the drowned fisherman, and I cowered under the sheets, in spite of the heat, so as not to hear the fig tree that kept creaking in the yard, so as not to hear the voices of the grown-ups downstairs, suddenly cruel like gigantic prehistoric birds, trying to peck out my eyes as if they were cherries. One of these days I'll ask for the key to the mansion and take you on the bus to Alentejo, to visit the village, the castle, the cemetery, the room where the electric train tracks are rusting away, the bed where my grandfather died seven summers ago, my secrets, my fears, the hand-carved angels and the copper sun that blinds the stray dogs on the steps of the church. Yes, I'll take you to that expired land where the clock hands are paralysed, but don't be surprised, when the cemetery is reduced to an indefinite polygon and the shadows of trees stretch out on the ground like sleeping arms, if then, without warning, I squat under the heavy old dining table to hide from the ghosts of the photographs. "Sit there and don't move," my sister ordered. "At least you can't get dirty if you stay put."

If I had a picture of her in my wallet, you'd see how much we look alike: same long nose, same bubble cheeks, same swallowed chin and same tawny, almost mulatto skin, inherited from our father, which she tempers with lotions and I disguise with my pubic moustache and scrub beard. I haven't heard from her since she left her husband and children to take up with a guy in Brazil who's my age and teaches swimming and apparently batters her systematically, breaking surfboard after surfboard across her back.

"Can't you sit still for one minute without excavating your nose?"

And yet as strange as it may seem, in spite of her severity and her aggressive gestures and her constant fault-finding, she's one of the few people in the family I remember well, and almost miss, and almost feel good about: she smelled nice, she sometimes gave me coins to finance my orgies of chewing-gum and mints, she'd come out of the bathroom looking troubled, with her eyes swollen under black mascara, and even today I'm convinced that if she could she'd crawl under the tables to be there with me, hemmed in by the giant legs of adults and biting our nails over a nameless affliction, the way you and I do in the months when our money runs out, and the Telephone Company disconnects the phone, the Water Company shuts off the water, the Electric Company cuts off the lights, the grocer cuts off our credit, the bottled gas runs out and we sit on the bed, in the middle of our shipwrecked existence, munching on stale biscuits and staring at the derricks on the Tagus River.

I remember, darling, that it must have been night, for a dimness subdued the trees in the paintings and the tree of my blood, while the profile of my sister, leaning towards the cigarette box next to the table lamp, shone like the faces of the women in the old paintings, gazing raptly at lit candles in an impenetrable serenity. Sitting obediently in the chair they assigned me, my feet reached vainly for the swirls in the rug as I waited for the two glass doors of the dining room to open, like the legs of a woman at the gynaecologist's; the maid would announce dinner, and past her, past the doors, there were more paintings, silver, cupboards full of dragon-stamped teacups, a tablecloth, glasses, utensils, potted plants, concealed lights that diffused a clarity as soft as stained glass, and the expectant solemnity of altars where humans are about to be sacrificed. My brother-in-law invariably entered the living room carrying a newspaper and a briefcase with patient files, offered his indifferent mouth to my sister's indifferent cheek, waved me an indifferent greeting as he set paper and briefcase on a glaringly polished table, and exuded his prosthetic odours everywhere, and as I looked at him and his affected nonchalance I always thought, I hate your guts, with such intensity that if he was leafing through a magazine he'd glance over at me in astonishment. My sister inhumed cigarettes in the ashtray, where her pile of lipstick-stained stubs reminded me of used tampons, and I suspected she shared my hatred of her spouse: there were times when her thinking and mine twirled in millimetrically precise unison, as in dance hall contests. The rumba of our contempt for the intruder no doubt deserved to

131

come in first, I reasoned, and as a kind of consolation prize I allowed myself the indulgence of inserting my finger all the way up my nose, as if it to screw it into my face, but my sister made a grimace, my brother-in-law returned to his magazine, and three bowls of soup, waiting close by, bubbled their chicken-and-vegetable lava.

"It's time to eat, go and wash your hands," my sister invariably required, walking as if dragging a princess's train towards the steamy spires continually dying and resurrecting from the dishes on the table.

And I would remain seated and speechless, my feet dangling like a hanged man's, looking up at her with the joyless eyes of a Dalmatian. Nuno would lay down his magazine and stand by the sideboard, bathing the silver with the disinfectant cloud that went everywhere he did, identifying him as a *bona fide* dental torturer:

"Your brother's probably still scared of the dark."

When I was eleven or twelve it wasn't only the dark that scared me, it was firecrackers, birthday balloons, sports events, sewer rats, Gym class brutality and my Geography tutors. I wanted to be a painter and musician, to shock audiences with my Liszt-styled hair, my dandruff, and my agile fingers. I wavered between violin and paints, dreaming of nude models and of fashionable women with jutting collarbones fawning on double basses in an ethereal atmosphere of eighth notes. I wound up doing abstracts (two purple lines on a yellow field) and playing flute in a second-rate rock group that occasionally performs at Saturday-night dances in country clubs. There, dressed in black leather along with the rest of the band and pressing my fingers on the holes of an instrument no one hears over the clamouring guitars, I watch couples move in dignified hops mirrored on the waxed dance floor while mothers and fathers nod their heads at the tables along the wall, holding on to their somnambulant children, startled awake by screeches from the organ. But back then, as a kid, my fear of the dark was so intense, much more than now, that I'd tearfully beg the maid who was tucking me in bed to leave a light on, and I'd finally fall asleep next to the ecclesiastical flutter of a candle wick, travelling in long-winded nightmares which only my mother's voice could silence. If I opened my eyes, the mirror over the dresser would duplicate the insignificance of my body, overwhelmed by wardrobes that leaned towards me in formal mahogany bows. The streetlights projected the slats of the blinds on the ceiling. The laughter and talk of the grown-ups echoed in a bottomless well, choked by ferns and moss. Uniformed in leather as I blow into a flute drowned out by two saxes, I see myself back in the apartments in Lisbon or in the Monsaraz mansion, shivering in bed, unable to sleep, haunted by the stolid black shapes of the dressers and by the moonlit outline of my own face, undulating in the window as if under an aquatic membrane. And I suddenly remember to pull the flute from my lips as the hip-twisting vocalist, wearing a silver suit and a chrome smile, leans into the mike.

"I'll turn the light on for you," my sister said, throwing her husband a glance of rancour or weariness.

The hallway in my sister's place went on for miles, the route being indicated by light switches which, if you turned them on, revealed dozens of consoles, Chinese vases, an almost life-size marble maiden overcome by an inexplicable grief, chests, closed doors, and finally, after a half-hour journey, the bathroom, just like the Chem lab at school: spotlessly clean, symmetrical shelves full of coloured powders, even the same wall tile. A transparent bird hung by a green ribbon from the ceiling. A basket with hairbrushes pointed silky and wiry strands in all directions. It wouldn't have surprised me to find lab reports, temperature graphs, set-up diagrams and mathematical calculations rolled up in the toilet paper. My sister turned on the spigot, which resembled a gaping fish-mouth, and I reached for the tentacle of soap, stretched out like a fakir on a bed of rubber nails. Bending over the running water without touching it, I stared in amazement at the fish's continual, turbulent, imperturbable vomit.

"What are you waiting for?" my sister nasaled.

I quickly stuck the tips of my fingers into the liquid that whirled in the basin (the soap escaped two or three times and tried to get away through the drain), dried them on a towel as furry as a dog, turned to go back to the living room, and noticed with astonishment, embarrassment, worry, and bewilderment that her face was shifting and coming undone, like a puzzle, as if she would cry.

2

In the early morning before the dawn, when we know the colour of the blinds is about to begin turning, when any minute now the furniture and our clothes and the cracks in the wall will emerge from the dark, trembling like a sunken ship resurfaced, poking forth the bedside lamp as a kind of mast, covered with the molluscs of sleep, when my body, hanging from yours like a baby baboon from its mother, begins to crawl around for a filterless carcinogenic banana, when finally everything has changed with nothing really changing, everything waiting for the lemon sun to appear on the platter of rooftops—then don't you hear, as this blank space of morning slowly paints its face with colours, not only the noises from adjacent flats, not only the pigeons and trees and clanging trams, not only the tobacco seething in our bronchitis, but also, coming from some unsearchable place beyond these walls and the streets of Lisbon, from an infinite distance of God knows how many photo albums, the whistle of an electric train circling among the shoes under the bed or plying between the broken hi-fi and the transistor radio in the living room, with my father—horn round his neck—waving his ridiculous flags from the window?

As soon as my sister and I arrived at Monsaraz I ran up the

stairs, pursued by the teetering leaps of the old bloodhound, to go and see my father, who was seated in a corner of the alcove, smiling at the freight cars with his stationmaster's gold incisor, tacked on to his gum by the dentist in Reguengos years before, as if it were a medal for his service to the railway that ran between the river and the mansion among grasshoppers, crickets, ants, and imaginary passengers coming and going, their hands full of luggage, in a phantasmic hurry. I stood there looking at him the way I look at you in the kitchen, amazed at how you manage to produce, in five square feet of greasy tiles, a bowl of soup or a roast chicken on one of our happy days when you get paid at the theatre or someone buys one of my oils or the vocalist hands me a ten or a twenty and we eat in silence, huddled around the pans, like the survivors of a plane crash devouring the stewardess's packets of jam. I stood there looking at him while in the lanes of the village the festival simmered with the heat: the cows at the castle mooed louder, band musicians spilled out of the taverns, reverberating from corner to corner as they dragged their instruments over the stones, agitated dogs barked at men and women dressed as ghosts, causing them to trip on the doorsteps, and stuffed animals were being hung from nails in the raffle stalls on the square. I stood there looking at him the way I look at you, in your robe, opening the jammed cutlery drawer and manoeuvring in the kitchen like a silkworm in its cocoon, until the bent forks and knives you take out grow larger, the cupboard with the plates expands, the stove inflates to fill up the doorway and your features blur, you become quiet, stuck to the wall, metamorphosing into a chrysalis, then into a giant butterfly vibrating its furry antennae while reciting the lines of a play at the wicker lunch table.

The light bulb shining from the ceiling made my father's baldness a second bulb, screwed into the collar of his uniform and

136

equipped with a filament of eyelashes that blinked on seeing me—"Hello there, son"—before instantly refocusing on the trains choo-chooing around the floor, while in front of the house a stray trombone was belching the sixteenth notes of too much barbecued pork. Someone (a servant? the steward? my uncle?) went out through the gate (its hinges whined in the night) and pushed the musician up the street until the notes and steps and voices dissolved in the stable odours from the castle and in the sheets of the ghosts on their way to the dance. I heard my sister in the store-room, which had once been full of chests and baskets and suitcases and my old wheelless tricycle and which was now full of erratic, mulish breathing noises and the pharmacy smell of sarsaparilla mixed with the perpetual smell of musty lace, I heard the servant, or the steward, or my uncle returning, I heard the figs of the fig tree smacking like lips in the darkness, I heard talking downstairs, and my father stopped the train, cupped his hand to call me over, stood up from the stool, pointed to the wall with his sleeve's gold stripes, and said, "Tomorrow I'm going to inaugurate a branch line to the bed where your grandfather's dying," at the very moment my mongoloid aunt began screaming in the hallway.

I remember how for years and years she and I were equally annoying to the grown-ups, because we both wet our pants, broke our toys, spilled crumbs, overturned teacups, and howled for the attention they wouldn't give us, and so we were both shut up in the stewy-smelling kitchen, where we banged on pans with wooden spoons. And for years and years, darling, I thought that that overgrown infant with her pinafore dress and wrinkly flesh and mop-head of grey hair was my age, and even today, if she comes to mind, I don't picture her as being any older, just as I don't see you as older, despite your teenage daughter who's pregnant by a sixty-year-old set designer, despite the fact that you could have given birth to me on the mattress where at night we sleep, intertwined like the letters of a monogram or the linked rings of an impossible Japanese puzzle.

My aunt started shouting, my brother-in-law kicked her in the bum to shut her up, my father said, "A branch line with a double track, son, The parts are on their way from Lisbon," the bloodhound barked then yelped as it skidded on the stone floor, and in the next room down my grandfather, lying with wide-open gums in a huge bed that obstructed everything, spat out incoherent phrases to my sister, who was propped against the syrups and pills and drops on the medicine table, answering him with grunts as if to imitate the moos of the festival cattle that were smelling of blood and cruelty and the spectators' cries before there was any blood or cruelty or cries or costumed ghosts going from house to house to scare and be scared by their ghostly counterparts. And it occurs to me that I live with you because here in your attic I feel at peace, swallowed by your thighs that shield me from fear. And when I hear you, when I feel your steady, tranquil, animal breathing, for a moment I'm convinced that I'll keep going for ever, alongside your body, breathing the morning sweat of your shaven armpits.

My father got down on all fours and chalked out the route of the new branch line, which began next to my grandfather's bed, bypassed the strait formed by his slippers, followed around the base of the wall and returned to the bed, petering out in the no man's land of the headboard, where the light from the ceiling lost itself in a web of shadows and the stench from the bedpan. My aunt's husband, who managed the family properties, whispered something to Ana while squeezing her waist, and the two of them exited into the hall, leaving me alone with a dying man and a stationmaster holding a red flag out of the window as if a locomotive under the fig tree were awaiting his signal to depart.

And in no time at all, in fact, a bed down the hall started to roll and gain speed, stirring up a wind that rustled the tree's leaves, my sister's headlight eyes illumined the tracks ahead of her, my uncle furiously shovelled coal into her flaming furnace, and my father rolled up the flags and observed his naked daughter coupled to his brother-in-law, the two of them lurching forward in the streets, scandalizing the penned-up cattle and disturbing the darkness with the tail-lights of their bouncing buttocks. I ran to the stairway, craning my neck to see them pass by, but my mother appeared and hauled me off to my room with its stupid toy soldiers, Donald Duck wall figures, and an imposing Christ whose lips were on the verge of uttering the tender and comforting words I'd waited for for so long and still wait for sometimes, when I'm alone and can't sleep, immersed in the spooky rattling of shadows, until you arrive and crash into bed—one shoe on and one shoe off—in an alcoholic daze. My mother pulled me out of my school clothes and inserted me into pyjamas the way a shop assistant wraps merchandise, tied my trouser string into a bow, said "Off you go," kissed my forehead as if licking shut an envelope, switched off the light, and turned into a blank profile that tiptoed away with the soft trot of foxes. I could vaguely discern her talking to my father in the hall, telling him about a train strike to get him downstairs, and as soon as he answered "If there were a strike they would have sent me a telegram," it was morning and I woke up.

And now, my love, after having lived eighteen, almost nineteen years, after endless nights of talk and drink and syringes, of God knows how many grams of pills and heroin, I return to the world at two or three in the afternoon, surrounded by your collection of old hats, the overflowing ashtrays and the smell of urine from the Siamese that struts over the covers while we sleep, I return with the weariness of a septuagenarian frog, my kidneys splitting with

139

pain as I flounder in a swamp of algae. It takes me for ever to collect aromas, thoughts, colours, like a blind man the coins in his cap. Where am I?, what's my name?, how did I land here?, and only after the third cigarette do I begin to realize who you are and that I live with you, that I'm five feet six and probably have identification in that coat over there, I recognize your strands on the pillowcase, your skinny body, your hacking cough. I swallow a capsule that helps me shuffle to the sink, where my erection dissolves in the beer foam I urinate, which in turn washes the fishbones from last night's dinner down the drain. There are always five or six turtle-doves on the roof, the only angels possible in a city where billboards hide, like bandages, the sores of an incurable wasting-away. Lisbon evokes a beggar in the sun, with sparrows instead of lice roaming freely in the thinning hair of its trees. And returning to bed I find you seated on the mattress, your cartilaginous outlines protruding through your blouse as you stare in the alarmed confusion of the resurrected when still in a state of hungoverness.

I like you, damn it, I really do. I like the colour of your eyes and your hands on my shoulders when we make love, your legs that wrap around mine and hold me, immobilize me, prevent me from kicking up and down as you pinch and bite and insult me, till suddenly you lose your wrinkles and die like a helpless insect in a cascade of anguished moans, your face twisted as if ready to cry. I like being older than you for just a few seconds, when I give you pleasure, when you humbly obey the rhythm of my pubis, when without warning my muscles dilate and I deposit a cubic inch of passion in your vagina. I like holding on to you afterwards, my chin resting between your breasts (you being taller, I always take the higher side of the pavement), and I like knowing that as long as I'm with you I'll be all right, in spite of the tough moments that come my way. And it terrifies me to imagine coming home after a concert, flute case in hand, to find the mattress vacant, vacated, bearing only the inscription of your back's curve, the thumbprint of an irreparable anxiety, like that of my mongoloid aunt the year my grandfather died and she was locked up in the pantry, screaming her head off among the jars of fruit and bags of rice at the same time that a din of band music, firecrackers and people hawking fritters and raffle tickets swelled and subsided in waves shaped by the clapping of tourists in the square.

It was morning and I woke straight up—with no guilt or worry or pain—and went down to the gloomy dining room, where my grandfather's empty chair presided over the family breakfast. My father periodically set down his toast to shake his flags at a train that whooshed by, parallel to the table, leaving us on the white linen platform, forgotten passengers with our luggage of sugar bowls and coffee pots. My other aunt stared at Ana with a knife-sharp hatred. The bloodhound's nose butted the biscuit tin. A maid brought the mongoloid her warm oatmeal and hung a torn shirt as a bib over her striped pinafore. My mother passed me the Ovaltine, the vitamins and the bread basket and said, "Eat something," at which point a girl my sister's age strolled in unannounced, followed by a redhead foreigner who wore gladiator sandals and looked like a Saint Bernard or an Armenian priest, his crystalline pupils beaming through the bushes of his beard.

She was the only one in the whole clan who dressed like you, love, with indigent Bedouin tunics, grimy jeans, wire bracelets, glass rings, and those necklaces sold in subway stations by emaciated Hindus sitting cross-legged by purple cloths with assorted junk jewellery and a cassette player whining out Indian music. I found out later that she was the mongoloid's daughter, and it seemed odd that I never saw her before or after the three-day festival; it was as if the firework mortars had made her appear for a fleeting instant—her and her body's intense odour, bits of wool stuck to her clothes, and a Saint Bernard brandishing Neptune's trident—with the celestial thunder of visitations. She walked around the table like a bishop around the altar, jangling her copper jewellery instead of a censer and shuffling forward in her strange prophet's sandals, while the Armenian apostle followed close behind, terrorizing the bloodhound, which growled from its hiding place under the tablecloth. The mongoloid, awkward and indifferent, ate her oatmeal with a pink plastic spoon and managed to spatter milky brown specks on herself, on our sweaters, on the maid's uniform and on the pictures. No one had asked my cousin to be seated, but she installed herself in my grandfather's place, offered a slice of cheese to the Saint Bernard, and, holding forth a teaspoon, demanded the sugar bowl, smiling throughout, the way my uncle sometimes smiled, with one side of the face absolutely rigid, as if dead or catatonic, while the other side radiated with scorn and sarcasm. The Armenian finished swallowing and dumbly pointed his colossal finger at a dish full of menstrual-red compote. Exploding fireworks marked the minutes. The band went straight from a toreador two-step featuring castanets into a funereally solemn tune for the procession, in which infant angels dressed in old scapulars batted their wings to open up paths through the mob of phantoms in white sheets, dusty jewellers peddling flamboyant earrings, and Spanish women selling almond brittle.

"Wackawackawacka," said my cousin in Turkish to the Saint Bernard, who immediately withdrew his submissive finger. The mongoloid finished her oatmeal in a typhoon of soggy morsels, and the maid used the torn shirt to wipe her clean before unstrapping her. The procession trampled over the already twisted, tortured lanes to the accompaniment of clarinets, trombones, and tambourines in a heart-rending display of

142

miserable splendour. The fireworks burst into luminous flakes in the air, and we only heard them once they were fading in powdery threads.

"What are you nosing around here for?" asked my aunt, her eyelids heavy with rage. "We got you that cabin and bought you the looms on the condition that you never again set foot in this house."

"Wackawackawacka," the Saint Bernard begged, lusting after the cheese.

"The doctor from Reguengos told me the old man's about to kick the bucket," my cousin said serenely, helping herself to more coffee. "The workshop's not working out, no one buys the blankets, so I need my share of the inheritance. I was thinking of opening a craft shop, or maybe an antique store, or an art gallery: landscapes, oil portraits, local delicacies, pottery, anything tourists will go for. Burt [the Saint Bernard puffed up on hearing his own name] is great with that kind of crap."

"Inheritance?" my uncle exclaimed. "You must be out of your skull. What inheritance? Your mother and your train-demented uncle have eaten it all up with clinics, Your grandfather had the bright idea of sending them to exorbitant hospitals in Spain, And now you've got the cheek to expect some inheritance? Do you realize that even the house we're sitting in had to be mortgaged?"

"I don't want you anywhere in sight when my father dies," declared my aunt as she pried the mongoloid's hands off her skirt. "Some people from Lisbon are coming, and I don't want them to have the slightest inkling that you're part of the family, is that clear? We've got plenty to live down without adding you to the list. Just look at your mother over there grunting like an ape."

"Not to mention her cretin brother who stands up to whistle in the middle of Mass wearing that preposterous uniform," added my uncle. "You want your inheritance? You want your precious little inheritance? Get hold of a cage, take these two with you, train them, and then show them off in the circus—you'll be a millionaire overnight!"

The music grew, swelled, deafened and transformed us into stingrays that move their jaws but make no sound. A teacup shattered on the floor in the mute clamour of dreams while the procession's thousand or so boots of five hundred or so farm workers centipeded past our door, along with the mortars, brass instruments, golden-shawled priest and a retinue of widows. The floor-turned-drumhead, pocked by knots, vibrated to where the goblets clanged in the china cabinet: "Is this what you want to inherit, you ninny?" my aunt shouted, "A ramshackle house surrounded by a few scraggly lemon and fig trees?, Is this the furniture you want to take from us?, These splintered chairs and tables propped up by folded bits of cardboard?", and my unkempt cousin kept right on eating and drinking in the old man's chair, waving orders to the Armenian and smiling at us while my aunt went on, "This broken plumbing?, this falling plaster?, these peeling walls?, these disintegrating cabinets?", the doorbell rang, a ghost howled through the front door and went away, "You want to inherit our loan obligations?" my aunt continued, "the overdrawn accounts?, the mortgages?, the unpaid bills?" and I imagined the sort of thing that happens to us: drawerfuls of bill slips tied round with rubber bands, creditors gesticulating on the stairway, tax officials appraising our flat, and that time I saw you on the landing, with a breast hanging out, getting rid of the pharmacist by saying, "We don't have any money, I'm waiting to get paid from the theatre, Go ahead and take it to court, Frankly I don't give a damn." "You want the junk in the attic?, the dead owls?, the leather trunks?, your grandfather's corpse?, Take it all, it's yours, Hire a pick-up truck and load everything up, Sell it in Evora and open a restaurant in Outeiro," and the music and bustling of the maids died down, the fireworks spewed their white guts over the olive trees next to the river. "Your grandfather's savings, the orchards, the vegetable farms, and the properties we had in Beja all went to pay for your mother's doctor visits," my uncle explained, indicating the mongoloid with an open hand and immediately shooing her away with a napkin, the cows' mooing would come and go with the wind, accompanied by the smell of dung and straw, "Some of the rooms upstairs are so bad they're missing window panes and floorboards, Go and have a look if you don't believe me." "Wackawackawacka," said my still-smiling cousin, reprimanding the Saint Bernard, whose knife was advancing cautiously towards the cheese. "It's not enough that I live in this disgusting attic," you complained to the pharmacist while flicking ashes that fell on your robe, "Now I have to have you harassing me over a few measly pennies." "I want to see the books," my cousin said, "I want to see what kind of scams my grandfather and you people have been up to all these years," and was it she or you that sat there like a rock, indomitable, still smiling?, Was it she or you that told off the money-grubbing pharmacist, and the butcher, and the man from the cigarette stand, and the wine merchant? "I'm calling the police to have her thrown out," my uncle announced, "She's going too far with these insinuations." "I'm not insinuating anything," she said as evenly as ever, "You may be as poor as church mice, thanks to your stupidity, but I'm still entitled to know what frauds you've perpetrated." "Francisco," said my flustered mother, "take your handicapped aunt for a nice little walk," and the procession must have gone back into the church, for there was no more music, only the howling of werewolves and ghosts in the bedrooms. "All this fuss to inherit a stack of debts!" my uncle said, "To inherit a dilapidated house in a mouldering village!", and I took the mongoloid and headed straight for the village walls, away from the bands and the drunks and the Spanish almond brittle and towards the river, passing by the dogs that crouched and whimpered in fear in the bushes, their noses pressed to the ground, waiting for the bull to be killed and the tourists to leave before going back into the deserted lanes, where they'd examine the ducks and chickens fighting over lunch scraps set out by the grocer, and halfway down the hill we ran into my brother-in-law the dentist, leaning against a cork tree and chewing on a leaf, his beard unshaven, and he barely lifted his nose to look at us, and the look was a quick and indifferent look, the look of a complete and total stranger.

3

At eleven or eleven-thirty, love, as I wait for you to get home
from rehearsal and I hear the voices of gay men entering and
leaving the sauna beneath our attic apartment on Praça Street
(and the darkness, obliterating the five-storey distance, makes the
voices so sharp and clear I sometimes think they're talking in the
kitchen or in the room next to ours, where your daughter sleeps
with a boyfriend or two), as I lie on the rickety brass bed whose
treacherous arabesques trap my ankles and I prepare myself for
you, for your body, I always find myself looking at the alarm
clock, adding up the time you should leave the theatre to the time
the bus ride will take, and I stare at the door, I hear the click of the
key, your coughing, your shoe stepping on the broken floorboard
that groans without fail, and I turn off the light, feigning sleep as I
spy you: a raincoat-clad octopus undulating among shadows and
shapes until you trip on a shoe, support yourself on the bed, then
drop off your clothes like a tulip its leaves, becoming a stalk that
bows low, fighting against your recalcitrant tights before donning
a robe and disappearing into the bathroom, where you gargle
with the dentist's insecticide-scented mouthwash. My urge to
hide under the dresser goes away, the laughing voices walk down
the street and die, the toilet flushes, the sauna employees lock up

for the night, you return barefoot from the bathroom and I peer at the window-framed silhouette of your head, your arms, and your trunk, which emanate antiseptic vapours, which try to get comfortable in the hollow of the mattress, which touch me, which move away, which touch me again. I run my finger over the whorled hairs of your thighs, over the moist, mossy gash that excites me, I unbutton my pyjamas, I lean into the roundness of your buttocks, I grope for the pleats of your anus, and I'm in Monsaraz, the first day of the festival, curled up in bed after lunch, with my grandfather dying upstairs amid fireworks and dance music and shouting as I squeezed against the pillow, swelling for the orgasm that didn't come.

My aunt trailed behind me through the cemetery and down the hillside like a mule behind its gypsy owner, snorting protests of fatigue. I still sometimes saw her after her death, walking four-leggedly through my dreams, as off balance as ever, always about to fall, and even today, every summer, I confront her odour in the hiking boots which I found between moth-eaten blankets and old sink stands in a junk shop on São Bento Street and which, when I wear them, endow me with the virile ruggedness of an explorer. But when I was eleven, love, I saw my aunt as a circus act, an obedient animal constantly searching my pockets for gumdrops I didn't have, and at night she'd start crying and banging her fists for no apparent reason, waking the bats and the wind in the fig tree. The adults were forever having me take her for walks so that they could freely slaughter one another over money and their jealousies and their grudges: irrational motives that none the less made their hatred-temperatures soar. So on almost every day in September, when the sun makes shadows stand vertical for hours, I'd drag that gigantic baby through the back door as she fondly licked my face and neck, and we'd sit and sweat on the village wall, surrounded by wasps, swinging our legs as if to kick the Guadiana River into Spain.

148

But seven years ago, in the part of the story they told me to tell, I was so frightened by the exploding fireworks, the white-sheeted ghosts, the band's strange tangos and the mooing from the bull-pen that I scampered around aimlessly, running into bushes and brambles that pricked me, clambering up slippery mounds, disappearing like a mole in the hollows and sliding along the muddy banks, in the hope of escaping the spent fireworks that fell from the sky, their wire knots blackened and stinking of dead gunpowder. My brother-in-law stared at the bursting mute flames in the sky that were echoed, an eternity later, by soft popping salvoes. A bottleneck poked out from his pocket like an antenna. With his hair all dishevelled, his jacket all splotched, and his breath pure alcohol, he reminded me of the tramps that wheeze under bridges or on fire escapes, immersed in debris and filth, sputtering through their lips to the waterfall rhythm of their lungs. I almost expected him to stagger towards us, holding out his hand to get enough spare change for another drink, with bits of dry dirt and leaves stuck to his trousers, and revealing, when he hiccuped, half a dozen rusty teeth. I saw him a few weeks ago in the street, in Campolide: fat, bald, unbelievably deteriorated, wearing glasses and an overcoat that slid back and forth over his body's bulges. He had a sandwich in his hand and was looking at some shoes in a grimy shop window with the same absent expression he wore while watching the festival fireworks seven years ago, and although he was relatively neat and clean-shaven, he had an air of inner abandon, as if the dirt and debris lined his insides, as if he were a beggar turned inside-out.

"Turn round and go back," he ordered without looking at us, absorbed as he was by the trajectory of a falling cone. "The schoolteacher's Alsatian has broken away and it's on the loose."

This was the same dog that barked in mad fury and pressed its nose menacingly against the fence at my school during breaktime, and the thought of it being somewhere in the woods was enough to make me race in panic towards the village, followed by my aunt the goose, who stumbled, sobbing, over the rocks of the hillside and looked for me among the cement angels of the cemetery, whose dead inhabitants occupy doorless, windowless homes, patiently fashioned—like doilies—by gravediggers.

"Wait for her!" my brother-in-law shouted from down below, near the eels of the river and the dead fireworks, in a shrill voice broken by the loudspeakers. I stopped obediently before the village wall, like his fat bald self before the shoe-shop window, hoping that the monstrous German shepherd would get stuck in the Guadiana mud when it tried to bite into the fluid transparency of a frog. And I remembered my grandfather upstairs in his room, without his vest, without his cigarette-holder, without his hair cream, and without his usual condescending smile, stripped of his grandeur and sarcasm, feebler and closer to death with each spoonful of syrup, as now I remember my brother-in-law amid the ugly and sad buildings of Campolide, looking at a dusty display of cheap slippers as he munched on a sandwich.

My aunt finally caught up to me, panting as her bell-shaped body tolled to the flip-flopping of her sandals, while the slipper admirer stood motionless in the background, reduced to a dark point in the ochre landscape of trees wafting in the heat, waving in and out as if anchored in an invisible water. The cement angels smelled of the cabbages and spinach from the adjacent garden and of the fritters being fried in the village, and the smells swirled in my hair with the delirious agitation of moths excited and blinded by electric lights. Pulling the mongoloid by the sleeve like a young bull by its nose ring, we arrived at the square. Over by the castle where the cattle kept on moaning their melancholy rage the brass band, scrunched together on a platform, began Ravel's *Bolero*, old ladies dressed in black flapped their jaws like the loose soles of worn-out shoes as they cackled ceaselessly, a fellow wearing a chequered cap hawked blankets and sweaters, and on the steps of the church, firework masters lit fuses as nonchalantly as cigarettes. The storks and falcons of the Guadiana River looked on so stilly I thought for a minute they were umbrellas whose points were poking out of the trees. An old man chased a chicken in the middle of the square, intent on decapitating the creature with his cane. Blind people sitting on benches, their faces pasty as those of church statues, contemplated us with the same sidelong seriousness. Drunks pushed and shoved and sang at the entrance to the bar, and I thought I saw my brother-in-law there with his arm around a beggar on crutches, as when I wait for you in the café on the corner, at the end of the bar next to the bathrooms, where I can see all the tables, and I think that every woman who walks in is you, has your curved shoulders, your bearing, your hair colour, your face, so I lift up the puff pastry and call your name but it isn't you, it's never you, it's a pudgy woman whose nose funnels into her orange drink, or a bureaucrat shuffling her papers, or a high-school student, or the linen-shop manager, all of whom respond to my call and my pastry with an indignant jerk of the head. And I hide my embarrassment in my neighbour's newspaper, under the wreckage of an earthquake in Tunisia.

Unnerved by the music, the crowds, and the noise, I was all set to take the mongoloid back to the house in spite of the grown-ups' orders to stay away while they bickered, and I thought, If we go round the back by way of the water pump and the tanks, we can enter through the kitchen, where there won't be anybody now, just a thousand plates weeping detergent in the dishwasher, and then we'll sneak into the pantry and hide among the empty wine jugs and instant soups and watch the cockroaches, fat from breadcrumbs, flitting over the floor and gaping at the pickle jars.

We walked along the building façades to avoid the fireworks and couples that danced in awkward hops, crashing into each other like bumper cars in amusement parks. The women's breasts seemed larger than usual, their tongues longer, their teeth like tusks, their smiles grotesque. A coloured star exploded about a yard from my tennis shoes and I jumped back, dragging my aunt into an alleyway where the vendor with the chequered cap was sprawled out in a deck chair with a bottle of booze.

"How much do you want for her?" asked the vendor, pointing the cork at my aunt, whose grey hair fluttered above mine like apostolic tongues of fire.

The man in pursuit of the chicken swung at it with his cane but missed, sending only a solitary feather into the air, and the bird slipped into a hole in the wall, which the old man furiously beat in vain. A guy with a monkey on his shoulder and an open suitcase at his side tried to get people's attention with a scarf-covered microphone, and the man with the bottle leaned forward to touch my elbow, offering me a conspiratorial swig.

"Three dollars? Four dollars?" he asked.

He had a unique aluminium-coloured tie, an imposing ring engraved with zodiac signs, a glitzy tweed sports coat and an irrefutable halitosis. The chequered cap hid one of his eyes and half his beard, and the head or tail of a snake crawling over his ribs popped out now and then from between his shirt buttons. The band took a break but the fireworks went on, bursting in the molten sky like pus-filled fistulae.

"Five dollars and the snake," the man offered, feeling around in his coat. "She adores mice, you'll have loads of fun with her."

Just the thought of that slimy creature lolling around in the vendor's sweat and strumming its frenetic string tongue practically made me puke, though I guess it would be useful here, on Praça Street, when we're woken by scampering from under the floorboards in the middle of the night. Or on Monday afternoons, when you don't have rehearsal and we stay in bed for hours on end—amongst magazines, books, trays of food, and sticky wet spots on the sheets—and we see a darting shape insert itself like a suppository in the space between two trunks. I'm afraid of waking up one morning with an ear missing, and sometimes when I get up in the middle of the night, hungry for a piece of last month's sponge cake, I find a heap of cake crumbs on the kitchen table, rat droppings on the floor, and teeth marks in the plastic water bottle, leaking like a slowly bleeding body. But I think by some miracle we'll be able to survive the rats, the lack of money, the switched-off gas and switched-off electricity, just as old folks in rest homes are able to overtake last winter's pneumonia with their slow but steady hobble to the linoleum lunch tables.

"You can be the one to bring her, and we'll split the profit after taking some out for food," said the man. "I know a guy in Alter who collects Eskimos."

The chicken, exasperated by the relentless cane, finally jumped out on to the street from a different hole, flapping along as fast as it could while the old man resumed his insults and swung away at it, always missing, until he plunged into the mêlée of drunks and dancing couples and the brass band, whose dented trombones he inadvertently hit. The outraged conductor grabbed a clarinet from a mouth in mid-blow and went after the chicken harasser. The mouth followed, respectfully extending its timid hand and asking for the instrument as it cautiously approached the tornado of cane swipes and false notes, around which the ghosts and werewolves were gathering in their wine-happy hope for some good honest gore. The escaped chicken came towards us, wagging its relieved belly. The dealer in mongoloids stretched forward with chameleon speed, snagged the chicken by the neck, and stuck it under his coat, from where an irate wing issued periodically, batting against a lapel.

"Don't worry," he assured me with an accomplice's smile, "the snake will kill it in no time. She absolutely loathes chickens. So where were we, buddy, in our little business deal?"

And it's not only rats that live with us in the attic. We've got a whole zooful of ants, mosquitoes, crickets, roaches, centipedes, spiders and termites that presumably feed on the same lack of food we do. And there are the moths that fry themselves on light bulbs, reducing themselves to a lacquery dust. And there are the pigeons. And the turtle-doves. And the boats, like slugs, on the Tagus River. And our neighbours in undershirts, unable to fly, crucified against their balconies' carnations. And their short-sighted, frizzy-haired dogs that try to pee on their pyjama legs, confusing them with the street's mulberry trees. And there's you and I, scrawnier and scrawnier, preparing our breakfast of a half-gram of heroin. And the butter that cools in yellow lumps on the toast. And our bones that embrace. And some part of me penetrating some part of you, swelling, engaging and contracting in short pulses of pleasure. It's not only rats. It wasn't only rats. Nor only spiders, nor only centipedes, nor only heroin, nor only toast and boats and ants and pigeons: there was also, when I touched you, the exalting itch of my love for you, that silly, idiotic, absurd feeling I still feel, especially at night, in bed, when I cannot find your legs, your pubis, your ribs, your breath on my shoulder, the wet clarity of your eyes. They make me shower every morning in a spick-and-span stall, and the nurse, almost always the same one, brings me a plastic cup with the methadone pills. And then, in the rustle of the other mattresses, in the shirts and faces and arms and legs that rise up as if by levitation, I realize how happy I was with you, and how happy I still am, and I stop and stare for hours at the wall, in the endless wonder of discoveries.

"We'll split costs and profits down the middle," proposed the

Eskimo broker. "How about it, kid? Or would you prefer a crisp ten-dollar bill right now and we'll call it a deal?"

The chicken wing trembled under his breast pocket, slid into his shirt, resurfaced and flapped viciously. Taken by surprise, the vendor bent over and ran his hand around his stomach, was yet more surprised, kept feeling around, unbuttoned his coat, and twisted and turned like a tapeworm. The man with the cane was being buried under a mound of brass B-flats. The bass-drum player dismantled his instrument over the skull of a ghost that fell on his back, right next to a werewolf engaged in thrashing the sexton. The church widows were pelting each other with stearin candles. The guy who lit the fireworks threatened everyone with a loaded mortar, until the grocer clouted him with a bottle of rosé. The entrepreneur, visibly distressed, ripped off his sports coat to find out what was happening: a chicken squawk blew out from his buttocks. The choir marched out of the other tavern to do battle with the band. The mortar shattered a window. The vendor pulled up his shirt in a storm of feathers and was astounded to find the chicken alive and kicking, and holding the dead snake in its beak: "How did this fucker do it?" he asked as the animal's red feet pedalled the air, "How did it finish off a poisonous snake that could hypnotize ostriches?", and he lay back in his chair, stunned, looking at the bird, until the old man with the cane broke free of the saxes and headed towards us, shaking his tireless weapon. "Fifteen dollars for the Eskimo and that's my final offer," said the man with the chequered cap before the cane bashed his nose in and made his pupils whirl clockwise as he plummeted slowly to the ground. The priest blessed the bloodbath from the church portal, undaunted by the menacing flute section. The Council President and his Vice went at each other in the cemetery, armed with marble slabs. The old man finally got hold of the chicken, sat with his back against a horse cart, lit a cigarette stub and began to defeather the bird between grunts of triumph and cackles of pain. I fanned the dead snake-owner but his orbs kept on spinning, now in cross-eyed fashion, and I said to my aunt, "Wait here a minute, I'll be right back," shoving her towards the old man, who was unfolding a jack-knife to behead the monster, and before it could utter its final cluck I'd circled behind the house to the kitchen door and crawled under the table, where I hugged my knees to my chest as the fireworks blasted and the legs of the maids moved over the flagstones and I thought of headless chickens and dead snakes.

Day Two of the Festival:

The Eve of My Death

I opened my eyes to find my son-in-law ransacking the desk, pulling papers out of the drawers, leafing through my correspondence and digging through bundles of stock certificates stored in metal boxes. He trampled on contracts, broke the lock on my diary where I never wrote about business, and forced open the safe, dispensing with his usual mask of polite deference, Yes sir, No sir, Of course sir, Whatever you say sir, and I thought If I weren't so weak I'd teach him with the rod the way dogs and children are taught, I'd yell "Sit!" and he'd crouch down whimpering in fear instead of flinging my diary against the medicine table, tipping over half the bottles, grabbing me by my pyjama collar and sticking his nose into my nose and shouting, "Where have you hidden the will, you crotchety bastard?, Where's the frigging will?"

And not only him but also my daughter, who was looking in the chest of drawers, in the wardrobe, and under the mattress, overturning objects, sifting through my underwear, rumpling my ties and pronouncing, in a tunnel voice of the Last Judgement, "He couldn't have swallowed the damn thing, so it's got to be here somewhere," and my son who, with a train horn around his neck and a pencil behind his ear, was laying tracks on the floor and moving his cheeks to make the Chug chug chug of connecting rods. "And what if the will gives everything to the family idiots?" said my daughter, "What if it cuts you and me out altogether?" "Even if the old codger left it with the notary in Reguengos, there are ways to fix things in our favour," my son-in-law answered, "And Leonor, leave the antique clock alone, Throwing things on the floor isn't going to get us anywhere," although he himself meddled in everything, shoving aside *bibelots*, knocking down pictures and smashing a white china dove to smithereens before landing his foot in the bedpan and extracting the diarrhoea-dripping fish of his shoe. "That's just what I needed, Jesus fucking shit," he complained as my son kept chug-chug-chugging and my daughter, smiling at me, said in a sugary voice, "Does Daddy remember if he left the will here or with the notary?, Can't Daddy remember where he put it?", and her husband, sitting on the mattress to clean his shit-soaked shoe, "The prick wants to take his money in his asshole to the grave, What he needs is a couple of gunshots, then I bet he'll talk," and my son spat "Sssssshhhhhhhh," putting on the brakes. My daughter's no-longer-smiling face pulled away, swayed in the air and dis-appeared, "I'll find that fucking will," she guaranteed, "I'll find it if it's the last thing I do," and there was a knock at the door, "May I?", it was the doctor. "Come in, doctor," said my daughter, scooping up papers and stuffing them back in the desk, "We've been trying to straighten out the files, You can't imagine how disorganized my father was." My son-in-law began tucking the covers around my body in a fit of ostensible tenderness. "In every household there's always one person who's a little more careless than the rest," the doctor assured, "In my family I'm the guilty one, according to my wife," and, having made this pathetic confession, he leaned over the bed and asked, "How's our patient doing, what with all the hullabaloo of the festival?" "I think he's actually a little better," my son-in-law said as he scraped a flattened turd into the bedpan, "Just five minutes ago he was railing against the Communists," and the doctor pierced my pupils with a needle-sharp light and checked my pulse while gazing at the photograph of my wife, hanging in her oval frame, proud of the cretins she generated. My son walked backwards with the slow caution of a manoeuvring locomotive and bumped into the chest of drawers as into a stray baggage car, while the doctor pricked my arms and legs without me feeling anything, hammered my elbows and listened to my empty insides with a brand-new stethoscope ("Your nephew and the dog finished the old one off," he informed my daughter). My son-in-law went through the metal boxes with renewed energy, rummaged in the nightstand with my slippers, and searched every inch of the chest of drawers, no longer minding the scandalized doctor, who was feeling my bladder and testing my liver, "The chequebook, God damn it, there's got to be a chequebook somewhere or other." My daughter, after witnessing the examination with eyes that hoped for death, poked through my socks, my undershirts, my berets, and my hunting cartridges: "Nothing," she reported in dismay, stepping all over my silk shirts, and her husband, looking behind pictures for a hidden safe: "Nothing my ass, We've got to at least find the receipts or something to help us figure out the son-of-a-bitch's accounts before our niece goes to Reguengos or Evora and screws us good and proper." The doctor inserted the thermometer in my mouth, looked at the mercury level, shook and reinserted it, and I felt the narrow coolness of the glass on my tongue and the doctor's donkey breath on my face. "Are you positive you didn't overlook anything in the office?" my daughter asked as she leaned into the gun cabinet and got tangled up like a mummy in the leather bandoleers. "One hundred and two," the doctor cried out in an auctioneer's voice: "Are there any antibiotics lying around?" "By order of the Transport Ministry," my son announced with a whistle-blow, "construction is to begin immediately on a grand central station under my father's bed." "Of course I'm positive," said my son-in-law, "All I found in the office were some corny love letters on pink paper with birds in the margins that your mother sent him a hundred years ago from Vendas Novas, before they got married." "Garages, waiting rooms, nine tracks and a restaurant-bar!" my son beamed as he bumped into the doctor, "An Italian painter will be commissioned to do the murals at the entrance, and there'll be a marble fountain in the main hall," but I was already with the steward, crouched behind the riverside thickets, my fingers grasping on to a double-barrelled shotgun that waited patiently for the quail, and I whispered, "The first one's mine, don't you shoot," twenty or thirty or forty years ago, when I could move my limbs and smoke cigarettes and give orders. The bloodhound, tense as a harp, quivered by my side, its neck reaching forward, ready. A flock of ducks sailed in a V far above us, southward, their wings almost lost in the white July sky. "Hear them?" said the steward, "Over there in the underbrush," and indeed some sort of commotion was joggling the bushes about twenty yards away. I aimed. The bloodhound, breathing as if no game were there, hung its imploring glass drops on my own, duller eyes. I pulled the trigger slowly, the steward deflected my arm with a panicky jab of his gun, the report made my shoulder recoil, and the branches of an oak tree intermingled for a moment before taking up their old places. The steward tore out in a run to the bushes, where he pulled out my son-in-law, attached to a strange naked animal I recognized as my mongoloid daughter, excrescence of my flesh, emblem of my wretchedness and shame of my blood, who must have escaped from the room she was locked in to go tramping in the mud among the frogs and toads, and who now threw up both hands to defend herself from the first furious, exasperated swipe of the rod.

Because it's the rod that teaches children. Because it was the rod that my father used to teach me, in Lisbon, in a house full of doors and shadows, in the hallway, thrashing me before the horror of the servants and the blindness of the old women that stood all in a row—my grandmother, her twin sister, assorted great aunts—all with tousled hair and pale eyelids framed by waxy deposits, all wearing robes and nightgowns with ruffles clasped by their blanched asparagus fingers, and the thwack of the rod sent me streaming by and into the sitting room, where I emptied into a pool of consternated ladies, not quite as old as the invalids but every bit as dismal, mumbling confessions through their holy veils. "Come back here, you rascal!" my father shouted, running by leaps while the rod cut the air into pieces, and my mother reached into her sleeve for her handkerchief of sorrows, and I slid in sideways between two china cabinets, ceasing to exist in the half-light of the drapes and linen cloths, while my father thrashed plates and pitchers, yelling "You've got to come out sooner or later, you little scamp!, You've got to learn your lesson!" amidst sobs, pleas, flying dishes, signs of the cross, and swoons, until he finally collapsed from exhaustion into the women's terrified laps, his switch still in hand and his moustache's moribund handlebars pointing to the chandelier.

Children are taught by the rod, and my increasingly paunchy and red-faced father taught me conscientiously all throughout grammar school and the summers we spent in Alentejo, with me hurling myself, day after day, into the safety of an eternal, immutable circle of gloves and whispers, until one afternoon, sixty or seventy years ago, after countless wars and earthquakes had passed and more would come, when he finally managed to hook his claws into my coat collar, push me up against a sacristy chest that still smelled faintly of candle wax, and raise his stick in a statuesquely heroic pose, then suddenly his features looked surprised, they distended, they froze, and a bead of blood paused on his lower lip before trickling down his chin in a leisurely scarlet. "Bring some water!" my mother called to the kitchen, "Bring some water, the major's having a stroke!" Someone came running with a glassful but the stick had already fallen to the floor, the shoes gave up trying to regain their footing, and the suit—without bones—dropped slow as pudding. My mother, assisted by a gaggle of solicitous lace gloves, poured the water through my father's plasticized lips as his lost eyes looked everywhere and at no one, and the corners of his mouth secreted new globules, red rivulets rippling off his wilting body on to the rug, and the dog licked his shirt front. "Go into the study and stay there, Diogo," they told me, and when I saw him the next day he was dressed up in a tuxedo and looked cramped in the coffin, surrounded by flowers and a few tears, a handkerchief veiling his infuriated nostrils.

Perhaps, like my father, I should have used the rod to teach my children and son-in-law, so they wouldn't now be yowling for the money that's not in my deathbed, so they wouldn't torture me with their electric trains that wander all over the house on snaky tracks, taking the butter from the breakfast table right as I'm about to reach for it, transporting my socks to the bathroom and offering a toothbrush or the shoe polish in exchange, whistling around bends, pouring out smoke, spilling off the tracks and spinning their wheels, persecuting me so doggedly that even the passengers painted on the windows shake their fists when I step on to the rubber mat with a towel around my waist and drip water on the trains chugging by the toilet bowl or the laundry basket.

I should definitely have used the rod on my wife, who didn't die, as everyone believes, or pretends to believe, or claims to believe, but simply walked out on me one fine day, decades ago, three or four years after the mongoloid was born and had begun grunting her sad monkey's complaint from room to room, when the sun was still high and I came home from partridge hunting to find her—my wife—packing suitcases and hat boxes. My shotgun was tucked under my armpit and my cartridge belt held four or five dangling birds that had interrupted their flight (the hounds fetched their riddled corpses) to fan my haunches, and I arrived at the bedroom door trailing dust from my boots on the carpet and smelling of gunpowder, the earth, the woods, and the blood of rabbits and turtle-doves, and my wife, who didn't look at me, was pulling dresses from the closets and laying them on the bedspread, folding blouses, gathering up underwear and shoes, and tugging on the leather straps of the open suitcases, knowing I was watching her—my gun in hand and my navel crowned with partridges, looking like a holy card of Our Lady surrounded by murdered angels—watching her move forward and backward and sideways in the mirrors, as if it were twelve instead of one that I'd married, until I asked, "What the hell's going on?" And as she packed up a set of brushes, as if we were talking about the weather, she answered, "I'm fed up, Diogo, and don't bother me now, because the bus is leaving in two hours and I've hardly started packing," and her bodies bent down and stood up and walked in the mirrors, carrying clothes or jars or framed pictures in their arms, arranging objects in the shelves of the trunks, carefully laying in slip after slip, the way she laid our kids in their iron cribs, and I pointed the gun at her and said, "You just take it easy," and she or one of her reflections laughed in amusement and went back to folding shawls and blouses, "No more scenes, Diogo, Fifteen years of them was quite enough."

And I was confused, I couldn't tell which of my wives was

speaking, because they moved simultaneously in the walls all around me as I tried to find the real one, over by the chest or the chair or the dressing table (and the dangling birds bounced against my thighs), but no, not there, nor over there, she'd stopped existing and yet was alive as the liquid shadow of fish, and when I aimed the weapon at an image of an image I heard the echo of her breathing, mocking me from I couldn't tell where in that army of exasperating, identical wives with identical movements, identical impatience and identical wearied frowns on their faces, so I whistled for the bloodhound, "Get her!", watched it skip into the room and stop short amidst the disorienting clutter of trunks and bags and suitcases and hundreds of reflections fluttering in the cellophane of the mirrors, again ordered "Get her!" and saw the confounded animal also go from chest to chair to dressing table, its jaws hanging open as when it chased shadows made by my hands—a wolf, a rabbit, a seagull, a house. "Get her!" I commanded as if the prey were a partridge or hare or duck, and I advanced like a blind man, following the dog's odour, until at last it nabbed a leg that belonged to my wife, busily cramming her cosmetics case with bottles and tubes and brushes and a wiglet and the spiders she glues on to her eyelashes, and she turned around, finally real, finally tangible, finally vulnerable to the shotgun, to say "What's this all about?" without even raising her voice, "What game have you come up with this time, Diogo?", and I, the master now, loaded two cartridges into the breech, saying, "That's exactly what I'd like to know," while the bloodhound chewed on her ankle as on goose-necks, mangling her tendons and wringing her flesh, "Get her!", and to my wife, "I'd like to know what kind of show's going on in this room, and what this crap is about taking off without a word of warning," staring at her, avoiding the mirror so as not to lose her or myself, pulling shut the breech, raising the gun, aiming, "So the bus leaves in two hours, huh?, So husband and kids can fuck themselves, huh?, So it's bye-bye because you're sick of us, huh?, So the moron can wriggle around squealing in the kitchen while her highness packs her bags as if she had nothing to do with the kid, huh?, Is that the idea?, That was a good question about what game is going on here," and I pointed straight at her: "Now let's see how you answer."

The dog let go and I roared "Bring her here!" as if referring to a bulleted prey that lay in the field, intermittently jerking a leg like a flipper. "Bring her here!" I commanded, grinding a dirty boot into the embroidery, cords, and sequins of a pile of blouses. My wife looked up from a suitcase: "Fifteen years of brutality haven't satisfied you, Diogo?, Will you only stop once this flea-infested creature succeeds in mangling my body to a mush?" The bloodhound, anchoring its paws into the floor, tried to pull her towards me with a furious tug. "Tell this beast to let go of me at once," said my wife, twisting around on her knees and removing a canvas strap from one of the bags, "or I'll whip it with this buckle," and I held my aim, thinking, I already knew about your indifference towards me, but now I've discovered your hatred, not only in you but in this mirror and that one and that one and that one, Now I know the rage built up in you during all the years you've been silently detesting me night after night, putting up with me in bed as I tickled your navel and exuded my detestable sweat of dead partridges' blood and fondled your breasts, your thighs, kissed you, lay on you breathing like an ox, and when she tried to hit my arm with the strap I raised the gun slightly and pulled, it fired, the boom flooded the room and deafened me, glass fragments showered the clock and ornaments above the fireplace, one of her images gave way to a cracked and discoloured rectangle of wall, the hound backed off barking, clawing the door to get out, I kicked it goodbye, closed and locked the door and put the key in my pocket and said, "Now we're going to have a little chat, you bitch, and you can begin by telling your darling husband about this bus you think you're going to take," and as I flattened her against the rug with my boot and mashed her kidneys under the weight of my heel I flung a packed suitcase out of the window, pulverizing the panes and decorating the fig tree with garters, bras, and belts that hung from the branches like meretricious fruits, ripe with lace and elastic. The chickens in the yard nibbled on the rubble. The Guadiana storks perched in the olive trees and on the rocks along the bank like scraps of paper abandoned by the wind. From the height of the sun, night looked to be a long way away.

"You thought you could zip out of town just like that, did you?" I growled, stepping up on her back. "Thought you could leave your lackey behind to cope with the abnormal children you gave him, is that it?"

I booted her towards the bed and sat down in the rocking chair, smiling, allowing her to sit up on the floor and straighten out her skirt, and she stared at me with as much hate as ever but without any fear.

"So this is how marriage vows are fulfilled," I lamented, heartbroken, my nose pointing to the ceiling lamp, to its greenish Formica wafers. "So this is what I get for half a dozen disciplinary slaps during years and years of conjugal education."

My wife ran her hands over her arms, legs, and head, apparently to make sure she still existed. Leaning back against the bed, she'd inadvertently exposed a hunk of thigh, white and round, and I felt a hardness in my trousers as she grabbed the clock off the mantel and contemplated the cracked dial, propped up by a pair of bronze angels.

"The bus leaves in exactly one hour," she said, as if she hadn't heard me, as if she'd never, in all our life together, heard me. "One hour, and thanks to you I've got nothing ready."

I looked at the shotgun, wondering whether I should repay her insolence with some lead, and decided instead to broaden my smile, as if I were confronting a fickle child or the monkey capers of my mongoloid daughter. There was no breeze, and the overhead lamp's Formica wafers, held together by tiny wire hooks, scintillated their complicity. The fractured glass on the floor reflected a million things in a puzzle I would never be able to solve. I've never, for that matter, fathomed the jeering tortuosity of unbroken mirrors, which remind me of my childhood, of the glasses worn by know-it-all students for whom Maths problems and History work sheets shared the sinister quality of being disarmingly simple.

"So now what?, Are you going to sic the mongrel on me again?" asked my wife, who massaged her leg, looked around at the mess and proceeded to restack her blouses and skirts and underskirts. "Well, Diogo? Are you going to perforate my guts or not?"

Her round piece of thigh enlarged, and the hardness in my trousers got harder as I rocked in the rocker. A promontory pressed against my fly, yearning for more room, yearning to assert itself, yearning to crack through the shell with its beak, and I helped it by unfastening my belt, unbuttoning my trousers and sliding down my long johns until there was no more barrier and I could see, even without looking down, the penis-smokestack of my steamer-body, with my shirt-tail serving as flag. The maids and the steward jabbered in the yard, alarmed by the shot, as I kept swelling amid the scattered clothes and dried mud, dilating the purple veins of my desire. If it weren't for the mirrors that mocked and unnerved me I would have felt transported, back on the slopes, crouching on a terrace, trembling with excitement as I listened for a calling bird or a bounding rabbit. But the mirrors muck everything up when they send us back to ourselves,

stamped with dark splotches like packages returned as unmail-
able, and that's why I picked up the angel-buttressed clock and
assassinated every last one of those sardonic glass rectangles so
smugly set in their carved wood frames. My faces disappeared
from the walls as instantly as furniture when a light is switched
off, chinks in the paint and spots of mildew appeared in their
stead, gilded chips flew aimlessly through the room, bits of brick
and yellow powder rained on the floor, and I thought, It was my
mother who decorated the room, She was the one who put up all
the mirrors, after my father's death, so that she could at least have
the company of herself or, rather, of her undulating self-
deceptions, for she must have known that what we see when we
look at ourselves is as different as a stranger from the real us, with
a forehead that's different, cheekbones that are different, ears
that are different, unrecognizable, grave, and false, and I thought
Now not even my mother's ghost can appreciate, among these
chests and dressers, the nebulous and transparent illusions of an
old lady looking this way and that, with childish glee, at the rouge
on her cheeks, at her outmoded dresses, her outlandish hairdos,
and while my wife gathered up brushes, hangers, and cosmetic
jars and shut coats and scarves into trunks, I bashed away at the
mirror frames, still with that piece of thigh in mind, looking at it
the way a horny mutt in the park looks at a bitch's hindquarters,
and I observed her hair unpinned, her skirt in disarray, her ankle
gnawed to the bone, and I forced her to lie face up on the rug and
dropped the angelic timepiece to wrench open her legs, laughing
at her protests, her shrieks and her silly womanish punches, and
as I penetrated, punishing her with a smack across the face for the
scratches on my back and for her slippery eel's resistance that
refused my tongue and my caresses and my anxious male body on
her breast, she picked up the broken mantel clock, and I saw her
fingers around the marble base grow larger, saw her arm in the

air, saw her suddenly vengeful face, saw the clock hands approach with the slow-motion swiftness of a catastrophe, and I felt a different taste in my mouth, my eyes out of focus, an unexpected inertia, an infant weakness in my muscles, and after she got free of me, after she dragged me out of the way over the mirror and glass and frame remains, after she finished packing, without worrying about folding her clothes at the creases since the bus was about to leave, and after she lugged the suitcases to the door, then she called one or two maids to help her carry her things to the village while I lay there alone, unable to move but hearing and understanding everything and hating her, wishing the bloodhound would attack her on the stairs or ram her waist into the cabinets' wrought-iron hinges, and five or six years ago, when I heard she was living in Oporto with a married couple of half-blind cousins, I phoned to Reguengos for a taxi and got a prehistoric carcass that broke down just outside Portalegre, fuming burned rubber from under the hood. The driver and I stood to one side with our hands in our pockets and silently regarded the pitiful wheezing of the decrepit dragon, eructing hot water and dark liquids down its rusty flanks as its metallic entrails clanged and snapped, until the man announced, as we began walking towards town, "This heap of shit belongs in the junk yard, I'll sell it for a counterfeit dollar to the first gypsy I see," but there were no gypsies to be had, only the highway and trees and thistles, a chilliness that made us button up our coats and a cart that grumbled on a dirt by-road next to the asphalt. "The really sad thing," he said in a mournful voice, angling for a good tip, "is that I can't buy a new one, I'm flat broke, so now what?" Beggars, spongers and anyone who ejaculates tears for money irritate me almost as much as women, so I asked him with the friendly innocence of one who hasn't understood, "What did you do before driving a taxi?", and the guy snivelled, "I was a cook in a

171

café," and as we reached the first houses I said, "If I could just be a plain old cook, you've no idea how much grief I'd be spared," and, hearing an explosion behind us, we turned to see the holocausted taxi. I supportively slapped the scapula of the driver, who with the stillness of a china animal watched his car fizzle in a series of elongated flames and writhing, buckling metals, "Don't worry, they'll take you back at the café, maybe not to cook but at least to wait at tables or to sweep the floor and clean the toilets in the morning," and when the taxi had been reduced to a pork crackling whose charred edges still smouldered, I added sweetly, "Since you didn't take me to Oporto I guess I don't owe you anything, One of these days I'm sure we'll have the pleasure of meeting up in Reguengos, and do take it easy till then," and I walked quickly into the town, because personal misfortunes disgust me as much as women's menstruations and make me feel equally, indignantly impotent, and I wish I could have forgotten the nauseating wreckage and its cry-baby owner, standing there gazing with the hunched-in body of a cat that's just been castrated.

I took the train and the next day I was in Oporto, which is larger than Evora but sunless—brown and black like a rotten tooth—and it was raining the melancholy waters of a geriatric autumn, of a second-hand November bought cheap at a flea market. The blind cousins lived near a park on a road with trams, in a basement flat whose taps all dripped in unison into cement or rusty enamel sinks: taps by the dozen, lurking behind partitions and photographs and tureens, raining their own mini-autumns in the abominable odour of last night's meatballs. The male cousin opened the door, probing with his glasses and smelling the silence, asking, "May I help you?" I elbowed him aside, groped in the shadows and shouted, "Adelina, come here immediately! Adelina!", and as I got used to the darkness I realized that everything there was ugly and mangy and cruddy and repugnant. A cape dangled from the hat rack like a hanged bat. Blue-violet reindeer pranced in the rug. A leg-short cabinet tottered in its corner, next to a handful of umbrellas buried in a tall pot like *banderillas* in a bull, while the taps continued their Chinese water torture, doing their damnedest to drive me insane with the slow persistent monotony of their dripping. The elfish cousin, about half my height and weight, planted his glasses in my navel as he climbed up the buttons of my vest.

"Adelina," I called, swatting him away, "get your butt over here or else!"

A woman clenching a mop appeared in the hallway and without hearing or seeing me informed the elf, "There's a foot and a half of water in the kitchen and casseroles are floating into the dining room, Should I call the plumber or what?"

"Adelina," I bellowed, "am I going to have to drag you out by the ear?, Is that what you want?"

"It's too late," said the blind cousin, perched on my shoulders, "The phone swam past a couple of minutes ago, Can't you hear it ringing on the steps?"

The umbrella urn wavered, lifted up several inches, tipped on its side, rode the current through my legs and, reaching the landing, bubbled its last, desperate drowning gasp. Through a bedroom window I could see rain and more rain, some old buildings, a statue, and the birdlessness of perpetual winters. "I put the tape measure up against the wall," the woman's voice called from the kitchen. "Twenty-one inches and still counting."

The husband hopped on top of my head to scan my face with his glasses and hot breath until he concluded, "You're Diogo, aren't you?", during which time pictures and platters whirled around my waist, the exultant voice announced "Twenty-three inches, Filipe," the floor settled in successive creaks, a lamp was caught up in the storm, followed by an earthenware cat with a broken paw, and finally the leg-short cabinet started reeling. "You're Diogo, right?" the blind man insisted as he imprinted his glasses into my neck, my cheeks, my eyes, "Adelina passed away about a month ago, One evening she didn't come out for dinner, which we thought was odd, so we went to her room and yup, seems all her stomach veins ruptured at once." "Twenty-eight inches," rejoiced the wife, her exaltation muffled by the gushing water. Only one or two taps close to the ceiling still dripped, inaudible next to the cascades coming off the dressers. "Three feet eight inch—" yelled the woman, abruptly stifled, no doubt crushed by a mahogany reef full of dishes and silverware. Wooden spoons and plastic forks streamed out of the kitchen, and as I sat down in the train that would take me back to Reguengos, the cousin with glasses, shiny shoes and a tie floated flat on his back down the station platform, colliding haphazardly into waving handkerchiefs, into Coke and sandwich machines, and into the people saying farewell outside my window and looking fuzzy through the dust of many journeys, until we pulled out into the open air and into more rain, wedged between walls and buildings, with me all infuriated that I couldn't get revenge, that most of the people we hate make a point of dying right when we're about to lay hands on them, that I didn't even have the pleasure of going to your funeral, where I could have twisted inside with pangs of joy as your coffin was lowered, and a white-jacketed employee walked by to announce dinner with a jingling bell behind which staggered a troop of starved passengers. From time to time the lights of villages or factories showed through my reflection which was always there, bald and ugly, its teeth chewing on an empty cigarette-holder, its chin resting on a tie like a caterpillar on a leaf, and I dozed off, lulled by the dinner bell as I planned a week of celebration in Lisbon, in some whore-house or other where I'd stay all day and night, meals in bed, crumbs on the covers, lots of black lace, lots of lipstick, lots of imitation champagne, lots of expensive tenderness that would clean out my pockets, lots of forks bringing chicken and rice to my mouth, lots of furry hips, lots of laughter and exhausted tits, and on waking in the train I tried to get up and couldn't, I couldn't even budge my fingers, I was paralysed in bed, in Monsaraz, where my son was on all fours, bypassing the medicine table with curved sections of track, blowing through his train-whistle lips, and my son-in-law was saying, "I'll hop in the car and go to Evora right this minute if necessary, but we've got to find the old man's bank statement, even if it's buried in the trash, If that smart-ass niece manages to grab the mongoloid in the hubbub of the festival and take her away, then our goose will really be cooked," and my daughter, pulling me by the shoulder, was asking, "Where's the will, Father?, Where's all the money?, Who did you leave everything to?", and I, just in from Oporto, looked at her with a foreigner's bewilderment, unable to comprehend or answer, feeling only a remnant of blood swishing here and there in my veins, shoved along by a worn-out pump.

"Has the kid come back with the retard yet?" asked my son-in-law, fishing for the car keys in his coat. "Who was the idiot who let them leave?"

"Ask your feather-brained sister-in-law," said my daughter, who was tapping the furniture on the non-existent chance of a secret compartment.

Just like her mother, I thought. Just like her mother, whom I fetched in Vendas Novas to be my wife, on the basis of a photograph and my brother's letter, "Stepdaughter of a doctor, heiress of a rich family, plays harp, paints, speaks German, has more land coming to her alone than all of us put together, and what's more, she's got the finest pair of boobs in Alentejo, If I were in your shoes I'd at least have a look at her, What's there to lose?", and I went to have a look, not only because it was the slack season on the farms but because I was getting tired of lifting maids' skirts behind doors and paying more attention to the sound of my mother's footsteps than to the body I was fondling, and my brother met me in his lieutenant's uniform, extolling the merits of the photograph in the midst of pushes and shoves and train whistles, "Just look at her hair, Just look at that neck, And her shoulders, You'll see her in person soon enough, I'll point her out to you on Sunday when she comes out of Mass," and I was dumfounded by such selflessness, such enthusiasm, such insistence, until I found out years later that they'd been fucking each other for months, doing it pushed up against the piano during the regiment's dances and commemorative dinners, both of them with cake or glass in hand, sprinkling each other with flour as her rear end played a frenzied sonata on the keyboard, and that they continued to fuck, even after our wedding, until a grenade exploded during training and nine soldiers including my dear brother were sent fifty feet skyward in a magnificent firework display of bones, teeth, mangled entrails, and gold buttons, and on Sunday, true to his word, we were ensconced in a café opposite the church, waiting for the photograph to come out of Mass. Suddenly my brother shook me, jumping up from his painted metal chair, "Look," and it was you walking down the steps and greeting people before heading home, escorted by an old woman who kept spitting into a handkerchief and who ended up living here in Monsaraz for more years than I care to remember, eating millions of bowls of mushy cereal and complaining of her arthritis with her mouth full. I met you for the first time in that cruddy army town, where the wind lifted litter from the ground to drape it from the trees, "Over there, the tall one wearing blue," indicated my brother, poking his fingers into my ribs, "Where does she live?" I asked without any apparent curiosity, lighting a cigarette, and he, so unbelievably nice, paying for the coffees, "Just past the school, Come on and I'll show you," and we came to the gate of a huge dishevelled garden with a house in the middle, "You can go back to the base," I said, "I can do the rest by myself," and I pushed open the gate, walked across the shaggy lawn, and ten minutes later was in the sitting room talking to the doctor, who drank non-stop, nudging me knowingly on the knee without letting go of his glass, and after bottle number three he leaned back in the sofa and bellowed for Hortense. A hippo-sized woman wearing an apron stuck her muzzle into the room to ask, "What is it now?, Have you run out of white?", and the doctor said, "Let me introduce you to Adelina's husband—uh, I'm terrible with names, What did you say yours was?" The incredulous mastodon trudged across the rug, staring at us—me and the drunk—with her petite hippo eyes, "What kind of horse shit has the wine filled your head with this time, Ernesto?", and the dazed doctor, curled up on the sofa with his shirt hanging out, studying the wineglass against the light from the window, "But think how useful a son-in-law would be, Hortense, He could wash the car, fix leaking taps, laugh fifty times at the same joke," and the wife, to me, "You run along, young man, so I can take care of this idiot's health," while the doctor uncorked another bottle, reasoning, "Imagine how great it would be to have someone who only agrees with us, Hortense." "If you'll allow me, ma'am," I said politely as the doctor sank in a pillowy shipwreck, exclaiming, "This imbecile wants to marry Adelina, Hortense!" "If you'll just give me thirty seconds of your time, ma'am," I implored as I plunged the drunk's head under the cushions and sat on top of the human wine vat, which would occasionally raise my lapels in the air with its rippling, insisting "The nitwit wants to marry your daughter, Hortense, What are you waiting for?", and the voice gradually grew faint and distant, turning into the weak cheep of a bird in the rain, burbling then quieting then burbling then nothing, "Thirty seconds, ma'am," I said to the hippopotamus, crumpling the doctor's corpse with my thighs, "Thirty seconds so that I can explain my feelings for your daughter." The regiment's bugles rallied the soldiers to their useless exercises, my brother pinned flags on a map, and the woman hesitated, trying to gauge by the colour of my nose how many shots I'd chugged that morning. "I just came out of Mass," I swore to put her at ease, "a nice Mass like I go to every day, and today, when I was standing up after Communion, I saw your daughter in the pew across from mine, and it was like I'd walked into Paradise, into the presence of the Virgin herself." A maid entered and left, the doctor's corpse began to stink of cemetery under my hips, as if my armpits had traded places with my groin, and the woman opened the mossy cavern of her mouth in a formidable roar, "SCRAM," and it was three months later, after lunch, that I took the photograph to bed in Monsaraz, listening to the housekeeper play marching guard in the hall, back and forth like a metronome—a great help to smooth over my jerky ostrich thrusts.

"Going to Evora or Lisbon or anywhere else is a waste of time," my daughter said to her husband, turning the loathing rage of her nose towards me. "You really think you can find where this wrinkled waxwork stuck his will?"

And I thought, Children are taught by the rod, especially when we're almost sure they're not ours. By the rod, like mules, from the day they're born until the day we die, or become so crippled we can no longer move from the bed where they lay us, hardly seeing, hardly hearing, hardly understanding the meaning of their words and these fireworks blasting outside, this shouting commotion, this strange happy feasting, remembering my wife's

178

grief when my brother died, his lying-in-state in a narrow room full of uniformed visitors, the long and drawn-out funeral procession, olive tree past olive tree, dusty bar past dusty bar, while my son-in-law demanded the money I'd spent over the years in casinos and brothels in Lisbon, until finally he yanked me off the mattress, so that I lay on the floor in my pyjamas with the catheter bag dripping between my legs amidst the roaches, the ants, my slippers, and my son, who was placing a locomotive lovingly on the tracks, next to the bedpan station, his practised cheeks making a storm of saliva in which I could still hear a Chug chug chug.

Day Three of the Festival:

The Role of String-Pulling
in the Genesis of Schizophrenia

Chapter

The workshop was open for Sunday customers, blankets were displayed on the walls and the tables and the ground, and I was by myself, mending a rug, when the man walked in. The light from the windows faded the colours and refracted in the showcase aquariums, where objects carved from steer horns wavered like distant fish or hoopoes, and outside I could see the tea-leaf wings of kites dissolving in the teapot sky, whose aluminium distorted the houses and trees in twisted, protracted reflections. The man walked in and I could tell, even before looking at him, by a kind of instinct akin to the disquiet of animals prior to earthquakes, that he wasn't there to buy anything, that he wasn't interested in wooden figurines or blankets or rugs, and I could tell that he'd had to jump this way and that to avoid the scrambling chickens, and that the dust and wool strands hanging like tapeworms made him cough silently, and that he was wearing his usual car-nivorously amiable smile, waiting for me to lift my head and notice him standing there, between two looms, hunting in his pockets for his cigarette case. The firecrackers from the castle made the house shudder. The mooing of the cows came and went with the tides of the south wind, and so too came the spectators' wild shouting and the band instruments inside the arena blowing their random notes, identical to the pieces of paper that blow over the streets in winter, urging death to the bull. It must have been seven or eight in the morning because the sun still hadn't lit up the wall that was covered with pictures of saints and tin-framed photos of my daughter. From the door I'd have been able to see the Guadiana River below, with its boulders and shrubs, flowing down terraces or running aground on its way to the sea. The man struck a match (there was a flash, it died) and cleared his throat so that I'd look up, and I looked. Seated on my stool with a rug in my lap, a needle in the air and a eucalyptic serenity on my face, I looked.

"Where is she?" he asked.

The last few days had taken their toll, making him haggard like an autumn sunset, as if he were the sick one, as if he and not my grandfather were the victim of the medicines of the doctor from Reguengos, and his dentures loomed larger on his pleated face, like molars protruding from skulls. A stray dog paused on the doormat, sniffed the dust that hung in the air and ran away, and the smell of the man's tobacco, the same as I remembered, filled my nose as in the old days, when he lay naked on his back in my bed, smoking, his skinny feet evoking the skeletal ankles of martyrs in church paintings.

"The kid doesn't wake up till nine," I said as if I hadn't understood, cutting a thread with the scissors and mending the fringes, in the midst of glazed plates and cowhide belts. (The first mosquitoes began to hum.) "Unless you want me to get her up now. It's probably not a bad idea for her to spend a little time with her father."

The man couldn't find an ashtray, so he carefully extinguished the cigarette against the dirt floor, as if all the junk strewn about him (blankets, cloaks, wooden figures, vases) had taken on a mysterious and ironic importance. He went to the outside door to toss away the butt and I looked at him, wondering, How did I ever?, What on earth attracted me to such an old lummox? If the fireworks had stopped exploding, I could have heard the Guadiana waters siphoning through the rocks.

"I'm not interested in the girl," the man said, picking a piece of tobacco off his lip. "I want to know where your mother is."

The Guadiana waters siphoning through the rocks, the birds at the mill and at the drowned fisherman's boats, the fingers of the wind caressing the olive trees, and, behind everything, the morning silence. If the fireworks had stopped exploding, I could have heard just how irritated the man was. He stared at a blanket without seeing it, contained his rage as he regarded the crumbling ceiling, and smiled with my grandfather's smile of furious rage, which I'd slowly come to recognize over the years.

"Isn't she up at the festival?" I asked in surprise, still wondering, How could I let him? "She always hangs around in the square, fascinated by the gold in the jewellers' stalls."

How could I let him and how could my mother let him, even if she does take after a monkey, even if she can't talk, even if she is a mongoloid?, How could we both get pregnant by him, how could we let him near us, how could his wife let him, and how can my aunt still let him? A holm oak bowed and touched the front of the house and I thought The entire village knows I'm his daughter and that I have a daughter by him in my bedroom, The entire village knows that they set me up with this cabin in Outeiro to get rid of the painful accusation of my presence, which even disturbed my grandfather, and which even disturbs me when I happen to catch my face in a mirror and see them both perfectly—my grandfather and my uncle—as if their faces had been superimposed to arrive at my nose, eyebrows, mouth, and that forever mute, sarcastic smile.

"Nobody's seen her at the festival," the man said, apparently amused as he played with a stuffed cloth doll. "I thought you might be hiding her because of her part in the inheritance."

Now the workshop was shimmering with a greenish light filtered by the branches, and although the heat had not yet stirred, the chickens and ducks were already filing inside to escape the sun, settling into corners on beds of broken feathers. The first cow must have trotted into the ring, because the band started up and the screams of the drunk audience almost drowned out the firecrackers. I imagined them all, sitting on the circular stone steps inside the ruined castle, watching the teenagers wave cloths and coats before fleeing the animals' horns, while the bar owner, sticking out his enormous gut, marched out of the pen and towards the animals with the slow and proud disdain of cheap brandy.

. "Then maybe she's in the castle watching the bullfight," I said as I folded the rug and put it with the others, "hoping someone will offer her a caramel bar or some almond brittle. Did you send the steward to go and look for her there?"

A bird chirped in the naseberry tree to the left of the house. I've never been good at the names of plants or birds: I get them all mixed up in my head, the words seem alien, meaningless, with no resemblance to fixed roots or flying eyes. The man, who was still playing with the doll, swinging it by a leg like a dead hare, widened his amiable smile and I thought No, it can't be true, this son-of-a-bitch and I don't really have a daughter in the room in the back next to the cork trees that at night remind me of my dying grandfather's hair, with my uncle purring Chug chug chug under the mattress, surrounded by slippers and bedpans.

"In the castle my ass," the man said, tired of the doll, dropping it from the tip of its arm like a horse its cylinder of faeces. The doll smiled at me from the floor before it was crushed underfoot. "I know perfectly well she's here, The cripple in the choir saw her leave Monsaraz with you. Right now your aunt's got the notary holed up in the living room, keeping him amused with liqueurs until we get your mother there to scribble some monkey Xs on the mortgage papers."

The stuffed cloth doll bled sawdust from its charcoal-drawn mouth. The bird in the naseberry took off, to be replaced by a flock of pigeons. The mosquitoes around the laundry tank hummed their microscopic gluttony. Shrubs whose names I didn't know and grasses without any names at all were crawling through the chinks in the windows. The Australian diver was going down and coming up in the Guadiana River, snagging eels for dinner as his snorkel's ping-pong ball bobbed in the foam. A foreign couple armed with backpacks invaded the workshop, marvelling at the pottery and animal hides like the explorers of old before the Africans' ebony statuettes. A square of paper on the door proclaimed *English spoken*, and I approached the backpacks with the friendly unctuosity of tour guides: at the official exchange rate a tureen was equivalent to a couple of pork chops, i.e. to a few hours without hunger and the disgusting eels going rancid in the kitchen.

"If she's not at the house screeching, then she has to be in the castle," I said, pausing to listen to the clamour of the band, thinking This afternoon I'd like to go and watch the bull lose its head. "Why should I care about money you've already proved doesn't exist?"

The foreigners sifted through the rubbish with great interest as I hovered over them like a wasp, showing off my rubbish (*Look, look*), and for the first time I could feel the smell of the river sludge in the cabin, the seaweed smell of the fish we ate regularly and silently for dinner on a linoleum table next to the stove, fish still wet with their foetal waters. I felt the unpleasant aroma of shores where water has come and gone, identical to that of bodies on the edge of sleep after making love, sticky with fatigue, I felt the smell of the Guadiana crossing through the hallway to lie down at my feet the way animals do, and from some other world, with the river in my head, I pointed out a platter, a cruet-holder and a quilt (*Look look, Achtung*) to the two backpacks, which followed me warily, like explorers behind pygmies, through a labyrinthine forest of blankets. And as we turned the corner around a straw-seated chair (they gaped as if beholding a baobab), I saw the man lift his boot and rest it against a stand full of pottery objects. Bowls, cups, casseroles, pots, amphoras, jars, jugs and speckled animals slowly tilted towards one of the looms, slid off the shelves and shattered on the ground, to the delight of the backpacks, who no doubt felt privileged to be witnessing a primitive ritual, executed in their honour by a member of the tribe. My daughter began whimpering in the back room.

"Either you tell me where she is," explained the man in a gentle voice, applying his sole to a second stand, "or I'll finish off every last piece of this shit."

I felt the smell of the river's fish and sludge and dead frogs, the smell of things that decompose and decay and putrefy under water, like the diver who daily dwindled in size, reduced to a pair of flippers, a rubber tube topped with a ping-pong ball, and a basket with eels writhing in the slimy straw bottom. The smell was of the goat carcasses carried by the rapids from waterfall to waterfall. The foreigners were approaching a pile of hides when the second stand took a bow and followed the first one to the floor, crashing into a case of rugs that wagged their paleness like ailing tongues. I thought about hitting the man, I thought about screaming, I thought about going to get Burt, but how could I ask for help from a deaf plastic ball that moved up and down in a swirl of circles? My daughter called me. The backpacks were enthralled by the curious local custom of a man bashing looms apart with a stool as he repeated calmly, "The mongoloid isn't entitled to anything, and if you don't hurry up and tell me where you've hidden her, I can guarantee you'll be on the street begging for your next meal." The chickens and ducks ambled away, shaking off dirty eiderdown feathers that rose up weightless in the growing heat. As the man proceeded to cut up the blankets with a pair of scissors he waved the backpacks away (*Allez allez*), and the foreigners floated in zigzags towards the road, towards the sea, like the corpses of livestock during the December floods. "You can't imagine how I hate doing this, but she's nowhere to be found in the castle or the village," the man regretted, going at the quilts with a razor knife, "It pains me to ruin my own poor daughter, all because of a measly X we need from your mother on the notary's papers." The workshop was turning into a rubbish heap where I coughed on feathers, wool scraps and sticky lumps of dust. "Really and truly it pains me to ruin my own daughter," the man lamented, "particularly since there's nothing worth fighting over in the old man's estate." There was no one I could resort to, no one that passed by the open door except for a dog or two with drooping eyelids, and the ping-pong ball kept bobbing in the river with a maniacal perseverance, far away and oblivious to me. The ever smiling man waded towards me through a high tide of debris: "Well, young lady? You're not going to force me to hang around here all day waiting for your mother, I hope." He kicked the door shut, knocked over the only stand that was still standing ("Now it's just you and me, darling, So have you stuck the mongoloid in a trunk or what?"), and I realized then that he'd lied to me in my grandfather's office as he'd lied to me the entire time he slept with me and murmured "I love you" in my ear so that I'd go further with him, so that I'd give him more pleasure, more thrill, more orgasms, so that I'd let him push my head against his thighs, "Swallow it, baby, swallow, that's right," I realized that not everything was squandered, sold or mortgaged, that there was still money in the bank, or in land, or in buildings, and that he and his wife wanted to get it before the Communists did, before a scruffy mob of farm workers armed with rakes and knives and shotguns broke into the living room in a whirl of unreasonable, inflexible demands. I took a couple of steps into the hallway that led to the still dark end of the cabin, from where my daughter was calling, and the man said, "Not so fast, sweetie, not so fast, We're going to inspect every inch of this place," and he grabbed me by the elbow with the claws of a bird (a bird as nameless as the plants and other birds), dragged me into the kitchen and promptly smashed the doors to the china cabinet and the glassware inside it, knocked down the chairs, opened the refrigerator, turned over the margarine and the cottage cheese, tore open and emptied the plastic bag full of eels, whose horrendous smell brought the sea to my nostrils, poured out the detergent, the olive oil, and the wine, and I watched him as if in a trance, without anger or protest, trying to figure out what they'd done with the money, "So tell me, how are you going to put everything back together?" asked my uncle, who then, very calmly, cracked the sink with a flat-iron, "Would you rather have the Communists?, Do you want them to line us up against the church wall and shoot us all tomorrow?", and I followed without trying to stop him as he emptied out trunks, tore up photographs, and flung papers around, I had the sea in my mind, stretches of deserted beach, fishing villages perched on the cliffs, and the placid sunset purpling the waters, "Don't you realize that we need the dough to get over the border?" my uncle asked, "Don't you understand that we'll be made into mincemeat if we hang around here any longer?", and I imagined a legion of red flags coming after us with their hoes while my uncle penetrated a cubicle replete with empty wine jugs, which were soon awkwardly swinging their wicker-covered buttocks, stumbling on their handles as on defective legs. My daughter, several rooms down, called "Mummy!" from her bed in the troubled voice peculiar to nightmares, the festival band stopped playing then started, and the next cow charged into the ring behind children, men wearing caps who took cover in the dug-outs, and drunks who lurched blindly, smashing into the boards. The Communists nestled a pistol into my grandfather's ear and fired as an old mouthless woman, with a priest's narrow eyes, tragically and terribly held up a crossed hammer and sickle in the churchyard. The man ransacked the linen closet (a white cotton Guadiana covered the floor with sheets and towels and washcloths), he toppled over a small chest on which pictures and a piggy bank had been sitting, "Are you too stupid to see that they want to kill people like us?" he argued, "Can't you get it into your thick skull that I want to save your mother from being raped for days on end by every bumpkin within a fifty-mile radius?", and I envisioned farm workers ripping off her striped pinafore with their grubby hands, I imagined her hairy legs on the mattress and a peasant unzipping his trousers with glee, and I thought Preposterous, it's just a cheap trick to extort what they want from me, and I thought In any case the workers don't obey like they used to, they demand better wages, they grumble, they protest, they don't smile politely, they turn their heads, and my uncle ferreted through all the rooms, sniffing, pawing, circling, recircling, ravaging, and asking, "You want to see your mother dead, is that it?, I bet you want to see us all dead!", and reddening with fury, still sniffing, pawing, circling, and ravaging, he said, "All dead, in a gruesome bloodbath, with pitchforks planted in our guts, our arms sliced off, our genitals mutilated—is that what you want, you fool?", and far below, indifferent to the man and indifferent to me, the ping-pong ball obsessively climbed and descended the current. When the frog-man comes back, I thought, with his beard dripping like an oversized pubis, he'll bring ten or twelve pounds of eels and find us—my daughter and me—impaled by the Communists or crouched behind a pile of bricks waiting for him. My uncle returned to the kitchen and kicked the insect colonies which inhabited the tiles, which perched on the water taps and gas burners, which deposited eggs and excrement in the pots and pans, pecked their way into the bags of rice, and skipped out to the yard in contralto sniggers. "This place is revolting," the man said, inspecting the shelves shielded with screening to keep out the flies, "I honestly don't understand how your daughter doesn't get hepatitis in this cesspool." The people in the castle applauded, the music swayed along with the tree branches, "How can you make a soup in all this filth?, How can you prepare fish in such a pigsty?" A chicken peered at us from a crate. The man squeezed into the midget-sized pantry, battling jars of vinegar and canned sardines. "Mummy!" my daughter kept calling monotonously in a neutral voice like a perpetual pendulum, mum-mee mum-mee mum-mee mum-mee. The Communists, with machine guns on their shoulders and wine on their breath, would rape her as well, pulling her hair and dragging her by the neck out to the turnip patch, murdering my geese, my turkeys, and my chickens, and I thought, in the way my mind used to think as a child, when my cranium was a vacant sky with just a tiny cloud of desire inside, This afternoon I want to go to the bullfight, and I saw the knives being thrust into the bull's backside, then falling out, to be thrust in again, I saw a huge crowd, the beast's slow gait, the gleaming trumpets, the crumbling battlements, "I guess you wouldn't feel at home in a place that was moderately clean," the man said, looking over the bedroom, and there was no more ping-pong ball on the river, now the frog-man was on his way back, getting his flippers caught in the gorse, losing eels that fell out of the basket and crawled every which way, like desperate intestines, drowning in the brush, and now he was pushing open the door with the eel-spear and standing on the doormat surveying the shambles. My uncle pulled aside the curtain and was met by the perfect miniature of his own face sitting up in the bed, with an expression that matched his, dispassionately repeating "Mummy, mummy, mummy, mummy, mummy" as if there were a broken spring in her larynx that made her get stuck on the same two syllables, and I was alone, hardly aware of them at all, thinking It would be fun to go to the bullfight this afternoon, to be in the middle of those smells, the laughs, the shouts, the cheers, the sweating and breathing of the audience, The man rushed straight at me and shook me by the elbows in anger and fear, saying "Do you think I want to end up in the hands of the Commies like you?, What I want, all I want, is for the frigging mongoloid to mark an X for the notary so I can get some money and clear out." The band began the two-step for the next cow, "Just tell me where you hid the brainless chimp and I won't lay a finger on you," he proposed, "I'll even send you some dollars from Brazil so you can put this place back together and keep selling these damfool blankets if that's what you want," and his fingers bit my bones, something snapped in my shoulderblade like a globule of air or a stick when it breaks. "Don't be such an idiot, The Commies are everywhere, Can't you smell them?, If you want to be killed by them, that's your business, but if not, then for Christ's sake bring the retard and come along with us." "Mummy," my daughter said in her marionette tone, and two equal faces were staring at me, "I've already told you to try at the festival," I said, "at the castle, at the jewellery stalls, the almond brittle, the fritters," while they—father and daughter—looked at me in silence, disbelief, and unmoving rage, as if frozen in a gesture, or on the verge of one, and the chicken coop retreated under the shade of the trees, and next to the coop the woodshed, and next to the woodshed the lean-to that stored old looms, some pruning shears on nails, brushes and cans of lime and the scythe for shaving the scrubby area behind the cabin. The two-step halted but the fireworks' blasts and the man's fingers kept up their slow, frightful, inexorable slaughter, shredding tendons and cartilage, while a rooster pecked the black hen and immediately got bored of her, "If the notary heads back for Reguengos before I locate your mother," my uncle said, "then so help you God, don't even try to imagine what I'm going to do to you," and I wasn't sure if it was the man or my daughter speaking, both so grim, threatening, stark. Someone (the ping-pong ball? the rapists? the murderers?) knocked on the door at the other end of the cabin and my uncle said, "Tomorrow at the latest we're crossing into Spain, and you can come with us if you want, but if your mother doesn't show and the notary balks, then we won't even have enough money to buy lunch," and my daughter seemed to be agreeing with what he said or to be saying it herself, in the annoying, homophonic tinkle of a goatbell, and the man looked casually out the window, then at me, then the window, then me again, as his pupils changed size, heavy with suspicion, "At the castle, huh?" he said slowly, "At the festival with the drunks and the fireworks, is that right?", the knocking at the door continued, there was shouting, the ping-pong ball appeared in the window like a celluloid sunrise, and below the ball there was a rubberized head with a foggy oval mask that asked "Wackawacka?" as my uncle leaped out of the window, passing the frog-man as if he weren't real, as if he were nothing more than a bizarre, bearded crystallization of a cartoon character, weightless and worthless. My uncle threw open the door to the woodshed, stepping on pine cones and logs, I sat on the edge of the bed, my daughter hushed up, a few seconds later he reappeared, brushing off straw and cobwebs and dragging behind him a little grey-haired woman whose tongue hung out and whose pinafore was too tight and who squealed like one of the pigs on the slope leading up to the village, and the stupefied Australian merely stood there, hugging on to the basket of eels that brought the odour of ocean, whiff on whiff, into the bedroom's stagnant quiet.

Chapter

They talk about their money, but they have no money. Whatever money they had is gone and even the clothes they're wearing look a bit shabby, second-hand, as if bought at clearance sales in Reguengos or Evora. They may have servants and silver and paintings and factories and land and the largest house in Monsaraz, but they have no money, everything was mortgaged to the hilt by the old man wheezing in the bed upstairs. The old man, he had money, or so they say, before I or any of these people were born, and as long as he was in good health he managed to keep up appearances through a million and one legal and illegal strata-gems: deferring payments, extending credit and renegotiating terms while simultaneously spending in Lisbon what he didn't have, selling the same farm twice or the same apartment three times, and inventing, when necessary, other properties and other buildings in a juggling act that was as effective as it was confusing, because it pitted person against person, bank against bank, and they all gave in, because no one's convinced they're entitled to anything in a nation where hardly anyone has anything nor can expect anything, and certainly not anything from the deceased, who on leaving this world leave us nothing but debts, an angry nostalgia where their dinner plate once sat, and a few photographed smiles that fade with our memory. Which is why these people who dragged me to their house don't have any money. But they're determined to play out their own poorer version of the old man's farce, so I was forced to travel ten miles and put up with teas and chit-chat and sweets that were hell on my dentures while they hunted for some mongoloid or other to thumbprint a document entitling them to enough money—if they're lucky—to buy food for three days before having to graze on the cabbages in the cemetery or else double-hock the already hocked furniture. They found me playing dominoes at a friend's house and I fell for their sob story, as I'd forgotten about the festival and they conveniently forgot to mention it, so we inched along the road at five miles an hour behind God knows how many cars and buses, watching men and women pass us on foot, sweaty and solemn, dressed up for the Sunday Mass they weren't going to, and inside the village walls we were plunged into a labyrinth of music, fireworks, frying fritters, jewellery stands and shifty gypsy smiles until, after passing a barefoot African who walked on glass while swallowing and belching fire, we arrived at the house, almost as imposing as a church, with five balconies on the second floor, a skin disease in the window frames, and a woman in mourning (though the mournee hadn't quite yet croaked) who spied us from the door, twisted her head around to confide something to someone, and graciously moved aside to let me through, "Do come in please, The sitting room is to your left." She reminded me of the old man, but without his cigarette-holder and his sardonic verve, and I thought So this is the estate manager's wife, the one he cheats on every day with any woman who'll have him, even with the oddball niece who sells bedspreads in Outeiro and who, according to the rumours, has him to thank for the asthmatic daughter that plays in the shop with scraps of wool. I sat in a huge velvet-covered chair, embarrassed by my sheepskin boots and work trousers (I weed the vegetable patch every Sunday), and the woman and her manager husband placed a teacup in my hands and stuffed my mouth with cookies, and as I chewed I gazed at them with the cheerless expression of a stable animal, irritated by the fireworks, irritated by the music, and irritated by their nervous anguish, and I could tell from the lighter-coloured rectangles that some pictures were missing from the walls, thus confirming that the family had begun dumping artwork and silverware on the antique dealers in Evora to pay the doctor and the butcher, both equally expensive, bloody and unnecessary: what with so many herbal teas to cure kidney stones which will eventually get pissed out, and what with so many hares just waiting to be caught for lunch in the fields, spending money on butchers of whatever sort is as incomprehensible to me as the tides of the ocean and the phases of the moon.

"Do forgive us for taking you away from your game," the woman apologized, squirming on the sofa like a hamster as she offered me more crackers and cookies in her plot to permanently stop up my body's plumbing, "but I suppose my husband has explained our urgency. We're going on a business trip to Spain this evening."

There was a whirring from the ceiling that I couldn't make out too well over the fireworks, but it sounded as if something electric was moving over the floorboards, and I looked at them again—the couple in front of me—ageing in furious and acidic fashion, probably still sleeping in the same bed but without ever touching, and I thought They don't have any money, They don't have and will never have any more money, except maybe a few crumbs from a creditor that feels sorry for them.

"I explained it all on the way here," the husband assured her, "—how we have to settle the inheritance immediately, before your father dies, since he left no will. All that's necessary is for everybody to sign, but now that your mongoloid sister for once in her life is actually needed she's disappeared. I've sent the steward and two servants to look for her, but so far no luck."

The whirring increased, delineating an ellipse of sound before it waned. Werewolf howls cavorted through the lanes, frightening the geese. The woman reopened her choppers, lined with bristly whiskers like a shark's:

"My brother will be easy," she said, "Just go upstairs, tell him where to sign, and presto. My retarded sister is another matter. But if you would be so kind as to wait a bit, I'm sure we'll round her up in a jiffy."

The husband went up the stairs, the whirring stopped, and soon I was confronted by a man dressed up as a station chief, who had war crosses and tin medals pinned on to his coat, a horn around his neck, and two flags—green and red—tucked under his armpit, and who stared at us and the baggage on the tea tray with the disapproval accorded to late passengers at a rural station, lost among pine trees, with a scale on one side and a urinal on the other. He blew the horn and advised us to carry the cakes and teacups on board while pointing to an imaginary clock on the wall behind the chandelier: "Three minutes behind schedule, Make it snappy, ladies and gentlemen, Lisbon's waiting for us." He spoke with such force and conviction that for a second I thought I was in a real train, with a locomotive beyond the kitchen tooting its whistle and groaning forward among the trees, passing through tiny unmarked villages, where I waved back to the women and children that motioned from their wagons before the red and white gates of level crossings. The engines shook the furniture, a pile of newspapers trembled, and the castle ruins evaporated in the heat behind us. We passed a way station with flowery letters in a ceramic-tile frame, "Do you have the documents?" the woman asked, and since my mouth was too full of sugar and flour to answer, I opened my briefcase and handed them over while my tongue whittled away at a huge gingerbread plug. She flipped back and forth through the pages to find the place for the signatures. "There where the date is," I spluttered, spitting lumps and crumbs through my dentures. "There has to be a dotted line somewhere or other," helped the husband, pulling at the folder. "I've had enough of looking through this crap, I can't find a dotted line anywhere in these pages," she said, "I bet this chap zipped through this just any old way and forgot about it." I drank some tea to wash down some cake, but a sweet, sticky piece of dough stuck to the roof of my mouth like a stubborn barnacle, "No one's forgotten anything, Give it here," the husband said, "The very first thing a notary does is make the lines where we have to confess our full names." The station chief, squinting his eyes in the direction of the chests and cabinets, saw that an express train had arrived beyond the drawers. "Take your grubby hands off it," squealed the woman, "He screwed up the document for me not for you," and I thought, gagging, As soon as I get rid of this blasted biscuit I'm going to fly out of here, If only I'd never got into this prick's jalopy to begin with. "There it is," said the husband, "don't turn the page again or you'll lose it," while I sat there quietly, trying to free myself from the flour, trying not to choke to death as I gulped on the hard bits like revolting Communion wafers, afraid that this beggarly couple who pretended wealth by hiding behind costume jewellery and a tie would rip up an entire week's work, until finally the woman took hold of the gold-striped sleeve of the station chief (who was busy manoeuvring some invisible freight cars and who looked at me from way far away, as if coming out of a nightmare or a long flight) and held his hand to the paper, saying, "Sign on this line, Gonçalo," and to me and her husband: "Anyone have a pen handy?"

"Is this today's freight traffic report?" asked the suspicious railwayman. "Because I'm not signing anything unless it's official."

"Of course it's the report, Gonçalo," his brother-in-law promised, grabbing my ballpoint out of my coat pocket, "You think we have time to play games on duty?"

The fireworks and the brouhaha rattled the windows, and in spite of so many maids and seamstresses and stewards, even the flowers in the vases looked dusty and tobacco-singed like the tired curtains. Through the old warped cupboard doors I could catch timid reflections of light off the dishes, immersed in the bottomless darkness common to caves and oak desks. A bloodhound peed nonchalantly against a carved column, and the golden pool that spread over the floor complemented the ornamental leaves and grape clusters. Looking at the cracks in the plaster, I thought One of these days this three-storey piece of shit is going to cave in and crush everyone and everything in it, One of these days it'll fall flat to the ground, leaving nothing but a pile of ammonia-scented dust, with a dying howl or two hovering over it.

"And what about the grand central station I want to build at the foot of Dad's bed?" the railwayman said as he handed back the papers unsigned. "I've drawn up some plans and a preliminary budget to send to the offices in Lisbon."

I thought, It's not just the cracks in the walls, the crumbling furniture, the woodworms in the rafters, the pictures that shudder when we walk past, and this rusty silence behind all the words, it's the cracks in their faces, the rottenness in their muscles and in the fig tree's ossified roots, and the cookies kept on coming, I picked crumbs off my trousers with a spit-moistened finger while the woman held out another plateful of crackers, filled my teacup, dumped in some sugar, "Don't be shy, there's plenty more," not just the splintered and threadbare furniture but the reigning cadaverous quietude, the yellow air, the sounds from outside that puncture the brick and cement like cardboard, a maid brought another teapot from the kitchen, the hound lay down on the rug in its own urine, the woman leaned towards me with the slanting, unsettling, sarcastic smile of her father, "Drink up, drink up." This piece of shit's going to cave in and crush us all, "This document authorizes us to begin building the station," the husband lied, "Here's the pen, What are you waiting for?" "I don't see anything in here about stations," the brother-in-law answered, "just a lot of talk about buildings and land." "Don't be shy, have another bite," the woman insisted as she approached my chair with a plate in each palm. "I see you know nothing about how government works," the husband retorted, "Don't you understand that we can't talk about these things openly until the President makes them public?, Don't you see this is written in a kind of code?" The railwayman looked at the papers again, moving his mouth like church women reciting rosaries, seized the pen, and pressed it against the dotted line, hesitating, "That's right," encouraged his brother-in-law, "Sign your full name on that nice little line and next week you'll receive a card of thanks from the Prime Minister and be nominated for a medal." The woman motherishly brushed sugar crystals off my shirt, "Oh dear, you're all covered," she said, "You must be famished, I've never seen anyone with such an appetite," and more pastries, and sandwiches, and dried fruits, and almonds, and drool running down my chin and spotting my shirt, inundating me, as the station chief stuck his tongue out to help him write better and then went back up the stairs going Chug chug chug until after the last step where the chugs were absorbed into the electric noise of locomotives rambling around like exhausted rats. "One dimwit down and one to go!" his brother-in-law announced, holding up the signature like a bullfighter waving his hat to the crowds, "Now all we need is your mongoloid sister." It's not the house that will do me in, I thought, unable to budge, It's the crackers they keep cramming down my throat. "Bring some currant juice for our guest," the woman said, and a pitcher containing a maroonish fluid and a wooden spoon arrived: "This will help your digestion," she clarified, "Now I want all of this straight down the hatch, and no buts about it." "Where the devil's your sister?" asked the man brandishing the papers, "Did one of you let her out of the pantry this afternoon?", and the maid stared at him apprehensively, the fireworks burst and whistled, the cows mooed from inside the castle, "Did someone let her out of the pantry after lunch?" the man repeated about ten times as loud. "Who would let her loose against your orders?" asked the woman, pouring the currant glop and some pinkish ice cubes into a tall goblet, "Particularly with her daughter running around out there trying to rob what's rightfully ours." But the man sprang up with lit pupils, charged towards the kitchen and, after a whirl of orders and expletives and excuses and insults, returned, scarlet with rage, smacking the document against his leg, "Hold on to him with the currants," he instructed, as if the juice were a high-walled prison, "Hold on to him, because your dear sweet sister-in-law had her son take the retard for a walk, and I have an idea where she might be." The woman listened, her body frozen with the goblet in mid-air: "That little cunt offspring of the steward," she said, "That little cunt my father married to my brother so that we'd all be miserable," and her absolute loathing was uttered so softly it almost seemed she was praying. The husband tossed the papers on top of the cookie-laden plates, "Relax, I'll have her here within a half-hour, Just don't let the notary get away, Force-feed him cookies, aim the shotgun at him, tie him up, squeeze his balls, anything so he doesn't escape," and as currant morsels swished around my mouth I thought Hoodwinked out of dominos to have it all end here, and I thought of Sundays in my garden, of the vegetables that needed weeding, of the work that was waiting on my desk, of the wills and deeds and articles and decrees, I thought To have it all end here, stuffed to death like a suckling pig, and the man stormed out of the front door, the hound looked at him sleepily, tried to raise up on its front paws and dropped back down on to the rug, probably also stuffed to the breaking point with crackers and tea and cookies and currants, while the house agonized along with the old man, as if it would be senseless for one to outlive the other, as if they shared the very same aged, musty, moribund blood, "Now you just keep drinking and I'll be right back," the woman said as she went up the stairs, "I don't want to see a single drop of juice left in that jug," and she returned with one of those old-fashioned flintlock pistols, using both hands to point it straight at my head, "Eat up," she ordered, "Eat until you puke your guts out if you like, but don't stop eating," I reached gingerly for a sandwich with my fingertips and the pistol, which followed my every move, wiggled in her hands as if a puppet were wielding it, a puppet dressed up like a fat lady and seated on the sofa in front of me. I thought, Bet the house tumbles down before this Russian roulette's over with, and I imagined beams dropping down, sheets of plaster, powder everywhere, smashed furniture creaking at the joints, maids caught by the wings of their aprons and squawking like scared chickens, a locomotive that chugged to the safety of the front garden, too many hours on the clocks inside, and I don't know how much later it was that the man marched victoriously into the sitting room, dragging an ageless creature by its striped pinafore, "I found this beauty in a woodshed in Outeiro, The smarty-pants blanketeer can't even hide something," and as the woman momentarily lowered the flintlock pistol I asked meekly, between two slurps of pineapple syrup, "Would it be possible for me to use the toilet?"

"I hope you gave the blanket queen a good spanking," the woman said, shovelling a bowlful of pine-nuts down my gullet. "A whack or two never hurts when you're trying to teach an imbecile."

"I demolished her joke of a shop," the husband assured her as he chased the mongoloid away from the door that led outside. "Ever since this creature went strolling on the square, it seems nothing will stop her."

"Do it in your pants like everybody else," suggested the woman, fanning herself with the gun and pointing to the example of the bloodhound, which was twitching in its sleep at visions of partridges. "And polish off the juice, because I can't bear to look at it any more."

The man withdrew a bottle of ink from an ancient desk drawer furrowed by penknives like an old man's forehead, poured out the black liquid—as opaque and unreflecting as the September asphalt—in a port glass from the sideboard, dunked the retard's thumb into the ink and pressed it in the space below the signature of the station chief, whom I'd heard about years before because of his train mania, so acute that he'd even go to Evora to wave his flags at houses whose façades answered back with indignant or impassive stone looks. I'd heard of him years before because everyone in these parts knew who he was, including the dogs and chickens and other animals that would saunter in the burning afternoon heat along the deserted village lanes and witness the horn-blowing which signalled departures, obliging the buildings to rumble with the sounds of connecting rods and brake pads and to hiss on down the hillside, steering clear of the olive trees, with stupefied invalids and quiet-nosed children looking out of the windows of the stuccoed and tile-roofed passenger train until they finally arrived at the station in Lisbon, next to a huge port full of caravels and cranes and doublet-clad navigators whose beards still gleamed from typhoons, spices, and coconut trees as they slowly died of scurvy on the benches lining the Avenue, submerged in the silky blond curls of transvestites. On certain nights a police van would round up the transvestites and viceroys and haul them in to the municipal jail, where the employees seated behind metal desks were surprised to hear threats of banishment or the gallows yelled at them by admirals with red-wine breath in a medieval Portuguese that captivated the men-turned-women, whose torsos tilted on the wooden benches like flowers in vases as they picked the lice out of their false eyelashes and pencilled beauty marks. And morning would arrive like a sea-tragic dawn, drowning the rings under the surviving navigators' eyes in café au lait and stale bread, and they'd lie stomach-up on the taverna floor like poisoned seals on a ship's deck, snoring off their ration of rum.

"You can let the notary go now," the husband said, showing me the papers with the flamboyance of gypsies flashing their phony silks. "We're now the sole owners of the old man's estate, right?"

I tried to answer him, but my voice was thwarted by the currant juice, by a denture dislocated by so many cookies, and by the growling of the bloodhound at my ankles. The moron stumbled from corner to corner until settling down next to the staircase with her knees curled against her chest. Her eyes reminded me of the greenish bubbles of seaweed that the Guadiana carries on its shoulders across stones and rapids and sand to the sea.

"What exactly do we own?" asked the woman as she pulled a pair of glasses from her apron and sceptically studied my notebooks. "According to what's written here, we're the sole owners of a pile of debts, you fool."

206

The whirring from the ceiling swelled and subsided like the buzzing of voices in a bar. An employee at the police station said "Who the hell are you?" to a sailor wearing breeches, carrying a cutlass and hanging on to a bottleneck as to a mast in the storm. The bloodhound, which looked to be pregnant, rubbed its furry teats on the floorboards as it licked my shoelaces. The incredulous husband glanced over his wife's shoulder at the typed pages and shook his head.

"Debts, debts and more debts, and you and I are legally responsible for every last one of them," said the woman, pointing to paragraph after paragraph with her indignant little finger. "Congratulations, you've succeeded in making us millionaire mortgagors."

"Christ, There's got to be something," the man murmured as if in prayer. "After all the trouble to get the signatures there's got to be a little something for us."

"And indeed there is," replied the woman, who tossed the papers disgustedly on top of the table. The retard's eyes looked softly, serenely emptier than ever. "Overdue loans, unpaid bills, clinics threatening to sue, pawn tickets, the mortgage on the house. Show this to the Commies and who knows, maybe they'll take pity on our poverty." The cows at the castle mooed in between fireworks and the songs of the band.

"Now that you've got what you were after, do you think you could take me back to Reguengos?" I managed to ask, my tongue floundering in a sugary slime.

"I don't believe it, I can't believe it," the husband said as he leafed through the documents, shoving aside plates and glasses, one of which tipped over to drip its thick currant blood on the floor. "You know the old man, He's got something socked away somewhere or I'm a monkey's ass."

Forgetting about me, the dog went for the currant juice, cocking its snout in the air as it waited for each new drop with the quivering anxiety of wire. The man leaped furiously through the pages like a horse jumping hurdles, snorting foam through his nostrils.

"All squandered away in casinos, whore-houses, hospitals and doctors for the two idiots," the woman said, shrugging. "There's probably not even enough for the funeral. For all I care he can rot upstairs in the attic and infect the whole damned village with the sores on his limbs and the worms and flies in his belly. The way my grandmother infected the village when her time came, so that the commissioner had to order the coffin to be sealed with lead before it was lowered."

"May I go back to Reguengos?" I insisted, thinking of my vegetables in the garden. "I don't suppose you need me for anything else."

The mongoloid, her face veiled by grey hair, nestled in her corner like a sick turtle-dove. Her hands and face melded into the grey stripes of her pinafore. A firecracker exploded on the veranda and a rabble of pans clamoured in the kitchen.

"Go ahead and set a match to the papers, but don't let the tablecloth catch fire," the woman told her husband without listening to me. "All I needed was to inherit a financial mess."

The flame rose up from the table and frightened the bloodhound, which backed away barking, its legs spread apart, dropping a turd on the rug. Through the windows and past the veranda's broken flowerpots, in the fields that sloped down to the Guadiana River, spice ships from invisible Indies were shoring in. The oak trees were swaying when I stood up, sailors roosting in the olive trees folded and refolded the sails, a kite seagulled over the roof and the mongoloid halted on her way up the stairs, entranced by the fire or by the throng that was rushing towards

the docks at the old water mill as she smoothed her grey strands
with her mole-brown claws.

Chapter

My mother, at night, would sometimes play the harp in the sitting room. I remember how her fingers seemed to be saying farewell to the strings and how I liked to rest naked against her chest, close my eyes, feel those fingers on my back and hear the slight, fragile, sad sound of my skin and bones fading from lamp to lamp and dying at last in the curtain's shadows, like the moths in the pleats and in the so still, so black branches of the fig tree. My father would read the newspaper and occasionally pull on the chain of his watch: round and silver, and with a cover that closed over the hands, hiding the time, the way an oyster closes its calcareous eyelids over the secret of its mystery. When my bedtime arrived they would take me upstairs, put me into pyjamas, tuck me in, blow out the light and go back down, and a breathing, fluid body—silence—rose around the bed, and my neck would stretch towards the door in a vegetable creaking, like a sunflower stem that twists towards the sun, hoping for the improbable dawn of a chord from below. I could hear the turning of newspaper pages, the dogs' bronchitis, the kitchen screen door as it swung on its hinges, the wings of the owls over the village and the anxious rumbling of my girlish blood, until I began spiralling, leaf-like, into the deep well of the sheets, and the waters closed over my drowning white eyes, and the morning, pianoing the harsh notes of daylight on the windowsill, brought me back to the surface: a beach of sandy furniture and shelves full of dolls adorned with skirts, ribbons, frills, laces and eyes that regarded me with perverse innocence.

My uncle from Vendas Novas visited us on Sundays. My mother would spend all Saturday afternoon locked up in the bathroom with a maid while the steward brought tub after tub of hot water to the landing, and in the midst of the foggy steam, during the few seconds the door stayed open to exchange the empty tub for the full one, a pinkish leg or elbow or shoulder would emerge from the bath and offer itself to the maid's sponge with the bored languor of a sea anemone. Two glass breasts, whose dark nipples I thought of as grapes, were eventually enclosed in a Turkish-towel pod, but her navel and pubis remained uncovered, vulnerable, soft and tender, and a tiny vertical mouth with thin lips showed through the V-shape of curly hairs as the maid perfumed her back and her sides and then dried her feet, one toe at a time, with a jeweller's care. My father's hunting dogs barked in the yard, bobbing their spotted snouts all along the fence, the snap of the silver watch cover drifted in from the porch, a coughing crown of dead partridges with a cigarette-holder stepped between us—my mother and me—and soon I was sitting at the dinner table with my sister who never talked and my brother who was pushing an already wheelless locomotive between knives and forks, using his tongue to make the sound of the engine. My father unbelted the partridges in the pantry and entered the dining room with bugging eyeballs, right behind the cook's buttocks, which bounced along faster under the platter of rabbit meat balanced on her shoulder, and at that moment a harped arpeggio dissolved the noise of the cutlery and I could see, beyond a constellation of lamps softened by the March twilight, a silhouette leaning into the strings, indifferent to the hounds curled up on the rugs, to my sister's grunts, and to my father's lascivious tentacles pinching the maids' knees, massaging their kidneys and vanishing under their skirts in a flurry of laughs and squeals, "Stop it, sir, I'm losing the tray, Stop it, sir, the children might see, Stop it, sir, the missus will fire me," but he was deaf, he went right on touching them, tugging them, and squeezing them while his free hand held a rabbit leg that dripped blood on his waistcoat or else opened and reopened the pocket watch, as if he were expecting a visitor who was late, who wasn't coming.

On Sundays when we got back from Mass, however, there was always a visitor—my uniformed uncle—ensconced in the sofa with a lit cigar and a smile of military tenderness over which his moustache fell abruptly, like a curtain after the final act. My nervous, thrilled mother spilled ashtrays, overturned bottles and knocked into half-columns with vases, while the dogs paced in circles, warily sniffing the intruder who once a week brought an added disorder to the normal disorder, who flustered my mother, who excited the maids, all clustered behind doors to get a look at him, who ran his hand through the hair of my untalking sister, making her flee like a frightened animal, who gave my brother toy cars and trucks which he banged against the walls until they became dented oblongs of tin that kept him amused in a corner for hours, who gave me sweets that I never ate, letting the ants and the roaches have them, who talked and talked and talked, telling anecdotes from his army life and laughing hysterically at his own jokes. My father brooded behind the newspaper in his usual chair, reaching periodically into his fob, obsessed with time, obsessed with the wild rabbits and birds in the fields between the Guadiana shores and Reguengos, sitting here like a fool, listening to dumb army jokes and watching my kids getting bored, my wife all jittery and the maids in a frenzy, as if this asshole had more

212

power than me over my own household, as if this asshole were a thief come to rob what's rightfully mine, keeping me away from the turtle-doves in the woods, from hiking with a gun on my shoulder and the steward at my side, breathing the smells of earth and the brush and forgetting the fact that my wife wasn't a virgin when I first touched her naked flesh and the tunnel of her body which lay there inertly, with eyes open and not a single sigh of pleasure, desiring only that I caress her as little as possible, that I kiss her as little as possible, pound her as little as possible, that I finish quickly, get up quickly to wash and urinate, fall asleep quickly, staring at me in disgust, horror, resignation, pity, so I had to turn to the maids and to the farmhands' wives to appease my anxiety for tenderness, throwing them down on our double bed, without even bothering to roll down the sheets, so as to get back at you, so as to stain the bedspread with two or three drops of my frustrated desire, as bitter and lonely and unsatisfied as before I met you, as from the earliest moment I can remember, forever flipping open my watch in the hope that my children will grow up and leave me, that my wife will make up her mind to move in with my brother on the base and leave me, that the bloodhounds will die and leave me, that the maids will leave, that the steward will leave, that all the people who depend on my pocket will evaporate, and not only the people but the house, the church, and the village, so that I can grab my shotgun and cartridge belt, walk out of the no-longer-existing yard through the no-longer-existing gate and head south along the Guadiana River, towards the quail and the ocean I haven't seen for years, sit down on a high rock and watch the owls transformed into seagulls by the rhythmic rage of the floodwaters, and decide—why not?—to make everything harmonious by pulling the trigger on the anchored boats, sprawled on the sand like wooden whales. At the end of the day my uncle waved us goodbye, rubbed his condescending thumb across the dogs' hindquarters, kissed my mother on the forehead, shook my father's hand and told one last joke on his way to the front door, we heard his chuckles and his martial footsteps, the whining of the hinges, and then a silence both piercing and empty, inhabited by the smoke of his unextinguished cigar, and the mosquitoes and moths flitted in the bedrooms and the living room, the fig tree darkened, and before I heard the harp, before I wanted only to rest naked, eyes closed, in the music's mellow sorrow, I could still distinguish, through a crack in the drapes, the castle battlements melting blackly into the night as the pregnant moon hung over the rapids, tied to the river or to the land or to us by the stalk of a boxwood or the branch of a cork tree.

On the afternoon when every photograph of my mother disappeared from the house and my father, dressed in black, called me and my brother into his office to announce my mother's death while my sister who never talked was busy examining the strings that had no more fingers to say farewell, I can remember the desk and the furniture and the books all neatly shelved—like hens at sunset roosting in rows inside their coops—better than I can the face with which he spoke to us, grave and understanding, a priestly face, as he opened and closed his watch without ever looking at the hands, as if time had lost its reason for being or he realized it had never possessed one. I can remember the absent picture frames better than I can the words he spoke, just as my memory of the statues in church was always more vivid than that of the priest's sermons, but there was nothing I could do to get her to like me the way she liked my sisters, because I was male and looked like my father, and after I explained that their mother had died I called one of the maids to take them to breakfast, confident that no one in the kitchen would tell them what had really happened, not because they pitied me but because they feared. I locked the door and didn't eat or drink all day but sat in a stupor in the middle of my office, annoyed by the swelling on the back of my head, seeing over and over the steward's boot next to my face pressed flat on the ground, feeling him pulling on my shirt-tail, "Sir, Sir, What happened sir?", As if you didn't know, you bastard, I thought, still unable to move, As if they didn't tell you everything. The steward rolled me on to my back like a bale of hay, "How are you feeling, sir?, Are you all right, sir?" and I heard other steps, whispers, oohs and aahs. "The missus hit him in the head with the angel clock, cracking the marble base, look here at the blood, Should we call the doctor or what?" I tried to please her by drinking my milk before my sisters did but that wasn't good enough, I'd wash my hands before sitting down but she'd make me rewash them, "And leave that mangled train car in your room, Gonçalo, Honestly I don't know how you manage to spoil everything you touch, Look at the example you set for your sisters, You're already nine years old, before long you'll be in the Navy, Sit up straight, Gonçalo, What about your napkin?, Don't you know what your knife's for?" "He's no more about to die than I am," said the steward, his foot nudging my ribs, as it might nudge a mule, to make me react, "Can't you see his chest moving up and down?" "Don't eat with your mouth open," my mother scolded, "You think I want to look at your chewed-up food?, I wish someone would tell me where you learned your manners, Even your mentally deficient sister behaves better than you." "I'm going to fetch some water in any case," said the cook, "to wipe that dried blood off his neck," and I began to make them out, one by one, their faces, their odours, their torsos, legs, shoes, as if I were lying among the pedestals of a bunch of quiet statues. "No more dessert for you, young man," my mother decreed, "Go to your room and play with your broken trains." The hound's wet tongue was licking my jaw when I came to, still on my back, returned from some faraway place, from a disturbed and disturbing dream, the steward lifted my head and I felt the water in my hair and down the canal between my shoulders, "He's blinking his eyes," said a maid to the cook, "Now he's moving his legs a bit, Bring another bucket and we'll really wake him up." "Fold your napkin before you leave the table," my mother yelled, "I can't for the life of me understand your indulgence with this child, Diogo, I can't understand why you always let him have his way," and my father just kept on mutely smoking at the head of the table, flicking cigarette ashes into the rinds and pits that were piled on a plate, "I don't understand how you manage not to lose your temper with this brat, Diogo." I tested my head, right and left, shrugged my shoulders, clenched my fingers, flexed my muscles, and my nerves obeyed me but with a time lag, lackadaisically, like a drunken body which, sprawled over the sheets, takes a seeming eternity to pull itself back together. The steward's boot let off tormenting my ribs as my eyes, like hard-to-adjust knobs on a microscope, put him into focus: "Everybody shut up, he can hear us," the cook said, "Shut up before he fires us all!" I opened my mouth and the saliva tasted sweet on my palate and around my teeth, slithering as a runny jelly down my gullet, so I folded the napkin, pushed it through its ring, and was surprised when my father spoke, softly and calmly and without shifting position but extinguishing his cigarette with unusual caution against the rim of the plate (and the lamp hanging between us illumined his tie while throwing his face in the shade), saying "Maybe because this is the only child I'm almost certain is mine." The steward's face moved closer, spraying me with a vinegary, red-wine vapour, "Do you feel better now, sir?, Can you stand up now, sir?", "What?" asked my mother as her eyes got rounder, "What?" A dog that didn't belong to us was barking outside, and the infuriated bloodhounds raced to the foyer growling. "You heard what I said," said my father, "I'd bet my life

216

that the two girls don't come from me but from the balls of my brother, that uniformed pansy who has to pester us every single Sunday, boring everybody except you with his hot-shot sergeant talk." "Captain," my mother corrected and it gave me the willies to look at them, I felt something terrible might happen and I wished they'd shut up, I wished for a silence more violent than the night's, I wished she'd scold me like she did my brother and send me without dessert to my room, where my dolls would be waiting for me, sitting erect in their weary, rose-coloured glee. "Captain of a pile of horse shit," my father said sweetly as he cleaned his cigarette-holder with a toothpick. The dogs clawed the front door on their hind legs, the maids came and went with catastrophic fervour, a black and yellow beetle adhered to the overhead lamp, blinding itself, and I couldn't care less about the pudding, I left the dining room chug-chug-chugging like a train. "The girls are not yours?" my mother said with syllables that weighed a few tons each, "Do you consider me to be some kind of whore, Diogo?", and he put the cigarette-holder in his pocket, and smiled, and said, "Of course I do, my dear cocotte, Why do you think I lured you away from Vendas Novas?, Why do you think I married you?, A nice little slut, and rich to boot—what more could I ask for?" "Sir?" said the steward, waving the maids away, "Do you feel all right now, sir?" The beetle was slowly roasting on the lamp, my sister who never spoke was digging her fork handle into the tablecloth, the steward held my arms so that I wouldn't slip out of the chair, and I said: "Go home and get your shotgun. Tonight we'll hunt rabbits in Reguengos."

My father went into mourning for an entire year, and during the first few weeks he religiously reserved an hour after lunch, the hour when the village was crumbling from the heat and kites were accumulating in the ivory basin that couched the sun and the Guadiana was only a current of sand shining with quartz and an occasional puddle, an hour when neighbours could make sympathy calls in the living room, where they'd find him by the harp as if by his wife's coffin, resting his left arm on the instrument, solemn and sorrowful, sniffling in spite of his dry, mineral hunter's eyes, and when important visitors came, one of the maids also dressed us in black and led us into the shadow of the drapes, where our despondent silhouettes greeted the Council President, the Provincial Governor, the bishop's representative or the sad and supportive assemblymen, who were deeply touched by the sight of three orphans hanging on to each other in timid fear. My father listened to the consoling words and expressions of grief, offered visitors a liqueur from the cabinet, and sighed as he gazed at the deserted square, where cats hesitated before placing their tender paws on the burning stones. The square in front of the church, the hills waving blue on Monsaraz's eastern side, and the partridges hiding in bushes or grazing the earth's tummy with their own firm tummies, searching for a cooler shade in the gorse. The flies chased each other in the curtains. My father longingly plucked some strings, producing a dissonant scale, "The sacred love of family and the angelic love of music," observed the priest, buttoned with black buttons from head to toe, and there was something suspicious in that death without a burial, in that sudden disappearance, in the exaggerated sorrow of my father, who continued to pounce on the maids, lifting their skirts and nibbling their crests like a rooster, oblivious to their refusals, their squirming, their pushing, and their pleas, and full of contempt for them once he was through, shaking their broken feathers from his coat, letting them flee in terror to the kitchen, terrified of my mother or, now, of her absence, as if the harpist and her head full of curls could still reproach them—she who'd needed to do no more than lift an eyebrow and say (on the days before my uncle's visits), "My bath," and I'd go to watch as she combed in the mirror, her mouth full of hairpins, and she wouldn't get angry, not even annoyed, she'd look at my face in the glass for a moment, then pick up her brush, and I'd look at her face, blemished from where the silver backing had peeled.

And one Sunday, perhaps in September, perhaps in October, five or six weeks after my mother's death, there was a different kind of knock on the door: brusque, peremptory, imperious. The snoozing dogs lifted their heads off the floor to yawn, cross with fatigue, and in charged my grandparents, I mean my grandmother and her husband the doctor, whose pockets were stuffed with mini-bottles of wine. The cook, who had opened the door, was promptly shoved aside by my grandmother: "Get my son-in-law over here immediately." My grandmother's husband fixed his gaze on the maid's buttocks, which bounced alternately, like the pans of a scale, on her way to the office, until the old bag pulverized his liver with a resounding slap, "What are you gawking at, you worm?" The dogs ran around her skirt with their snouts bowed low, submissive. "Nothing, Hortense," replied the doctor, "I just happened to notice a nice painting." My sister, mixed in with the hounds, also sniffed the couple out, and I thought One of these days someone will train her to go hunting at night for the hares in Reguengos. "Since when have you been interested in art, you numskull?" my grandmother snorted while the doctor cringed and began to shrink in size and my father finally appeared in the hallway, snapping shut his watch, with a nervous maid trailing behind. "Adelina is at my house," boomed the old bag, scaring off the dogs, "so what's all this rigmarole about pretending she's dead?" My brother passed by, whistling like a train. The cook trotted towards the pantry, admired by the doctor, whose yellow eyes bobbed in their sockets like gelatinous sea creatures in jars of alcohol. "If you don't cut out this

219

mourning crap, then I'll take her to Evora, Montemor and Reguengos to prove to everyone that she's alive." "And well," added the doctor. "Shut up, you clown, and take the harp to the car." The doctor got himself tangled in the strings, pushed the instrument with his knees to free his fingers and got his foot hung up in the B-flats. The oldest bloodhound had lost its fear and started barking as the doctor, still with his hat on, battled the harp which was swallowing him like quicksand or a carnivorous plant. A D-string snapped and thrashed. "Help me out of this contraption, Hortense," begged the doctor, "Hold on to the frame while I try to work myself loose," and my father hauled him out like a drowned man, set him on his feet, straightened out his jacket, looked at the silver pocket watch, reloaded the cigarette-holder, and announced with all politeness, as if he'd heard nothing of what his mother-in-law had said, ignoring her threats, her ultimatums, her mammoth proportions: "The harp stays, madam. It's one of the few mementos I have of the lately deceased."

"And how about if the deceased comes for it herself?" my grandmother asked. "How would you like it if she shows up in Monsaraz, goes to the church, talks to the priest, enters the café, strolls around the square, and knocks on your door to give her children a hug?"

Outside, the steward made the water pump squeak like beds when they writhe under the nocturnal, carnivorous battles of two bodies. The skin of the figs, pecked by sparrows, popped with the sound of rounded lips. The doctor brushed himself to dry off the clefs, breathed like a wet turkey, and rummaged in his pocket for a mini-bottle. My sister who never talked, sitting on the floor, looked at us with a pair of irises borrowed from the china dolls in my bedroom.

"She won't come back," my father said in an affable tone.

"Correct me if I'm wrong, but I believe no corpse has resurrected for some two thousand years now. If her ghost should come around, I'm afraid people here are so touchy that they'd probably shoot at it. We have enough problems as is with the werewolves in the village."

"Your mother isn't dead, is that clear?" the old bag told my sister, who stared at her vaguely, emptily, with the transparent eyes of moon-men. "Your mother couldn't put up with your father any more—with his slaps, his insults, his punches, his eating away of her inheritance. Understand, kiddies?"

"Let's go, Hortense," the doctor prodded, his vigour and diplomacy rejuvenated by the wine. "You won't get anywhere with this sort of talk."

"Shoot?" shouted my grandmother, stepping backward and on to the tail of a dog, which tore off yelping into the coat closet. "You dirty scoundrel. You mean to tell me you could shoot the mother of your own children?"

"Gonçalo," said my father to my brother, "run to the office and get me my revolver."

The maids, whose clothes he regularly ripped away like a bird gone berserk in the darkest nooks of the hallway, were peeking in twos and threes from behind every possible door. Occasional coughs were smothered in their aprons or in the drapes over the doorways. My brother set down a contorted train and skipped down the hall. The revolver was tiny, shiny, and pretty, like an innocuous Christmas present. The first bullet sparked a fleeting flame in the barrel and punctured the rug about six inches from the old bag's ankles.

"I could sue your daughter for attempted homicide, for adultery, for incest with her brother-in-law, for abandoning her home, her husband and her children, and for neglecting a mongoloid child that just may not survive without the care and presence of her mother," said my father. "I could sue her for all that and much more, and you can be certain that any judge around would decide in my favour."

He lifted his arm, there was a second fleeting flame, a second bang and a second orifice in the rug, a couple of inches closer to my grandmother than the last. "I'm getting out of here, Hortense," the doctor said, swivelling towards the foyer, "I'm perfectly willing to accept your son-in-law's reasoning." Panicky profiles squawked a retreat from the doorways, the smoke-excited dogs barked and rubbed against my father's legs, and the swollen teats of the pregnant hound quivered while a front paw hung in the air, ready for attack. "And what about her money?" asked my grandmother, defending herself with an umbrella, "What about the lands she let you manage and the capital she put into your businesses?" "Gonçalo," my father said to my brother, "take the gun back to my office," and smiling at the bag: "When someone dies, madam, generally the spouse and children are the inheritors, Her will is in the safe and I'd be happy to let you have a look, It's as instructive as a book on political economy or the resistance of materials." As she turned the doorknob, my grandmother's lips vibrated spasmodically, the fall of her dainty hat vibrated, her entire enormous, enraged body vibrated. "I just hope to God I live long enough to see you burn in hell, you scoundrel." The door hinges whirled, the gate clacked. My father helped up the harp as if it were a decrepit senior citizen: "Remind me to phone to Evora tomorrow," he told me while staring at the broken strings, the cracked wood, a split volute. "There's got to be someone there who can fix this shit."

Chapter

The bull was bigger and fatter than in past years, its hide was spotted instead of black, it had unequal, lopsided horns like uneven eyelids, and it didn't want to cooperate: they had to goad it with sticks and tease it with assorted coloured cloths before the beast would move forward, slow and squeamish, through the stone corridors of the ancient walls and into the castle arena, where it advanced as far as the dug-outs and froze, dazed by the music, the fireworks, the whistles, the clapping, and the shouts, gaping dumbly at the bodies that rushed past with coats and shirts to rile it up and that tripped, fell down, scrambled to their feet and fled, challenging it from a safer distance, taunting and insulting it, a massive muscular bull with a bearded penis hanging from its belly like a painter's goatee, a tormented bull, shipped to the village in a cage made of logs strapped together with rope and twine, two days on a truck without touching its feed, defecating cones of silvery excrement that were coated immediately by cones of blowflies, and when the Chairman of the Community Chest invited me to have a look at the animal in its pen, we found it lying in the straw with its front hoofs tucked under its bulging girth, never moving except to swing its huge, contemptuous head in our direction before going right back to sleep. A drunk old man with a blanket and a jug of wine, presumably there to guard the bull, pissed on its flank through a chink in the boards.

"What do you think, doc?" asked the Community Chest Chairman, an emaciated diabetic who worked in the office of the cellulose factory and had a hairy mole on his nose. His sickness invested him with the acetic perfume of manicurists. "Was it worth it or not to fork out a little cash for this sausage with horns?"

Whenever his sugar level shot up, his wife would call me in Reguengos and be waiting for me at the door, surrounded by a bevy of neighbour women and cradling a clay chamber pot of urine, sweet like the juice of rotten daisies:

"He ate too much cake, doctor, it was his best friend's birthday, and just look at the tea he peed in this pot."

And before she could extend me the flower-painted pot and say Won't you have a cup?, I hurried into the house, where in every corner there were wide-eyed children and pictures of saints, both so immobile I could hardly tell paper from flesh, and after banging my knees against various chests I made it to the bedroom, where the hairy-moled Chairman of the Community Chest smiled nervously out of a tangle of pillows and pyjama stripes and exhibited a reddish incision like a trophy:

"Three stitches, doctor, Three stitches for a measly cream puff."

"We'll have to see how it does in the ring," I said, noticing scars on its flanks from previous bullfights and a more recent sore with a crown of flies on the purulent perimeter. "This animal's been in fifteen or twenty fights, maybe more."

In the next pen over, a conglomerate of cows rubbed their bony haunches against the worn castle stones as the split hoofs of steers trod on their own shit, making the place smell like a colossal latrine. The old wino, confusing the buttons on his trousers with those on his shirt, eyed us with two elliptic wax depositories and a stately air:

"As a safety precaution, no one's allowed to get near the animals." And I realized he was one of the beggars who hold out cans on the church steps, offering holy medals made of tin in exchange for alms.

"All the better," said the Community Chest. "If it's seen action twenty times, then it's bound to know all the right tricks for mauling a man good and proper, and the more it sends to the hospital, the more the crowd will go wild. Imagine the fiasco if there wasn't any blood: everyone would go home. Who doesn't like to see other people suffer?"

Dozens of likewise drunk ghosts howled on all sides, leaping to the chaotic rhythm of the band, whose members, red-faced from alcohol, were blowing each man for himself on their antique trombones. I wondered if I was the only living entity in the municipality who was more or less sober, and I felt overwhelmed by the inevitable solitude of teetotallers, with their sad, arid virtue: I think of heaven as a clinic for depressed angels, and the apostles' moustaches as blotting paper for their tears. The fireworks boomed invisibly in the dark, prefaced by long slanting whistles wet with gunpowdery spit. I could feel the mute presence of the old ladies in the night, stonily installed on the doorsteps like prehistoric birds on telephone wires.

"Me," I answered. "More injuries means that much more work for me. After the last bullfight, I spent an entire week single-handedly sewing up faces and legs. And don't you get added to the list with your cream puffs."

"Can I have just a sliver of almond brittle?" the diabetic bargained.

The bull, immersed in its faecal stink, raised an eyelid and dropped it back down in disgust, like a train passenger obliged to share his compartment with a couple of giggly schoolgirls.

"Arrange the funeral with the priest and you can eat anything you want," I said. "It's been ten years now that I've been sticking my nose in your chamber pot, and I'm getting a little tired of it, quite frankly."

The medal-hawking beggar, who achieved the improbable feat of smelling worse than the cows, suddenly spoke from the shadows where he sat wrapped in his blanket like a Roman emperor:

"What's so special about his pee?"

The hint of a wind blended the aromas and dispersed the music. There was a full moon, and the whites of the steers' eyes glistened with a watery sheen that seemed to flow over their dark boulder bodies. Clouds like the skims of warm milk bleared the sky. The firecrackers rattled the carious walls. The Community Chest Chairman's wife, forever hugging the chamber pot, with one foot on the street and the other on the doorstep, offered the fragrance of her piss-filled teapot to anyone who passed by:

"Just look at this miserable urine, Dona Teresa."

"Roses," I explained to the tramp. "My friend here carries the Holy Queen of Heaven in his bladder."

And it was in anticipation of the bruised and the gored that the following morning I instructed the hospital attendant—a sassy girl with a chequered smock who was arguing with a broken leg over whether there was or was not a cockroach in his milk at breakfast—to sterilize some tools and syringes and to place the rubber gloves and jars of gauze pads near the examination table, which stood like a bier amid the ceramic tiles of an ancient bathroom in whose broken toilet there still swam a tenacious Neolithic stool.

"If this isn't a roach then what do you call it?" the broken leg demanded, holding a drowned insect in his palm.

The phone started ringing at the back of the ward, in the minuscule consultation room where patients went on Thursdays and Saturdays asking for cough syrups, cold capsules, and ointments to soothe back pain. IV balloons hung from chrome scaffolds in a macabre carnival, dripping turbid tears into cirrhotic veins. The office manager, preceded by the curative waft of garlic pills, walked out of the horror chamber of X-rays where bones glowed in a reddish atmosphere.

"A crocodile," answered the hospital attendant. "As big as that thing is, what else could it be? A lizard, maybe? And take it easy with that crutch or I'll bash your head in with it."

I jogged down the hallway towards the ringing: since I've been involved with the widow from the funeral parlour my wife phones on the hour to determine my coordinates. So, for that matter, does the widow, her elbow propped on a coffin behind the counter, and this double vigilance explains why some of Reguengos's lately departed ride off to the cemetery with their backs concealing the naughty egg white of my passion. The other parlour went under for lack of customers and the shrewd widow, whose monopoly prospered, paid an Arab emir, in cash, for a luxury hearse with air-conditioning, crêpe curtains, a refrigerator with mineral water for the inconsolable, and Chopin's funeral march on the cassette player. We drove it down to the Algarve in August, with the widow purring embalmed obscenities in my ear. At night we anchored it in a campsite, drew the crêpe curtains, lit the electric candles and presto, we had a home on wheels. The Chopin march was great for getting a rhythm going, and the Germans in the surrounding tents, buttered with sun lotion, were fascinated by the phenomenon of weeping widow orgasms. As I neared the phone, I tried to guess by its *didilidileeng* whether I'd pick up to the strident bitchiness of my wife or to the lustful, vulturous melancholy of the motor-home widow, willing to give one more chance to the bankrupt pallbearer, which was her nickname for me, her way of insulting me when she called from the dank caverns of cafés where she drank the pawn tickets of her frantic decadence.

"Call the creature whatever you like," the broken leg immediately and imploringly answered the aide. "All I ask, for your own health and well-being, is that you don't dare touch my cast with the crutch."

I opened the door to the back pains and cough syrups and skirted the desk to reach the phone. The window showed me the usual buildings—yellow and squat like hepatitic dwarfs—and the usual parrot enunciating expletives from its perch while staring at me sideways with the stupid persistence of policemen. One of these days I'm going to bring my son's air rifle, aim it across the street and watch the bird ding-dong, head downward, from the chain attached to its foot, until it comes to a standstill, transformed into a feathered stalactite, with a final superlative swear word rolling slowly off its tongue.

"You bastard!" yelled the attendant. "You throw the lung cancer's inhaler at me again and I'll stick a syringeful of air into your vein so fast you won't know what hit you!"

"Hello," I said to the plastic pinholes while I lifted my middle finger to the parrot, which looked straight at me, filled its little breast with air and squawked, "Cocksucker." It was ten or eleven o'clock and I was already sweating from the heat: my wife, who makes me leave my shoes on the balcony, once confided that she first had a crush on me, years before, because I was the only person she knew who perspired in the shower. My armpits would probably even get wet at the North Pole. And I like sweating, I like smelliness: what excites me about the widow is her funereal fragrance. I guess I'm sexually aberrant, like sickos that get their thrills from infected corns or bearded women.

"I'm calling from Monsaraz," said an unrecognizable howl, trying to be heard over the drums of the band, the barking dogs and the detonating firecrackers. "Have a little more patience with us, doctor, I'm afraid my grandfather's heart is failing."

Patience is one of those words that's bound to grate on the nerves of any man going on twenty-four years of unhappily married life. One of the few, I think, because we gradually get used to the rest, after interminable arguments that finally give way to interminable silent evenings in which the clicking of needles substitutes for the tick-tock of clocks, and a new and profitable way to tell time is born: a knitted vest is equal to a week, a child's cap to a day, a scarf to two Sundays, a turtleneck sweater to a month, and the time it takes to put your elbows into it, a year. So marriage does have the advantage of turning alarm clocks and calendars into superfluous relics. Along with husbands, who hock mucus from their lungs into the bathroom sink in the morning, uncombed and unshod, "You've got to take something for that bronchitis, Alfredo, You kept me and the kids up all night with your coughing."

I informed the hospital attendant, who was pursuing the shrieking broken leg with a needle, of my trip to the castle in the name of patience, the Hippocratic oath and the fee I charge for house calls, and I told her to phone my back-up, an imbecile with an incredible flair for killing off patients. I phoned the widow myself, apprising her of the hopeful scenario so that she could get some extra coffins ready, I asked the front desk for the ambulance keys ("It's official business") to save on fuel and my car's tyres, I could faintly hear the innocent surprise of the aide back in the ward, "The guy with the broken leg's just now keeled over dead, And he was so nice, I wonder what on earth happened?", and I thought sadly, The poor girl doesn't have anyone left to torment—the cancerous lung is on its last huff and puff and the two strokes can't so much as budge a finger, and I thought, Hatred is vital to good health, and I thought, To find ourselves in harmony with the world is a lethal infection.

I turned on the siren to enliven my fellow earthlings' ingenuous spirits with a stimulating trail of noisy unhappiness, I ran over a cat at the edge of town and witnessed, in the rear-view mirror, its conversion into a bloody heap that dwindled on the asphalt until I forgot about it, and once all the houses had fallen out of sight I found myself surrounded by the brush, the heat, and the sparse trees of September, the twisted and battered and dry olive trees, gutless, lymphless, muscleless, lungless, reduced to rusted pleats of bark with hollow medullae where insects copulate, reproduce and deposit their teardrop eggs. How many times, O Lord, did I hold my ear against the trunks of trees when I was a boy, hoping that through their roots I'd discern the choral groan of the world below, of the invisible animals that hide in holes, the beetles, moles, mice, the quick eyes of rabbits, the supple silk of foxes, the harsh sandpaper of ponies, the boars my father always talked about but which I never saw, not even their tracks, and the high stone walls of Monsaraz emerged, and then the church and the bull, which advanced as far as the dug-outs and froze, dazed by the music, the fireworks, the whistles, the clapping and the shouts, gaping dumbly at the bodies that rushed past with coats and shirts to provoke it and that tripped, fell down, scrambled to their feet and fled, challenging it from a safer distance, taunting and insulting it, a bull with a bearded penis hanging from its belly like a painter's goatee, a bull that was spotted instead of black, that had huge dark testicles tucked between its thighs, that finally trotted a few steps, halted, hesitated while sticking its snout in the dirt as if it would bury its face in its hands, galloped ten or twelve or fifteen or seventeen or nineteen or twenty yards, knocked over a drunk man waving his hat, a teenager swinging a rag attached to the end of a stick and a bunch of workers from the cellulose factory dressed up in their Sunday best, tumbling one on top of the other at only the slightest butt from the horns, a bull that was suddenly alone in the middle of the castle arena, with all the spectators looking on in fear, a bull as alone as the old man on his oversized deathbed, his mouth hanging open, his cheeks sunken to nothing, his eyes regarding the ceiling without actually seeing it, regarding the walls without actually seeing them, regarding his children and grandchildren all gathered around, even the little one, even the blanket-maker from Outeiro, even the gigantic Australian who's always dressed in rubber and dives in the river with a comical ping-pong ball on a comical tube and uses an eel-spear to catch seaweed for dinner, the old man who trembled ever so slightly at the sound of barking from the first floor, where the bloodhounds were likewise stretched out motionless on the rugs, defecating without even spreading their haunches, tense as on the morning before a hunt, leaning forward and showing their teeth as if ready to take off running, a church, an old man and a bull, the three of them all alone in the village, in spite of the relatives that smoothed down the sheets, in spite of the cellulose worker that tried again to grab the beast's head and that fell and bled and crawled away and that carried off one or two or three fainted farmers to the undulating applause of the drunken audience, sitting on the drunken stone steps of the stands, and beyond the stands the drunken hills followed one after another into Spain while the drunken Guadiana meandered towards the sea, drunk like the band, the peddlers, the jewellers, the beggars, the chickens, the family and the dogs, and I took the old man's pulse in search of the faintest half-beat of life. The drunken bull whirled around on its drunken hoofs, scaring off a second or third or fourth or fifth pack of challengers, just as the old man's eyes—pausing on his son, on his

son-in-law, on his granddaughters or on the dentist husband of
the less ugly granddaughter—made the audience stand back in
fright, as if he could still dominate them, crush them, give them
orders, mock them, assign nicknames and take them away,
according to his whim of the moment, his mood, his fancy, his
temper, and at that moment the Chairman of the Community
Chest put his hand on my shoulder, and I confronted the hairy
mole on his nose and the acetic perfume of manicurists.

"So what do you think, doc?" he asked as I reached into my bag
for an ampoule of cardiac stimulant, unbuttoned the old man's
pyjama top and felt for a place between his ribs to stick the
needle. "Was it worth it or not to spend cash on this sausage with
horns?" And I noticed the tramp with the blanket pissing in the
corner against the medicine table. I felt the old man's heart thump
softly, like a small contractile membrane, under the tips of my
fingers, and I saw that the family had even been afraid to clip his
nails, afraid to touch the bull at all, in spite of the prize the village
awarded to the one who caught it, afraid of a man and an animal
they were preparing to kill, and it was as I took a rubber cord
from my case to tie around his arm and make his veins show that
they lassoed one of the horns and dragged the beast towards the
dug-outs to lasso the other, a bull who'd been in ten or fifteen
fights, maybe more, his pyjama top open, breathing (when he
breathed) deep, irregular gasps like gusts of wind, and the
daughter, not the mongoloid but the one married to the manager
that mostly managed the pudenda of the farm workers' wives,
stuck her sleeve under the bedspread and pulled out the
transparent catheter bag:

"Look at the colour, doctor, You'd think it was tea."

"When I was ten or twelve years old my father brought me to
the festival," I told the Community Chest Chairman, who was
proudly observing the rock-bodied bull, stretched out in front of

232

the feed it ignored, "and the thing I remember best is the trip back to Reguengos, when I asked him the reason for killing the bull and he answered, 'No real reason.' Just like that. Absurdity summed up by a travelling salesman—that's what my father was—in three simple words: no real reason. And I was struck by a sudden, strange sensation that my life had just begun, as if I'd just been born. Funny, isn't it?" As if the ten or twelve years on my ID card were all a lie, and the pictures of me crawling naked over a pillow were of some other baby. As if my existence only became real on the day I learned there was no real reason."

"And the smell," said the daughter, "Even dog piss isn't this bad."

My father, who hanged himself for no real reason about a month after I graduated, stood up to cheer: a mob of people stampeded towards the roped animal, which was still lunging at some body or other that dodged it, at a red scarf that eluded it, at the boots that kicked its testicles and its penis. One of my wife's cousins, wearing a straw hat, pounded the bull's head, its rump, its flanks, its loins, unfolded a switchblade, plunged it into the creature's dark flesh, pulled it out and plunged it back in, and again, and again, with the rhythmic movement of a blacksmith. The son-in-law seized a knife and stabbed the old man in the shoulder, my father cheered, the daughter grabbed the syringe from my hands and drove it as hard as she could into the patient's neck, one of the bloodhounds howled in agony in the living room, the station chief buried a screwdriver in his navel, the bull retched blood from dozens of mouths as it tried to escape the ropes, the knives, switchblades, and sickles, and it sank under brilliantly flashing metals, under cries, under laughs, under roars of triumph, it kneeled, it fell over, and the little grandson cut off an ear with his mother's scissors and held it up to the audience, who waved their handkerchiefs and caps and broad-brimmed hats.

"He's dead," I announced to the family while I straightened the old man's pyjama collar, and I gathered up my instruments and was ready to leave the bedroom, go down the stairs, face the bloodhounds and drive back to Reguengos in the hospital ambulance. "Dead," I announced. "Drag the body from the ring, tie up its hoofs and cut up its meat to sell to the butcher, you can get drunk for two or three days with the money from the deceased," that dumb stiff massiveness that bled and bled without the least shred of dignity. "What do you think, doc?" asked the Community Chest Chairman, "Was it worth it or not to fork out a little cash for this sausage with horns?" "Go ahead, son, get in the station wagon, what are you waiting for?", and I stood still, holding on to the ambulance door handle, gazing at the fig tree and the mansion before sitting in the ripped vinyl seat impregnated with the nauseating smell of the cardboard cartons my father sold from store to store, from Covilha to Aveiro, and when we arrived in Reguengos I told my mother I didn't want any dinner, I went up to my room, lay down without taking off my shoes and was only dimly aware of them covering me with a blanket and placing a mug of herb tea on the table, and of their silhouettes dancing around me on tiptoe, emitting worried whispers that expired, at last, in the immeasurably distant kitchen.

Chapter

I told them to start packing up the luggage, the paintings, the china, the jewels, the cutlery and what remained of the silver service, and whatever else we hadn't already pawned to the Jew in Evora, tucked away in his narrow shop full of fiddles and alarm clocks, I went to the cabinet in the office to get my father-in-law's cartridge belts and the two shotguns, I called the steward and told him to take the old man's dogs, which wouldn't obey me, which never obeyed me, to the abandoned mill, since otherwise the Communists were sure to use them to sniff out our trail, across the Guadiana and into Spain if necessary, so they could have the pleasure of lining us up against a wall and Ready, Aim, Fire while uttering their usual blasphemies against Family and against God and their usual lies against us, and Long live abortion, Long live the revolution, Down with the rich, and we without a penny in our pockets, slumped on the ground and stomped on by their work boots. The steward walked into the living room snapping his fingers and whistling for the hounds that were ensconced under tables or stretched out coughing on the rugs, and when it was almost twilight we left through the kitchen door and down the slope, whose slowly purpling trees were as sharply defined in the bleached pre-autumn and pre-night sky as the veins of old men in their thin-skinned hands. The steward led the way, wearing the beret he always wore, no doubt even when he washed his hair, tilted over an eyebrow, talking to the hounds with the tenderness rustics bestow on their animals instead of their wives, and as I followed him, with a hunting gun under each arm, I thought, He's probably an informer for the Commies, Probably as soon as we get back to Monsaraz he'll go and tell them our plan to cross the border and head towards Madrid, Probably a good idea to kill him after killing the dogs, to Ready, Aim, Fire and watch him slump down, hands gripping his stomach, beretless at last, with the grey locks of his temples interspersed with splotches of vitiligo or mould.

As is apt to happen when night is falling, the water slipped without sound through the rocks, slower and clearer and deeper than at sunrise or midday, and while the steward and the dogs filed into the mill I trudged along the muddy bank in my awkward shoes from Lisbon, examining the two or three flattish, leaf-shaped boats that had belonged to the fisherman—drowned years before—and that no one used for fear of incurring the wrath of his ghost, two or three boat fossils eaten by time and fish and successive winters, reduced to the spine and thin ribs of their frames and bearded with algae, far too decrepit to carry us across to the cork trees on the opposite shore, meaning we'd have to walk over the sludge and eels, in water up to our necks, as they yelled at us in the dark, pursuing us like in the movies, with searchlights and machine guns from Moscow.

I approached the water mill and paused at the door. It was a ruined structure, about the size of the old quarantine stations, with high windows and slanting sills facing both sides of the fields, and a hatch in the floor that dropped into the cascading Guadiana River. All that was left of the roof were gutted, crisscrossing beams, covered by a thatch of clouds the colour of lizard bellies and by a threat of rain from the north: a grey mass that smothered the outlines of hills as it advanced towards us in an oppressive, fevered sweat. The steward was sitting on a grinding stone, scratching at his thin, licy hair through the cotton cloth of his beret. The bloodhounds sniffed the walls for the ancient urine of deceased dogs or else looked at me with their annoyingly soft, submissive, clear brown eyes, capped by yellow lashes. A large wet rat scurried along the wall and vanished into a crack. I opened the gun breeches and placed two cartridges in each. None of the dogs, not even the pups, paid heed.

"But sir, are you serious about killing them?" asked the steward, still seated on the grindstone and pulling a rolling paper from his vest. "Your father-in-law would never have allowed it—he spent an awful lot of time training these dogs."

"And we spend an awful lot of time washing their piss off the rug every damn morning," I answered. "For almost thirty years now I've been living among dog stench and dog turds. They even crap on my pillow, even on my dinner plate."

"I'll buy them off you, sir," said the steward, stretching wide his arms. "Tell me how much you want and I'll buy them. I'll keep them at my place and you'll never have to put up with their smell and their pee again."

I set one of the guns down and aimed the other at the pregnant bitch, whose claws scratched through dirt to the cement floor as her nose searched the crack where the rat had escaped. I pulled back on the trigger and the bitch doubled into a species of somersault, then limped towards the steward, her tail drooping, but the second shot did away with her neck and the animal collapsed *en route*—one or two yards from the grindstone—into a bunch of canine components spread flat over leaves and branches and the sundry debris deposited by the annual floods. The steward stood up, wringing the beret in his hands like a wet hankie:

"I'll buy them off you, sir, I'll buy them all. Just name your price, Don't shoot any more, I'll bring you the money tonight."

One of the dogs licked the nape of the dead bitch, while the rest whimpered in panic behind the stone cubes flanking the windows. I pulled open the breech and inserted two new cartridges.

"Five grand," I said, aiming the barrel at the next victim, a hound that glared at me, baring its fangs and peddling its scrawny paws. "Do you have five thousand dollars handy?"

"Five thousand?" the steward's voice echoed and the stones re-echoed. "Did I hear you ask for five thousand dollars?"

"I didn't ask for anything," I replied. "You're the one who asked to buy. And the five thousand isn't just for your scabby mutts, it's also for your own hide, you fucking Commie pig."

The mill walls trembled, a stone shook loose and dissolved on the floor, the fangs put on lips, the glaring eyes went dark and turned away, and the body sank without sound, down through the hatch and into the silt-thick river, dragging with it a powdery black sand. I swallowed to make my deafened ears pop, one after the other, until I could hear the mulberry leaves that swished from rock to rock in the water below and the breathing of the stupefied hounds, whose pink eyes looked to the steward for a protection that wasn't forthcoming. There were no more festival fireworks and no more little round clouds flashing on and off in the now green sky. The storks were returning, flying flat as postcards and gauging the wind's direction with their beak antennae, returning to their gigantic nests in the tops of the cork oaks. By now the Communists, led by Czechoslovakian agitators, would be cramming into trucks and tractors in Beja and shouting their dumb slogans as they made their way to Alandroal, Arraiolos and Monsaraz, setting houses on fire and decapitating livestock and townsmen.

"What's five grand to you?" I asked as I changed guns. The walls returned my violence in concentric waves, simultaneously near and far, like those of pealing bells. "Moscow must have paid you a lot more than that to spy on us all these years."

I fired again, but the bullet ricocheted off the corner of a rock, a second rock, a rusty post, and out of a window into the night. Maybe it hit a stork, or maybe it fell at the end of its trajectory—inoffensive and useless—at the foot of some Commie or other. Maybe I should have been killing Reds instead of dogs, lying on my stomach, taking cover behind a holm oak, and showering all the cartridges on to a tractor. The steward put his beret back on and held up his spread fingers:

"Stop it, sir, please stop it," he said in a high-pitched but unafraid, unangry voice. "I'll be lucky if I can still buy food at the end of the month."

The river water turned black, the trees turned black, the evening's first crickets trilled their metallic eyelid wings, and the earth lifted slowly to the rumbling of the grasses which cranked it up until it touched the dark sky, trapping the birds: only the yellow-eyed owls flew freely in the treetops, hooting their frantic infant cries. The headlights of the Bolshevik trucks had reached Redondo and were already seesawing over the bumpy road—in a concert of Party songs and invectives—on their way to Monsaraz. One of the Czechs was consulting a list that had our names underlined.

"Are you trying to tell me you don't know that in one or two hours, at the most, your Cuban pals will descend on the village? Did you show the atheists exactly which house is ours, or are they going to skewer everybody with their scythes and their rakes?"

Troops and civilians all mixed together, receiving their instructions from the Russian Embassy, from the Cuban Embassy, from the nauseating bearded leaders of the revolution, whose beady eyes burned like those of the schoolteacher's German shepherd as it rammed its snout and paws into the gate.

"I don't have the slightest idea what you're talking about, sir," the steward said, scratching his beret, bewildered. "Cubans? Who are these Cubans? Excuse me, sir, but maybe you drank a little too much at the festival."

The night was now full, though the turbid round moon had still not risen from the brush. I could tell that the streetlights in Monsaraz were on, because a glowing halo crowned the walls, which resembled the thin cardboard of those church nativity scenes with mangers lit by tiny bulbs. The maids piled boxes and suitcases in the hallway. The mongoloid stared blankly with her usual stunned innocence as my wife removed her pinafore and strove with the help of the cook and our niece to get her into a sweater, a skirt, and some shoes that didn't fit her flipper-shaped feet with their scrunched-up toes, bulbous like the Guadiana's pebbles. The drunken survivors were snoring in the square in fits and starts, like horses with colds, fenced in by the barbed wire of their wine breath and their vomit. Barefoot tramps explored the rubbish with their walking sticks, competing with stray cats for the bones and rinds and greasy scraps of bread. The steward and the bloodhounds, engulfed by the shadows of the mill, could only be identified by the faintest of noises—a rustle, a crushed leaf, a soft growl, a grazing paw—and I understood the resentment of blind men towards the world beyond their dark glasses, towards the sunny days they cannot see.

"You went a little heavy on the brandy, sir, and it's brought out your mean side," said the steward, who seemed to be speaking from five or six different points in the mill. "Are you satisfied now? Have you committed enough atrocities for one day?"

A swift, whetted bat fluttered next to me for a second, arrowed up into the air, and was gone. One of the Czechs, with the butt of his rifle, cracked open a child's head like a rotten egg. In Outeiro the soldiers machine-gunned the windows or tossed home-made bombs on to rooftops. The people raised their arms to protect themselves from the firing Cubans, who laughed in scorn: I have to get back to the house, I have to round up the herd of freaks and whores I inherited from the old man and drive them into Spain.

"Come here, you Commie," I ordered, groping with the shotgun in the shadows, finding a shape, shooting, yanking open the breech, inserting more bullets, shooting again. "Come here, you son of a bitch, so I can teach you to respect your superiors."

And I must have hit a dog, for I heard the squeaky yelp of a wounded animal, a flurry of paws, growls of solidarity. The stone structure sang like a seashell, and the sounds, rather than fading away, collided like moths into the crumbling walls. My eyes smarted from the gunpowder, but my ears kept avidly listening for the steward in that hive of echoes, which seemed it might break away from the bank at any moment and drift downstream towards the sea, taking with it the slimy tentacles that clutched the foundation. Probably, surely, there was a hidden rudder and a sail in the ceiling topmast, and with these we could navigate between the rocks and the rapids, disembarking in Spain on a rickety dock full of puzzled fishermen. To my way of thinking, every house and every village counts as a boat: the ship of Monsaraz, for instance, began to moulder on its hill when the Guadiana spring tides withdrew from the slope. The vegetables in the cemetery have a coral texture and the surrounding hamlets are whitewashed shipwrecks, inhabited by sullen fish carrying hoes over their shoulders. Communists. Communists with posters of Lenin in their bedrooms. Communists lying in wait to finish us off: an injection in the carotid, a gun in the head, a knife in the lungs.

"You've lost control of your senses," said the steward's elusive voice, almost fluid, confounded with the river's. "In fact, you never had any to begin with. You're the one they should have put in the hospital in Lisbon. You even screwed around with the mongoloid in the woods. If I hadn't pushed your father-in-law's shotgun wide, I wouldn't have to be here now and watch all this."

And I remembered my retarded sister-in-law's body with its slack tits that were bigger than the schoolteacher's, and I remembered the schoolteacher's bedroom full of veils, thick drapes and necklaces hanging from the mirror's wicker frame, and her German shepherd clawing in fury at the kitchen window, "How am I supposed to get out of here with that monster going berserk in the garden?", and her urgent hand on my back, on my bottom, "Relax, I'll hold it by the collar, Come on, don't make me wait any longer, Stop worrying, Come over here," her lean thighs receiving me, her cheap perfume, the radio announcer reporting the news as I came inside her, station identification, two a.m., "If I don't get home soon my wife's going to make an incredible scene," "I won't let you leave, I won't hold on to the dog, Look at the way he's jumping all over the place, Stay a little longer, darling, I want more, I need more, It's been months, years, since I felt a man's weight on my body, Hold me tight, bite my neck, stick your tongue in my ear, Weeks and weeks waiting for this, Oh gosh, are my earrings hurting you?", and bed slats cracking like skeleton bones, how strange to kiss a mouth with dentures, to run into slick plastic and tiny wire hooks instead of impression-able flesh, "You can't imagine how lonely I feel here, When classes are over I come back, make dinner, knit, I don't even bother with TV, and then I go to bed, I see no one, talk to no one, I don't have a single friend here, my parents live in Faro, Don't be afraid of the dog, darling, he won't bite, Here, Hitler!, Come on, boy, settle down now, you want to get a good thrashing or what?, that's better, See, love?, He doesn't hurt anyone as long as they

242

don't hurt me," her hand securing the collar, the animal growling at me with phosphorescent jaws and tall, stiff ears, "See you tomorrow, You'll come back tomorrow, right?, You are coming back, aren't you?", dashing up the hill, tearing off my clothes and slipping into bed, and "Where have you been?", "Who, me?" the light came on, "At the schoolteacher's I'll bet, that little whore," "I hardly even know her, dear, it's just hi and bye, how absurd, Turn off the light and let's go to bed," "You stink of the most abominable perfume I've ever smelled, your face is covered with lipstick and you're all sticky with skin cream, God how disgusting, Tomorrow morning I'll ask my father to talk to an official and get the bitch transferred," "Don't be ridiculous, dear, what lipstick?", "What lipstick, You even have the nerve to ask me what lipstick, Look here, If this isn't lipstick on my finger then what is it?", "I don't know, I can't see anything, honest I can't," "This," "Oh, that there, it's hardly visible, Who knows?, I must have brushed my cheek against something, it could have been a million things, how am I supposed to know?, You're always imagining I'm in bed with other women, Come on, don't be silly, give me a kiss, Don't go and start crying," "Who's crying?, You think I'd cry over a louse like you?, I'm just sick and tired of playing the fool for twenty years, The only reason you didn't sleep with my own mother is because you never met her," "That's going too far, Leonor, Now turn off the light or I'll turn it off myself, You're so damn stubborn, you've got it into your head that I'm cheating on you and that's it, nothing can convince you otherwise, You think I don't have other things to do?", "Good question, very good question, So why don't you answer it?, What else do you do besides . . . besides fucking whatever comes along that's fuckable?", "Where do you keep your hankies?, you're all weepy and runny-nosed, you're going to wake the whole house with all this carrying on, Cut it out, God damn it, I hate seeing you this way, I hate it when you torment me like this without the slightest justification, If I'd actually done you wrong, then all right, you'd have something to whine about and I'd accept it, I'd have to accept it," "I want a divorce, is that clear?, and I want you out of Monsaraz tomorrow." "My God, dear, what's got into you?, You must have had a bad dream, a nightmare, Just try to forget it, it happens to us all, Tell me where the lipstick is now, You see?, it only exists in your head, Leonor, If you have to invent rivals then at least pick a woman that's halfway decent, The schoolteacher and me—it's too preposterous to take seriously, That you could even think to be jealous of a creature like that, dear, makes you look utterly ridiculous," "You're the one who looks ridiculous, You'll go to bed with anything and everything that has a vagina, even my sister, even my sister-in-law, I bet you've even slept with my nieces," "Stop it right there, Leonor, your imagination is getting just a teeny bit out of hand, you're saying absolute nonsense," "I know very well what I'm saying and you know very well what you've been doing all these years, because it's been years since you last touched me, years since you loved me," "After arguing like this, how could I possibly want to make love?, how could I possibly get it up?", "What does my retarded sister have that I don't?, And put your hand down or you'll regret it, What on earth did you see in that pathetic creature?", "Stop it, Leonor, I said stop it, it's almost three o'clock and I'm exhausted, Do you plan to go on like this all night?", "Slap me all you like, that's the only physical contact I get from you, Go ahead, give me another one," "I don't want to hit you, I want to sleep, let me go, let me go, Let go, what is this?, let go," I shouted at the steward I couldn't see, I could only hear his breathing and the seething of his sweat and of his smell of earth and no bath and the hissing of the dogs that would obey him and bite me, "Let go of the gun, you Commie, or I'll shoot your guts out," and they pushed me, I stumbled, I fell backward, I smacked my hip against a stone stair, I couldn't get up, and the footsteps of the steward and the bloodhounds retreated unhurriedly in the undergrowth, dark figures in the thick dark of a night teeming with wings, with insects, with twittering creatures, with the flight of vampires and owls, with rustling bushes and branches of trees and the noise of the Communist tractors and trucks far away as the moon finally rose, spotted and stained, a disc of crumpled paper that woke the broken arms of the olive trees, enlarged the pallid profile of the mill against the ashen profile of the slopes, illuminated the cemetery, the village walls, the gravedigger's black vegetables, the steward who now was there now was swallowed in the curtain of shrubs and the undulations of the earth, and I crawled towards the outline of a rock, tried to kneel upright, sat on the ground, tried again, Maybe by supporting myself on the shotgun, maybe by sticking the butt in the ground, or better yet the barrel, I can get my balance, and it wasn't only my hip that hurt, it was the nerve in my thigh muscle that burned like an incandescent wire, fanning pain out into my knee's cartilage, I won't be able to walk, I thought, I won't be able to budge from here, the Communists will apply an injection behind my ear and kick my dead body into the river, or the rats and locusts, flies, ants, and crickets will slowly feast on my flesh until someone discovers me, a faceless withered root, with cruddy shreds of clothing flapping against the bones of my corpse, as cankered and as trashed and as hollow as the old man's, abandoned in the room upstairs, without a soul or a candle to keep watch. Clouds distending like yawns glided past the grindstone moon and disappeared while I dragged myself on hands and knees across the two miles from the river to the house, all the while fearing the wild ponies and calling for help, yelling for the schoolteacher, yelling for the steward, yelling for my

245

nephew, "Help me!", and everything was frozen on top of the hill, everything perfectly hushed and menacing and still, like after explosions or natural disasters, when the dust begins to settle and we see, through the smoke, the corpses and the twisted, melted metal. The Czech pulled the pistol from its holster and lifted my chin with the icy barrel. Startled rabbits or partridges darted away from me through the brush, a soldier grabbed me by the shirt, "This is the landowner, kill him," and on reaching the wall, on the castle side, there were only my two aching legs, shoulders, kidneys, hands, and, inside the village, a few dead remains from the festival but no living soul, not even a lingering drunk, nor dog, nor chicken, nor light turned on in any of the houses. The moon chromed the fig-tree branches and the water-pump pillar and the fuzz of the geraniums next to the fence: I banged on the door, banged on the door, banged on the door, the trucks and tractors from Moscow were coming, I banged on the door, I heard a murmuring of dogs on the other side, something soft fell out of the fig tree and burst at my side, fragrant and aphthous, I banged on the door, the porch light came on and the steward's daughter, the train fanatic's wife, dressed in black and clasping her jacket against her chest, opened the door slowly, and I saw that there were no more paintings on the walls, and no more silver in the cupboards, and no more porcelain on the marble tops of the sideboards. They'd pushed aside a bookcase to empty out the safe. A broken wineglass in the chinaless china cabinet splintered the ceiling light into hundreds of colours.

"They all left for Spain ages ago," the short woman said softly, as if to beg pardon, in her shy, reticent, humble way, helping me to crawl up on to the leather sofa that faced the television, disconnected, "and I thought you might need me."